Improving the Economy, Efficiency, and Effectiveness of Not-for-Profits

WILEY NONPROFIT LAW, FINANCE, AND MANAGEMENT SERIES

The Art of Planned Giving: Understanding Donors and the Culture of Giving by Douglas E. White

Beyond Fund Raising: New Strategies for Nonprofit Investment and Innovation by Kay Grace

Budgeting for Not-for-Profit Organizations by David Maddox

Charity, Advocacy, and the Law by Bruce R. Hopkins

The Complete Guide to Fund Raising Management by Stanley Weinstein

The Complete Guide to Nonprofit Management by Smith, Bucklin & Associates

Critical Issues in Fund Raising edited by Dwight Burlingame

Developing Affordable Housing: A Practical Guide for Nonprofit Organizations, Second Edition by Bennett L. Hecht

Faith-Based Management: Leading Organizations that are Based on More than Just Mission by Peter Brinckerhoff

Financial and Accounting Guide for Not-for-Profit Organizations, Sixth Edition by Malvern J. Gross, Jr., Richard F. Larkin, Roger S. Bruttomesso, John J. McNally, PricewaterhouseCoopers LLP

Financial Empowerment: More Money for More Mission by Peter Brinckerhoff

Financial Management for Nonprofit Organizations by Jo Ann Hankin, Alan Seidner and John Zietlow

Financial Planning for Nonprofit Organizations by Jody Blazek

The First Legal Answer Book for Fund-Raisers by Bruce R. Hopkins

The Fund Raiser's Guide to the Internet by Michael Johnston

Fundraising Cost Effectiveness: A Self-Assessment Workbook by James M. Greenfield

Fund-Raising: Evaluating and Managing the Fund Development Process, Second Edition by James M. Greenfield

Fund-Raising Fundamentals: A Guide to Annual Giving for Professionals and Volunteers by James M. Greenfield

Fund-Raising Regulation: A State-by-State Handbook of Registration Forms, Requirements, and Procedures by Seth Perlman and Betsy Hills Bush

Grant Seeker's Budget Toolkit by James A. Quick and Cheryl S. New

Grantseeker's Toolkit: A Comprehensive Guide to Finding Funding by Cheryl S. New and James A. Quick

Grant Winner's Toolkit: Project Management and Evaluation by James A. Quick and Cheryl S. New

High Impact Philanthropy: How Donors, Boards, and Nonprofit Organizations can Transform Nonprofit Organizations, by Kay Sprinkel Grace and Alan L. Wendroff

High Performance Nonprofit Organizations: Managing Upstream for Greater Impact by Christine Letts, William Ryan, and Allen Grossman

Improving the Economy, Efficiency, and Effectiveness of Not-for-Profits: Conducting Operational Reviews by Rob Reider

Intermediate Sanctions: Curbing Nonprofit Abuse by Bruce R. Hopkins and D. Benson Tesdahl

International Fund Raising for Nonprofits by Thomas Harris

International Guide to Nonprofit Law by Lester A. Salamon and Stefan Toepler & Associates

Joint Ventures Involving Tax-Exempt Organizations, Second Edition by Michael I. Sanders

The Law of Fund-Raising, Second Edition by Bruce R. Hopkins

The Law of Tax-Exempt Healthcare Oganizations, Second Edition by Thomas K. Hyatt and Bruce R. Hopkins

The Law of Tax-Exempt Organizations, Seventh Edition by Bruce R. Hopkins

The Legal Answer Book for Nonprofit Organizations by Bruce R. Hopkins

A Legal Guide to Starting and Managing a Nonprofit Organization, Second Edition by Bruce R. Hopkins

The Legislative Labyrinth: A Map for Not-for-Profits, edited by Walter Pidgeon

Starting and Managing a Nonprofit Organization: A Legal Guide, Third Edition by Bruce R. Hopkins

Managing Affordable Housing: A Practical Guide to Creating Stable Communities by Bennett L. Hecht, Local Initiatives Support Corporation, and James Stockard

Managing Upstream: Creating High-Performance Nonprofit Organizations by Christine W. Letts, William P. Ryan, and Allan Grossman

Mission-Based Management: Leading Your Not-for-Profit In the 21st Century, Second Edition by Peter Brinckerhoff

Mission-Based Management: Leading Your Not-for-Profit In the 21st Century, Second Edition, Workbook by Peter Brinckerhoff

Web Site

As a purchaser of this book, *Improving the Economy, Efficiency, and Effectiveness of Not-For-Profits*, you have access to the supporting Web site:

www.wiley.com/reider

The Web site contains copies of many of the forms, checklists, exhibits, and working tools for you to use in conducting your own not-for-profit operational review—all easily downloadable. In addition, there may be other pertinent information and updates not shown in the book. You may want to visit the Web site prior to starting the book or as you proceed through the book and once again after completing the book.

The password for the Web site is: Reider

Improving the Economy, Efficiency, and Effectiveness of Not-for-Profits

Conducting Operational Reviews

Rob Reider, CPA, MBA, PhD

John Wiley & Sons, Inc.
New York • Chichester • Weinheim • Brisbane • Singapore • Toronto

Library of Congress Cataloging-in-Publication Data:

Reider, Harry R., 1940–
    Improving the economy, efficiency, and effectiveness of not-for-profits : conducting operational reviews / Rob Reider.
        p.   cm.—(Wiley nonprofit law, finance, and management series)
        Includes index.
        ISBN 0-471-39573-0 (cloth : alk. paper)
        1. Nonprofit organizations—Management.   2. Strategic planning.   I. Title.
    II. Series.
    HD62.6 .R45 2001
    658'.048—dc21   00-046266

About the Author

**Rob Reider, CPA, MBA, Ph.D,** is the President of Reider Associates, a management and organization consulting firm located in Santa Fe, New Mexico, which he founded in 1976. His area of expertise encompasses planning and budget systems, managerial and administrative systems, computer processing, financial and accounting procedures, organizational behavior and theory, management advisory services, large and small business consulting, management information and control techniques, and management training and staff development.

Rob has been a consultant, member of the board, and volunteer to numerous large, medium, and small not-for-profit organizations in the aforementioned areas. In addition, he has conducted many and varied operational reviews for not-for-profit entities as well as training internal staff and external consultants in these techniques. He is considered a national expert in the area of performing operational reviews together with internal and external benchmarking studies.

Prior to starting Reider Associates, Rob was a manager in the Management Consulting Department of Peat, Marwick in Philadelphia. Rob is the course author and nationally sought-after discussion leader and presenter for over 20 different seminars that are conducted nationally for various organizations and associations. He has presented over 1,000 such seminars throughout the country and has received the AICPA Outstanding Discussion Leader of the Year Award.

Rob is the course author of nine self-study courses marketed nationally. He is also the author of the following books also published by John Wiley & Sons, Inc.

- *The Complete Guide to Operational Auditing* (with annual supplements)
- *Operational Review: Maximum Results at Efficient Costs*
- *Benchmarking Strategies: A Tool for Profit Improvement*

Rob has also been a presenter at numerous professional meetings and conferences around the country and has published numerous articles in professional journals. He has been a frequent commentator on the educational videotape programs produced by Primemedia Workplace Learning such as *The CPA Report, The Governmental Update,* and the *Accounting and Financial Managers Network.*

Rob has earned the degrees of Bachelor of Science (B.S.) in Business Administration and Master of Science in Business (MBA) from Drexel University as well as Doctor of Philosophy (Ph.D) in Organizational and Management Psychology from Southwest University. He is currently listed in *Who's Who in the East and West, Who's Who in the World, Who's Who in Finance and Industry, Personalities in America, International Biography, Who's Who of Emerging Leaders in America,* and *Who's Who in Executives and Businesses.*

For more information about Rob Reider and Reider Associates, visit his web site at www.reiderassociates.com/otp/ or e-mail him at hrreider@ reiderassociates.com.

Acknowledgments

The author wishes to gratefully acknowledge all of those individuals employed at not-for-profit organizations that he has had the pleasure of providing consulting services. Without the input of these individuals, the author would not have been able to formulate the contents and examples used throughout the book. It was by working with these organizations that the author was able to accumulate the necessary knowledge over the years that went into developing this book.

The author also wishes to acknowledge Martha Cooley, his editor at John Wiley & Sons, Inc., who not only approached the author to develop this book for not-for-profit organizations but has been a guiding light and supporter in completing this book. Whatever success the book enjoys must be shared with Martha.

The author also acknowledges the support and contributions made by the following individuals in assisting the author in developing the case situations found between the chapters:

- New Mexico Suicide Intervention Project: Cynthia Gonzales, Executive Director and Apryl Miller, Program Director, Sky Center.
- Santa Fe Children's Museum: Ellen Biderman, Londi Carbajal, Ellyn Feldman—Co-Directors.
- Santa Fe Chamber Music Festival: Erich Vollmer, Executive Director
- Santa Fe Rape Crisis Center: Barbara Goldman, Executive Director

The author also wishes to acknowledge his wife, Barbara Reider, who has made working with not-for-profits personally profitable and who listened patiently to my complaints as this book evolved. A special acknowledgment to our dog Brandee who sat by my feet as I keyed the contents of the book into the computer.

Contents

Chapter Two: The Planning Phase   **57**

Preface

Not-for-profit organizations are generally considered those organizations that are established for charitable or educational purposes under Internal Revenue Code 501(a) and exempt from federal income taxes with contributions deductible by the donor as a tax deduction. Normally, such not-for-profits are supported by governmental entities, private foundations, public contributions, and fees. While these not-for-profit's are not permitted to make a profit, they are in existence to survive and provide the services for which they were established. Should a not-for-profit's revenues exceed expenditures for a period, the difference or excess (e.g., profit for a private business, accumulated reserve or net assets for a not-for-profit) is allowed to be carried forward to succeeding periods to be used in future operations. Accordingly, not-for-profits are in the business of providing services and increasing reserves for each period under operation.

Not-for-profit organizations include many different and varied types of organizations such as:

- Colleges and universities
- Providers of health care services
- Civic organizations
- Fraternal organizations
- Libraries
- Museums
- Cultural institutions
- Performing arts organizations
- Political parties
- Private and community foundations
- Private elementary and secondary schools
- Professional associations
- Public broadcasting stations
- Religious organizations
- Research and scientific organizations
- Social and country clubs

- Trade associations
- Zoological and botanical societies

It does not cover those types of entities that operate essentially as commercial businesses for the direct economic benefit of its members.

NOT-FOR-PROFITS
ARE NOT NONPROFITS

This book is directed toward looking at how to help such not-for-profits operate more economically, efficiently, and effectively within the guidelines of maintaining their not-for-profit status. While it addresses the particular concerns of operating and surviving in a not-for-profit world, it does not specifically treat any individual type of entity as mentioned above. Instead, it addresses the general concerns of many types of not-for-profits in surviving and prospering in today's environment.

One of the dynamics presently going on in not-for-profit organizations is the public perceived aspect that such organizations are being managed by ineffective and incompetent management. These not-for-profit entities have, in recent years, seen a receding revenue base (contributions and public and private grants) and at the same time an increased demand for their services. Not-for-profit management, which may be used to operating with the opposite scenario, has been struggling to function more efficiently and effectively. Many of the old remedies—such as increasing fees and admissions or going after additional contributions (many times through the largess of board members)—are not as readily available.

Accordingly, these not-for-profits may have resorted to "creative" revenue-raising measures such as gambling activities, elaborate fund-raising events, special fees, business enterprises, and so on. At the same time, these not-for-profits in many cases have tried to come to grips with the demand for increased services through measures such as "pay as you go," curtailing of services, shifting of services, outside referrals, and so on. So, it may be that today's not-for-profit managers are not any worse than in the past—it may be more that the situation has changed and they have not changed with it.

Although the economy in general is continuing on the path of steady in-

---

CREATIVITY IN THE SHORT TERM
MAY ELIMINATE THE LONG TERM

---

creases, many of the economic factors continue to have an impact on not-for-profit operations, resulting in lower revenues and contributions, such as:

- Declining tax bases
- Below past consumer spending
- Less willingness to make charitable contributions
- Higher unemployment in certain areas
- Higher underemployment
- Decreases in federal domestic spending, resulting in less spending by state and local governmental entities for many not-for-profits

While the steady growth of the economy has been favorable for some state and local governmental entities, others still struggle with the pressures of providing funding for necessary programs such as education, health care, law enforcement, local property tax relief, complying with federal unfunded mandates (e.g., environmental), and maintaining capital assets and infrastructure. Many not-for-profits, however, have not been as fortunate. Federal domestic spending and related funding continues to be reduced (e.g., National Endowment for the Arts), providing less assistance to these not-for-profit entities. Individuals and corporations have also resisted returning to previous levels of contributions and have become more selective as to where they contribute. While consumer spending has increased in many areas, corresponding increases in not-for-profit giving has not necessarily kept pace.

In addition, competition among many not-for-profits for contributions and the providing of services (both paid employees and volunteers) has made many potential contributors wary of contributing at all. Once having contributed, many donors are wary of receiving too many subsequent requests for additional contributions—it may be better to just not give at all. There also is a perception by a large segment of the public that too large a percentage of money received goes to administration (particularly executive salaries and benefits) and not to direct services, which has created a further reluctance to contribute. The irony is that as total contributions and costs spiral downward, even where administrative costs remain the same, these administrative costs percentage of total costs goes up.

**PUBLIC-SECTOR COMPETITION
CAN BE AS COMPETITIVE AS
PRIVATE-SECTOR COMPETITION**

In today's many-faceted and multidisciplined economic environment, not-for-profit management has placed an increasing emphasis on increasing results or maximizing the delivery of services with fewer resources through the evaluation of the economy, efficiency, and effectiveness of the organization's operations. The operational review is the tool used to perform such an evaluation of operations—singly or as part of another procedure such as benchmarking, activity-based management, total quality management, reengineering, and so on. The purpose of this book is to assist the reader to understand the basic principles of planning and conducting such an operational review, as well as the fundamentals of which the reviewer must be aware, to understand operational review concepts.

The purpose of this how-to guide for not-for-profits is to help them to understand the basic principles involved in planning and conducting an effective operational review. Such an operational review takes a critical look (looking at good and not so good practices) of the not-for-profit's major and critical functions and activities. The review is directed toward the implementation of best practices (within funding and operational constraints) in all areas of the organization in an organized program of continuous improvements. It is not enough in today's not-for-profit world where each entity must compete for scarce public and private dollars and resources for the not-for-profit to merely survive; it must also prosper and grow. Not-for-profit management must define what such growth means to their organization and develop effective systems that ensure that the not-for-profit moves positively in that direction. It is the goal of the operational review to assist not-for-profit management in achieving such growth goals.

This book provides the information and fundamentals the reviewer must know to use operational review concepts that will enable the not-for-profit to operate most economically, efficiently, and effectively—that is, to maximize operating results and service delivery efforts at the least cost using the most efficient methods. This book is designed to meet the needs of the reviewer—within or outside of the organization—regardless of whether he or she (or a review team) has any prior experience in performing operational reviews. Both basic knowledge for those with no previous hands-on experience and reinforcement and additional learning for those who already have some prior operational review experience are provided.

Questions that will be answered include:

- What is an operational review?
- When should an operational review be performed?
- How can an operational review be performed effectively and efficiently, particularly within the constraints of a not-for-profit entity?
- How can positive change be effected as a result of an operational review?
- How can operational review tools and techniques be used to maintain not-for-profit operations in an economic, efficient, and effective manner on an ongoing basis?
- How can best practices be identified and implemented effectively within the not-for-profit in a formalized program of continuous improvements?

**I KNOW THE QUESTIONS—
NOW WHAT ARE THE ANSWERS?**

The materials presented in this book can be used by management (e.g., board members, executive director, program management, etc.), supervision, and other employees to perform operational reviews for their operational areas of responsibility. In addition, the tools and techniques presented can be used by others, such as internal and external consultants and auditors, to maintain operations in the most economical, efficient, and effective manner.

PURPOSE AND OBJECTIVES

In today's economic and social environment where individuals, businesses, and corporations are resisting the pressures for increased taxation by a combination of federal, state, and local taxation programs, not-for-profit entities are being forced to scramble for fewer public allocations for the services they provide. As such public taxing authorities are attempting to increase desired results with less resources, they are asking not-for-profit entities to do the same. At the same time, many individual and organizational funding sources are decreasing the amount of overall funding to these not-for-profits.

In such an atmosphere, not-for-profit management has placed more emphasis on increasing results with fewer resources through the evaluation of the economy, efficiency, and effectiveness of the entity's operations. The operational review is the tool used to perform such an evaluation, either singularly or as part of another procedure such as benchmarking, activity-based management, total quality management, reengineering, and so on. This book presents the basic principles of planning and conducting such an operational review in the not-for-profit environment, as well as the fundamentals of which the reviewer must be aware to understand operational review concepts.

The objectives of this book are to:

- Increase understanding of operational review concepts within the not-for-profit environment and the ability to use them effectively.
- Increase understanding of the purpose and mechanics of conducting operational reviews in the not-for-profit sector.
- Help identify the relationships and differences between operational reviews and other procedures that a not-for-profit entity may be using, such as budget versus actual reporting, program evaluation techniques, progress reporting, service delivery statistics and comparisons, and so on.

- Increase the skills and abilities needed to conduct operational reviews so that the review itself is performed most effectively without compromising good practices that may already be in place.
- Increase awareness of operational review opportunities and to help in their identification—even where not-for-profit management has their entrenched belief systems in operation.
- Improve the operational reviewer's capability to perform effective operational reviews within the constraints of the not-for-profit entity.

In many not-for-profit entities today, top management is seeking ways to become more viable—not just to maintain their level of services, but to increase their levels—and not just to survive. Not-for-profit management has sensed that many of their organizational systems may be detrimental to progress and have held them back from achieving organizational, departmental, program, and individual goals and objectives. Many times, they have borrowed management fads and techniques (e.g., downsizing, restructuring, total quality management, etc.) from the private sector, which have resulted in increased costs and upheaval without significant results. Other systems, which were meant to be helpful, have had the opposite effects; for example:

- Planning systems, long and short term, that resulted in documented plans but not in actual desired results
- Budget systems (mainly based on line-item budgeting) that became costly in terms of effectively allocating resources and controlling costs in relation to results
- Organizational structures, made up of paid employees and volunteers, that created unwieldy hierarchies, which produced systems of unnecessary power and control
- Management systems that produced elaborate computer systems and reporting (many times confusing and incomprehensible), which did not enhance the effectiveness of operations
- Expenditure forecasting and reporting that neglected the revenue side and assumed that the level of activity would remain static and that such forecasting should remain static as well
- Operating practices that perpetuated outmoded belief systems (e.g., "We've always done it that way," "It won't work here—we're not in business to make a profit.") rather than promoting best practices
- Management techniques, such as participative management, empowerment, entrepreneurship, self-actualization, and so on, which may have resulted in more frequent and longer meetings but no appreciable increase in results

Operational reviews, together with other techniques, are tools to make these systems helpful as intended and direct the organization toward its goals and reasons for being in existence. Theoretically, all organizations—in both the public and private sectors—should operate in an economic, efficient, and effective manner at all times. If such were the case, operational review techniques would be applied on an ongoing basis. However, with the passage of time, good intentions and initially helpful systems tend to deteriorate. Operational reviews are then necessary to help get the not-for-profit entity back on track by pinpointing operational deficiencies, developing practical recommendations, and implementing positive changes.

> ## HELPFUL SYSTEMS LEFT UNATTENDED
> ## CAN BECOME HURTFUL SYSTEMS

In the not-for-profit sector, where resources may be scarcer than what is necessary to accomplish all of its desired results, the reviewer would expect that operations are more scrutinized than in the private sector and that waste is kept to a minimum. Top management and each program or department manager would be expected to be held accountable for using the scarce resources entrusted to them to achieve maximum results at the least possible costs. The reviewer might expect that management embraces operational review concepts and applies them as they proceed, but this is rarely the case. More typically, not-for-profit management has to be sold on the value of operational reviews.

In selling the benefits of conducting operational reviews, it is important to stress that unlike other techniques that cost scarce time and money for uncertain results, operational reviews pay for themselves. Although there are no guarantees, a successful operational review should result in at least three to four times its cost in annual savings. These are not one-time savings, but ongoing—that is, savings year after year that can be used to increase the level of service delivery or increase the quality of existing services. With the success of an operational review, management may quickly realize that the more operational reviews performed and the more recommended and implemented economies and efficiencies, the greater the savings and results. In addition, the residual capability for performing operational reviews remains with the entity or the area under review, so operations personnel (employees and/or volunteers) can continue to apply operational review concepts on an ongoing basis.

The intent of the operational review is not to be critical of present operations, but to review operations and develop a program of best practices and continuous positive operational improvements by working with management and staff personnel. This can be accomplished most effectively by working with operations personnel in areas where they recognize deficiencies and are willing to cooperate. The concept of operational reviews should be sold as an internal program of review directed toward improved economies and efficiencies that will produce increased operational results.

It is important to understand that the not-for-profit is a business just like any other. Its mission is to provide desired services to the community in which it resides. If it can do this successfully in an economical, efficient, and effective manner, it will survive and prosper. It is the task of the operational review team to assist not-for-profit management in making this happen. This book is the how-to guide in conducting such operational reviews.

**A NOT-FOR-PROFIT IS A BUSINESS
JUST LIKE ANY OTHER BUSINESS**

CHAPTER ONE

Introduction to Operational Reviews

INTRODUCTION

This chapter provides an overview of operational review concepts and principles and terminology. In an ever-changing economic and competitive environment where not-for-profit entities struggle for funding and revenues while at the same time the demand for services may be increasing, not-for-profit management is looking for more than historical financial and service delivery data. These managers need and request information about the internal operations of their organization, and seek recommendations as to how they can manage and operate more economically, efficiently, and effectively—managing scarce resources for maximum results. The operational review process is most helpful and beneficial in the following instances:

- Identifying operational areas in need of positive improvement—looking for best practices as part of a program for continuous improvements
- Pinpointing the cause (not the symptom) of the problem—avoiding quick-fix. short-term solutions in favor of longer-term, elegant solutions
- Quantifying the effect of the present situation on operations—identifying the cost of present practices and the benefits to be derived through implementation of best practices
- Developing recommendations as to alternative courses of action to correct the situation—identifying best practices using internal and external benchmarking techniques in a program of continuous improvements.

Operational review results provide the entity—board of directors, top management, operations management, employees, volunteers, clients or customers, vendors, and contractors—with data necessary for effective resource allocation and the strategic focus for the organization. The operational review process provides for those objective measures to determine the success of the entity's internal goals, objectives, and detail plans as well as external performance measures.

Evaluating the entity's performance against stakeholder (all those who are dependent on the survival of the entity) expectations enables the entity to pursue its program of continuous improvement on the road to excellence. Effective operational review procedures encompass both internal and external needs.

Managers responsible for an operational area have traditionally maintained the operation as they found it. That is, they primarily accepted the organization, personnel, and functions they inherited. They were not allowed or did not understand how to make their assigned area of responsibility more efficient. Many times, there were systems in effect (such as overcontrolling bosses) that prevented such positive changes. The purpose of the operational review is to help managers and operations staff look at areas of responsibility from an operational viewpoint. What does "from an operational viewpoint" mean? It means that operations are viewed with an eye as to whether operations can be improved so as to be performed more efficiently, effectively, or economically.

Given today's increasingly varied and competitive environment for not-for-profit funding, management places increasing emphasis on the evaluation of the economy, efficiency, and effectiveness of operations. Often, the managers and employees of an operational area are too close to operations, too resistant to change, too enmeshed in daily operations, and so on to objectively review their own operations. Because both internal and external consultants have the fact-finding and diagnostic skills needed to perform such operational reviews, they are frequently asked to do so. In some not-for-profits that are large enough, a separate unit is formed strictly to perform operational reviews.

Operational reviewing got its start when management stopped being concerned solely with reviewing the reporting of information and started wondering why a transaction was made in the first place and if there was a better way to do it. Operational review is the process whereby the reviewer determines whether management is using the resources entrusted to them in the most economical and efficient manner, to achieve the most effective results of operations.

The objective of this book is to help the reader to understand the basic principles involved in planning and conducting an operational review directed toward the continual implementation of best practices in an organized program of continuous improvements. In addition, it will provide the fundamentals the reader must know to use operational review concepts to enable him or her to operate most economically, efficiently, and effectively—that is, to maximize operating results at the least cost using the most efficient methods.

The materials presented in this book can be used by management and supervisors and other employees to perform operational reviews for their operational areas of responsibility. In addition, the tools and techniques presented can be used by others, such as internal and external consultants and auditors, to maintain operations in the most economical, efficient, and effective manner.

The focus and scope of operations in the not-for-profit sector has changed in recent years. Management has increased demands for more relevant information on the conduct of its operations and related results than can be found in strictly financial and historical data. Not-for-profit management seeks more information with which to judge the quality of operations and make operational improvements. That is why operational review techniques are needed to evaluate the effectiveness and efficiency of operations.

GENERAL CONCERNS FOR NOT-FOR-PROFITS

With decreased government funding (federal, state, and local) and private contributions for the arts, education, and social services, many not-for-profits are trying to do more with less. As a direct result of this reduced or stagnant revenues and contributions together with the demand for increased services, there has been an increasing emphasis on the reliance on more efficient operations. This has resulted in changes in operational concepts as well as operational concerns by boards of directors, contributors, and other interested parties relative to not-for-profits. With this increased emphasis on operations and results, not-for-profit management and operations personnel must not only be aware of innovative methods of achieving results at efficient costs, but must also change their belief systems and emphasis. No longer can this area of maximizing operational results at the least cost be ignored by placing minimal reliance on operational controls and performance measures.

Outside parties are just as interested in the manner in which the not-for-profit entity operates—within a controlled environment—as they are in financial statements. Economic recovery has not yet reached the not-for-profit sector to the degree it has reached the private sector; as many not-for-profits continue to experience reduced funding and increased service demand. Particular concerns include:

- Potential donors (individuals and corporations) reducing their levels of charitable giving
- Reduced public funding (federal, state, and local)
- Steady (lower than the past) interest rates, resulting in steady investment returns
- Increased scrutiny by the Internal Revenue Service (IRS) as to not-for-profit status
- Increased compliance requirements by governmental and private foundation entities
- Reasonableness of top management compensation, fringe benefits, and perquisites
- Continuity of tax-exempt status
- Stagnant contribution level by private foundations—with more scrutiny
- Reduced funding by the National Endowment for the Arts and other such agencies

- Shift toward federal block grants to states has reduced not-for-profit funding
- Individual concern and skepticism about the economy, efficiency, and effectiveness of not-for-profits has slowed down (and stopped) contributions by individuals
- Increases in equity markets (e.g., stock market) creating attractive investment opportunities but potential risks.

The public also continues its attention on adverse issues relating to not-for-profits, such as:

- Reasonableness of compensation (particularly those at the top)
- Fringe benefits exceeding expected levels
- Perquisites afforded to senior management (e.g., automobiles, limousines, trips, etc.)
- Perception that expenditures for program services are a low portion of total expenditures
- Fraud, abuse, embezzlement, and illegal acts
- Worthless investments, assets, and receivables
- The amounts of assets held by the not-for-profit entity
- The portion of revenue earned from sales and fees for goods and services
- Pressure to maximize investment returns
- Make operations appear as efficient as possible, when they are not

Recent increased interest rates have also increased the return on some investments held by not-for-profits fortunate enough to hold such investments. However, such interest rate increases have increased the cost of certain borrowings—a more significant issue to many not-for-profits.

> ### THE PUBLIC IS CONCERNED
> ### ABOUT THE PUBLIC SECTOR

SPECIFIC CONCERNS FOR NOT-FOR-PROFITS

In looking at a not-for-profit's operations, the reviewer should first look at the entity's external environment, considering such factors as the following.

Revenues

The difficulty for not-for-profits to achieve past revenue levels to be able to continue to provide the same or increased level of services include:

- Difficulty in acquiring funds needed to provide services
- Charitable giving down by individuals with less to give
- Governmental units, with economic problems of their own, have reduced or eliminated their past commitments
- Willingness of donors to continue levels of contribution
- Low interest rates have negatively affected investment returns and expected funds for operations
- Riskier investment opportunities (e.g., stock market, real estate)
- Use of nonrelated business enterprises (e.g., flower shops, coffee shops, gift shops, tee shirts and sweat shirts, art sponsorships, and so on) to produce revenues

Expenditures

The increased demand for services with fewer resources, coupled with the increased cost of providing such services, has produced the following concerns:

- Consumer concerns as to compensation (including fringe benefits and perquisites) for senior management and others, as well as the use of funds contributed
- Concerns as to the economic, efficient, and effective operations of the entity, and their ability to provide adequate services
- The entity's ability to survive as a going concern
- Questions as to tax-exempt status of certain not-for-profits

Operations

Not-for-profits tend to be operated by a part-time volunteer board of directors, with members having various levels of skills, abilities, and agendas. In addition, the entity often is managed by a full- or part-time director, whose abilities may vary but tend to relate more to the service being provided (or fund raising), rather than operations and fiscal controls. Support- and service-providing staff may not always be at desired levels—in terms of both abilities and number of staff—and many times are working at less than equitable compensation. Adding a high proportionate share of volunteers to this mix can result in a difficult organizational atmosphere to manage and control.

Some areas that the reviewer should be looking at as the result that these factors may have on the finances and operations of the not-for-profit include:

- *Investment strategy*, as not-for-profits seek to increase their yields through various techniques such as risky securities and real estate investments
- *Revenue recognition*, as management is tempted to use "improper" practices to present more favorable results. Reviewers should review revenue recognition practices, including:

- Recognition of restricted support and revenue
- Recognition and valuation of donated or contributed services
- Valuation of donated materials and facilities
- *Expense classification*, relative to whether expenses are properly classified and program categories are properly presented in operating reports and financial statements
- *Use of more volunteers* in both management and operating capacities as well as getting by with fewer overall personnel
- *Management compensation*: considering whether the entity has enforced policies to assure that compensation, benefits, and perquisites are approved by the board of directors and are in line with like entities—not necessarily the private sector
- *Investments*: looking at aggressive investment strategies that result in issues such as valuation of real estate and other investments for which market values may not be readily determinable
- *Creation of affiliates and new revenue sources*: increasing the risk that the entity will undertake operations that are outside management's traditional understanding and control
- *Gifts-in-kind*: reporting donations of nonmonetary assets at agreed-upon overstated amounts; resulting in overstating net assets and contributions and program expenditures and distorting financial statement ratios
- *Environmental liabilities*: receiving property that does not meet regulatory guidelines for environmental safety
- *Endowment funds*: using such funds to finance current operations through interfund transfers
- *Deferred gifts with high rates of return*: receiving gifts with rates of return due to donors that exceed rates the entity is likely to earn on the gifts. The entity may be liable for making up shortfalls between amounts due to donors and amounts earned on the investments.

**REVENUES, EXPENDITURES, AND OPERATIONS
ALL OF EQUAL CONCERN TO THE NOT-FOR-PROFIT**

BALANCED BUDGET REQUIREMENTS

Most not-for-profits operate with a beginning of fiscal operating year balanced budget requirement, with review, approval, and oversight responsibility provided by a volunteer board of directors. The expectation of such an approved balanced budget by the board of directors provides assurance to the not-for-profits stakeholders (e.g., contributors, funding agencies, employees, vendors, clients, and the public) that the not-for-profit is well managed. However, such stakeholders also need to be concerned as to actual spending, its relationship to the balanced budget, and the results achieved for the dollars spent. This is where the operational review comes into focus—that is, to ensure that budgeted dollars are used economically and efficiently to achieve desired results or effectiveness. In reviewing the workings of balanced budget requirements, the reviewer must look at both the budgeted revenue as well as the budgeted expenditure side of the picture.

The balanced budget requirement has resulted in many instances in the overestimating of revenues and contributions that never happen and the underestimating of expenditures that become more than anticipated. When reality hits and revenues do not materialize and expenditures exceed the budget, the not-for-profit may be pressed to take more drastic measures than desired. These drastic steps could have been avoided with effective management control and related planning and budget systems. It is the operational review process that can provide such guidance to correct these procedures for the not-for-profit and keep them that way.

For many not-for-profits, although overall revenues and contributions decline, demands for services may remain the same or even increase, resulting in pressure to increase expenditures. This pressure is making it increasingly difficult for these not-for-profits to balance operating budgets. To survive, not-for-profits have been using quick-fix and one-shot adjustments to produce balanced budgets, such as:

- Delaying expenditure payments for this year's operating needs to the next fiscal year (i.e., robbing Peter to pay Paul)
- Transferring from other funds (e.g., capital reserve and restricted funds) to the general operating fund
- Selling off assets (e.g., furniture, fixtures, cars and trucks, etc.) that might still have useful life and could be used by the not-for-profit
- Restructuring debt by refinancing long- and short-term borrowings either at a lower rate or for a longer period of time
- Reducing scheduled contributions to employee pension funds or borrowing from these pension funds where permitted
- Deferring scheduled or necessary repairs or maintenance (including preventive maintenance) to property, plant, and equipment
- Using past years' accumulated fund balances or reserves that may have been earmarked for special purposes for current operations
- Delaying payments to vendors so as to conserve current cash but risking increased prices in the future as well as the possibility that certain critical vendors may refuse future dealings

While the above techniques may give the appearance of improving the entity's current financial position, it may be only postponing impending financial and operational disaster. The reviewer must appraise these measures and others found from an operational standpoint to determine whether any laws and regulations have been violated, the entity can continue on a going-concern basis providing the same level of services, and what revenue enhancement and expenditure cutting measures may be required.

> ### THE BUDGET MUST BE BALANCED
> ### EVEN IF THE NOT-FOR-PROFIT IS NOT

THE POLITICAL ENVIRONMENT

The reviewer must also be aware of the politically sensitive environment, particularly in the present economy, that not-for-profits currently operate. Contributor perceptions of improprieties have resulted in decreased contributions and skeptical acceptance as to the operations and results of some not-for-profits. With this increased public focus on accountability of not-for-profits on both revenues and expenditures, the reviewer needs to address areas such as:

- Conflicts of interest or ethics
- Competitive bidding procedures
- Use of restricted funds for nonintended purposes
- Restrictions on travel (and entertainment) expenses
- Private use of not-for-profit–owned property (e.g., automobiles, equipment)
- Political activities and lobbying
- Fund-raising activities (e.g., percentage paid to outside fund raisers)
- Nonrelated business activities
- Unreasonable compensation and benefits
- Use of volunteers (e.g., use and valuations)
- Valuation of in-kind contributions

IRS CONCERNS FOR NOT-FOR-PROFITS

The Internal Revenue Service (IRS) defines not-for-profit organizations as those organizations that are generally exempt from federal income tax under section 501(a) of the Internal Revenue Code as an organization described in section 501(c)(3). Normally, such organizations are considered publicly supported or private foundations. These organizations are liable for Social Security taxes ($100 or more per employee per year), but not liable for federal unemployment taxes. Donors may deduct contributions for tax purposes to such organizations to the extent that such contributions are gifts—with no consideration received. Such not-for-profit organizations are required to file Form 990, Return of Organization Exempt from Income Tax, if their gross receipts each year are normally $25,000 or more. There is no requirement to file a federal income tax return unless the entity is subject to the tax on unrelated business income, and then it must file Form 990-T, Exempt Organization Business Income Tax Return.

The IRS continues to review not-for-profit tax-exempt organizations, focusing on whether an entity's activities further its tax-exempt status, looking at such activities as:

- Political activities that may result in loss of exempt status or the imposition of excise taxes, penalties, and interest assessments
- Lobbying activities that may result in loss of exempt status, the tax on disqualified lobbying expenditure, and taxes on not-for-profit organizations' managers
- Unrelated business activities, the income from which may be subject to income tax, and excessive amounts of which may jeopardize an organization's tax-exempt status; such activities may also prompt state and local governmental agencies to assess real estate or reduce existing exemptions
- Violations of IRC prohibitions against private benefit and private inurement
- Classification of personnel as employees or independent contractors, improper use of FICA tax exclusions, improper payroll reporting, revenue from mailing list rentals, and associate member dues

---

**POLITICS AND THE IRS
AFFECT NOT-FOR-PROFIT OPERATIONS**

AICPA INTERNAL CONTROL CONCERNS

The American Institute of Certified Public Accountants' (AICPA's) Auditing Standards Board (ASB), in December 1995, issued Statement on Auditing Standards (SAS) No. 78, "Consideration of Internal Control in a Financial Statement Audit: An Amendment to SAS No. 55." This SAS revises the definition and description of internal control contained in the SASs to recognize the definition and description contained in "Internal Control–Integrated Framework" published by the Committee of Sponsoring Organizations of the Treadway Commission (COSO). SAS No. 78 is effective for audits of financial statements for periods beginning on or after January 1, 1997 (with early application). Internal control is a process designed to provide reasonable assurance regarding the achievement of objectives in the following categories:

- Reliability of financial reporting
- Compliance with applicable laws and regulations
- Effectiveness and efficiency of operations

COSO redefines the three elements of internal control per SAS No. 55—control environment, accounting system, control procedures—to the five following elements:

1. Control environment; including the following factors:
   - Integrity and ethical values
   - Commitment to competence
   - Board of directors and audit committee
   - Management's philosophy and operating style
   - Organizational structure
   - Assigning authority and responsibility
   - Human resource policies and procedures
2. Risk assessment; including the following internal and external factors and circumstances:
   - Changes in operations
   - Changes in competitive pressures
   - Changes in personnel
   - New or updated information systems
   - Drastic changes: growth or retrenchment
   - New technology
   - New processes, activities, programs, and so on
3. Control activities, such as:
   - Performance reviews
   - Information processing (general and application controls)
   - Physical controls
   - Segregation of duties
4. Information and communication, including criteria such as:
   - Identify and record all valid transactions
   - Describe transactions in sufficient detail on a timely basis to permit proper classification of transactions for financial reporting
   - Measure the value of transactions for proper monetary recording in the financial statements
   - Recording of transactions in the proper accounting period
   - Present transactions properly (and related disclosures) in the financial statements
5. Monitoring—assessing the design and quality of the internal control structure considering factors such as:
   - Timely assessment by appropriate personnel
   - Necessary corrective actions taken

- Ongoing activities or specific evaluations
- Internal audit activity
- External feedback (e.g., customer/client complaints)

ACCOUNTING PRINCIPLES FOR NOT-FOR-PROFITS

It is not the intention of this book to teach the universe of fund accounting principles that relate to not-for-profits. However, there are certain aspects of fund accounting that would be helpful to know in conducting an operational review of a not-for-profit. First, the reviewer should be aware of some of the similarities between fund and business accounting, such as:

- Consistency between reporting periods
- Measurement and valuation basis—that is, historical cost
- Matching of operating revenues and costs (but not to determine net income)
- Materiality and full disclosure

Then, the reviewer should be aware that fund accounting has some different characteristics form normal business accounting, such as:

- A not-for-profit does not operate on a bottom-line basis—in other words, it does not operate to earn a profit—but may operate to maximize additions to net assets or reserves.
- A not-for-profit is in existence to allocate resources (sources of revenue) to provide services (expenditures of funds).
- Legal requirements must be followed and compliance demonstrated.
- The approved budget and its related operating systems and procedures must be in compliance.
- The not-for-profit has the power to raise revenues through various types of fund-raising endeavors.
- Except in cases of non–business-related activities (e.g., store operations), there are no equity interests.
- Cost versus benefit relationships may not be relevant and may not exist.
- Use of fund and budgetary (usually static line item budgets) reporting.

The reviewer must also be aware of the not-for-profit's basis of accounting. Although accrual accounting is acceptable for not-for-profit (and generally accepted accounting principles [GAAP]) reporting, many not-for-profits (particularly smaller ones) find that a cash or modified cash basis is adequate for their accounting record keeping and financial statement reporting needs. For many such not-for-profits, the cash basis is more easily understood by their staff and governing body personnel. When this is the case, the reviewer must understand the differences between cash and accrual accounting and the effect on the not-for-profit's operations.

Asset classifications for not-for-profits are similar to for-profit organizations such as cash, accounts receivable, investments, prepaid insurance, and so on. However, there are some possible differences that the reviewer should be aware of, such as:

- Contributions, pledges, or grants receivable
- Allowance for uncollectible contributions
- Historic or restored buildings used for display
- Collections—art, valuable books, prints, collector's items
- Restricted and endowment funds
- Plant funds
- Investment pools (to be distributed to various funds)
- Property, plant, and equipment (valuation and ownership)
- Gifts and loans of objects (value, catalog, identify)

Liabilities such as accounts payable and loans payable are similar to those of for-profit entities. Liabilities that the reviewer should pay particular attention to include:

- Tax-deferred annuities for employees
- Interfund borrowings (temporary or permanent)
- Refunds due to third parties for amounts collected under reimbursement agreements
- Deferred revenue (earned but not recognized) (e.g., membership dues, magazine subscriptions)
- Deferred support (e.g., unexpended balances of gifts, grants)

The reviewer's objective in analyzing revenues is to be assured that these revenues have been recorded properly relative to amount, account, and period. Typical revenues other than grants and contributions that may be encountered in the not-for-profit's review include:

- Service fees, such as dues, admissions, tuitions, client fees, annual care (e.g., cemeteries), life memberships, and so on
- Sales of purchased items, such as books, magazines, advertising, souvenirs, concessions, events, auctions, and so on
- Income and gains and losses from investments
- Third-party reimbursements

Not-for-profits may present their expenditures as either functional with each significant program reported separately or on an object basis showing line items such as personnel, materials, supplies, and so on. Some areas that the reviewer should consider related to such expenditures include:

- Program services
- Support services
- Fund-raising activities
- Management and administration
- Expense allocations
- Indirect cost allocations
- Budgeting and expense approvals
- Charges to grants and contracts
- Use of restricted funds
- Grants given to others
- Taxes—unrelated business activities, excess lobbying, excise, sales

Other areas that the reviewer should consider include:

- Support: gifts, grants, and bequests
  - Restricted or unrestricted
  - Based on service performance
  - Restricted for endowment, plant, equipment, and so on
  - Form—cash, services, facilities, equipment, goods, and so on
  - Donated or contributed services
  - Valuation of in-kind contributions
- Affiliated organizations
- Related-party transactions
- Illegal acts, errors, and irregularities
- Cash versus accrual accounting (as discussed above)
- Going-concern capabilities

NOT-FOR-PROFIT'S ABILITY TO CONTINUE AS A GOING CONCERN

Many not-for-profits, in the past, were assumed to have an unlimited ability to raise revenues through public and private funding to support their operations and to continue to service their client base. However, the current external environment and contributor initiatives (as well as limitations on contributor resources) have reduced the ability of these entities to continue to raise and increase revenues. SAS No. 59, "The Auditor's Consideration of an Entity's Ability to Continue as a Going Concern," requires as part of every audit that the auditor evaluate the entity's ability to continue as a going concern for a reasonable period of time (not to exceed one year from the financial statement date). During the audit, the auditor's might identify conditions casting doubt as to the entity's ability to continue as a going concern, such as:

- Defaults on debt (e.g., revenues inadequate to repay debt)
- Diminishing revenues and declining contributor bases, for example, a declining contributor population; lower program enrollment; reduced per-capita personal income; and reductions in the number and value of individual public and private contributions
- Increasing reliance on external funding
- Large, unfunded pension obligations combined with decreasing revenues and a declining contribution base
- Reliance by a fund incurring large deficits on continued support from other funds to support its operations (e.g., general fund operations relying on support from a large contributor or the use of restricted funds)
- Omission of key items, such as salary increases or pension contributions, from the budget to avoid an unbalanced budget
- Elaborate financing arrangements designed to alleviate financial stress
- Sale of or borrowing against assets to ease cash flow problems
- Inadequate steps to address fiscal stress resulting from poor economic conditions that seriously affect revenues and expenditures
- Fiscal stress resulting from lost revenues and increased demand for services
- Bonding out current expenditures, delaying recording bills in the current year, or accelerating the recording of revenues that are applicable to a future period
- Ineffective planning, budgeting, and fiscal control systems that tend to overestimate revenues and underestimate expenditures, with inadequate and inflexible ongoing controls

The above items must also be looked at and evaluated by the operational review as part of the operational review of a not-for-profit. It is the objective of the operational review team to ensure that the not-for-profit continue as a going concern. Many of the review team's recommendations will focus on these concerns as to implementing best practices that will support the not-for-profit's growth and survival.

As not-for-profits continue to operate under uncertain conditions as to revenues and the increasing demand for services, it becomes increasingly important for these entities to conduct their operations under more controlled conditions. This atmosphere of uncertainty and diminished resources has pushed regulatory authorities to increase their emphasis on the review and evaluation of operations and related internal controls.

This has been evidenced by the recent and more stringent revisions for internal operational controls in both financial statement and program audits. The reviewer must become more astute in recognizing weaknesses in operations and in assisting the not-for-profit to correct such weakness so that it can operate more efficiently and effectively with fewer resources. The review team can also assist the not-for-profit, through their knowledge of operations and best practices, to operate more economically (more services for the buck), efficiently (use best practice systems and methods), and effectively (achieving maximum results with minimal resources).

AICPA AND OTHERS
AFFECT NOT-FOR-PROFIT OPERATIONS

COMPUTER PROCESSING CONCERNS

The advent of the microcomputer for business purposes has made computerization available to almost all organizations—down to the smallest not-for-profit entity. The reviewer, as part of the operational review, needs to evaluate computer operations and related controls in such a microcomputer environment. In addition, as these entities are processing their accounting and financial data as well as operating program data using such microcomputer systems, the reviewer must possess the skills and abilities to perform microcomputer control reviews as well as using "through the computer" techniques.

Most not-for-profits now have or are considering microcomputer installations to process their financial and operating program transactions. These entities, both large and small, are processing financial and operational transactions and maintaining account balances on which the reviewer will rely to come to findings conclusions as the basis for recommendations. Such microcomputer systems can be used as stand-alone systems, internal local area networks (LANs), part of a wide area communications network via modem (using laptops and portables), or as a front-end processor to an umbrella system (e.g., work stations electronically tied into an organization-wide computer network), or in some combination.

Because many not-for-profits have moved from manual record keeping to the use of microcomputer processing, the reviewer must be aware of the special considerations in performing the operational review in a microcomputer environment.

SPECIFIC NOT-FOR-PROFIT ISSUES AND DEVELOPMENTS

Some areas that the reviewer should be looking at as the result that the above factors may have on the financial and operational aspects of the not-for-profit include:

- *Management compensation*—considering as part of the operational review whether the not-for-profit has enforced policies to ensure that compensation, benefits, and perquisites are approved by the board of directors

- *Investments*—considering aggressive strategies that result in valuation of real estate and other investments in which market values may not be readily determinable
- *Creation of affiliates and new revenue sources*—increasing the risk that the not-for-profit will undertake operations that are outside management's traditional understanding and control
- *Gifts in kind*—reporting donations of nonmonetary assets to other not-for-profits at overstated amounts, resulting in overstating net assets and contributions and program expenditures
- *Environmental liabilities*—the not-for-profit's receiving property that does not meet regulatory guidelines for environmental safety
- *Endowment funds*—not-for-profits using such funds to finance current operations through interfund transfers
- *Deferred gifts with high rates of return*—not-for-profits receiving gifts with rates of return due to donors that exceed rates the not-for-profit is likely to earn on the gifts. The not-for-profit may be liable for making up shortfalls between amounts due to donors and amounts earned on the investments

---

**SPECIAL CONCERNS AFFECT
NOT-FOR-PROFIT OPERATIONS**

WHO IS THE OPERATIONAL REVIEWER?

An operational review can be performed by anyone with the appropriate skills. However, internal and/or external consultants, because of their knowledge of the operations and their analytical skills, are typically requested to perform such services. In some organizations, a separate operational review unit trained in operational review concepts is established. The most effective way in which to implement such procedures is to assign overall responsibility for implementing organization-wide operational review procedures, which would include the performance of operational reviews as well as training operations personnel in implementing these techniques in their areas.

The progress and ultimate success in achieving the benefits of operational reviews depend greatly on the reviewers' skills and what management and others think of them. Those assigned to an operational review engagement must possess the ability to review and analyze financial, management, and operational areas. The attributes of an effective operational reviewer include:

- Curiosity (imagination)
- Analytical ability

- Persuasiveness
- Good business judgment
- Common sense
- Objectivity
- Communication skills
- Initiative to develop techniques in such areas as work measurement, flow-charting, cost–benefit analysis, organizational analysis, computer processing, and so on
- Independence
- Confidence

Beyond those previously listed, the successful operational reviewer should possess the following attributes:

- The ability to spot the trouble areas—to look at a given situation and quickly determine what is getting in the way
- The ability to identify the critical problem areas, so as to avoid chasing mice when one should be chasing elephants

The application of the 80/20 rule states that operational reviews require 80 percent common sense and 20 percent technical expertise; and that 80 percent of the trouble areas cause 20 percent of the problems and 20 percent cause 80 percent of the problems.

- The ability to place oneself in management's position—to analyze the problem and ask questions from management's perspective

This is sometimes difficult because many times the reviewer has never been in an operational-related management position. Even when this is not true, the reviewer may have difficulty understanding the constraints under which the manager must work—in effect, what they can and cannot do.

- The skill to effectively communicate operational review results.

The success of the operational review is measured by the degree with which recommendations are implemented, and implementation is a direct by-product of effective communication. A rule of thumb in operational reviews is that the review team has been successful if it can convince management to adopt more than 50 percent of its recommendations.

OPERATIONAL REVIEW SKILLS AND ABILITIES

Although the attributes previuosly described would also be helpful to any manager, they are vital to an operational reviewer. While managers should have analytical ability, they may use it primarily to perform repetitive tasks. Operational reviewers, however, use these skills and abilities to assess a user's situations and recommend positive operational improvements.

The difference in required attributes for operational personnel and operational reviewers is similar to the difference between the left brain and the right brain. The left brain, which controls thinking and calculation processes, is more important to operations personnel performing repetitive tasks, whereas the right brain, which controls creativity and perceptual skills, is more critical to the operational reviewer. Basically, the operational reviewer needs a good balance of both, yet with a greater emphasis on the creative and perceptual side. This is why the best manager or operating personnel does not always make the best operational reviewer—and why things tend to stay the same.

To render effective services, the operational reviewer must have substantial knowledge of the total environment of the organization being examined and a high degree of skill and experience with the analytical techniques and tools needed to solve problems. The operational reviewer should also have sensitivity to, and understanding of, the values and goals of all the various people that make up the not-for-profit entity.

Someone trained in operating systems and procedures need not spend many years learning new methods before engaging in operational reviews—the basic techniques are the same. They mainly need to sharpen the problem identification and analytical skills they already possess. Operational reviews can be viewed as 80 percent practical analysis and common sense and 20 percent technical know-how.

The operational review requires the reviewer to possess a number of varied tools and techniques. The following are included among these review techniques:

- Planning and budget processes
- Cost analysis, such as direct, standard, and activity-based costing methods
- Preparation and analysis of systems flowcharts
- Development and/or analysis of computer systems and programs
- Evaluation of computer processing procedures and results
- Statistical sampling procedures
- Development and understanding of forecasts and projections
- Interviewing skills
- Organizational planning development and analysis
- Creation of goals and objectives and other performance standards
- Development and analysis of organizational structures
- Identification of best practices—both internal and external—and development of a program of continuous improvements
- Verification of the accuracy of data
- Determination of compliance with laws and regulations
- Use of sophisticated analytical techniques such as matrix analysis, linear regression correlation, critical path method, and so on

- Cost versus benefit analysis
- Communication skills; both oral and written
- Knowledge of current thinking and procedures such as benchmarking, to-tal quality management (TQM), reengineering, and so on
- Knowledge of specific areas of operations pertinent to not-for-profits, such as grants and contracts, fund accounting, restricted funds, program and project budgeting, non–business-related enterprises, and so on
- Use of volunteers—from both a board of directors and operating person-nel standpoint—including the recruiting, use, and rewarding of such vol-unteer personnel

Success as an effective operational reviewer is based on what is accom-plished—that is, recommendations made to management that are subsequently implemented. Operational reviews should be fascinating and rewarding to the reviewer as well as operations personnel. The individual's stature as an opera-tional reviewer, credibility of the entire review staff, management's and others' positive regard of the review staff—all will increase in proportion to the degree of success attained in the operational review.

Because of the number of different types and complexities of operational reviews and the varying skills required, supporting functional disciplines are often necessary to supplement the regular review staff's skills and abilities. However, it is not always practical to maintain personnel with all of the re-quired skills on the operational review staff. Thus, one should consider the skills that are necessary for the successful conduct of each operational review, and either make sure that such skills are available on staff or contract for needed outside expertise.

**THE OPERATIONAL REVIEWER
DOES WHAT MANAGEMENT HAS NOT DONE**

WHY NOT-FOR-PROFITS ARE IN EXISTENCE

Before the review team even thinks about performing an operational review of a not-for-profit, it is necessary to determine why the not-for-profit is in existence. When not-for-profit management is asked this question, invariably the answer is "to pursue our mission"—that is, to provide the services for which the not-for-profit was founded. Although this is true, the review team should be aware of the two main reasons the not-for-profit exists.

1. *The customer service business.* This means that the not-for-profit is in the business of fulfilling its mission by providing those services that its

customers or clients desire in the most satisfactory manner, so that they will continue to use the not-for-profit's services and refer it to others. The more demand for its services, the greater the demand for funding sources and contributors and volunteers to want to be part of the not-for-profit's operations.

An organizational philosophy that correlates with this goal that has been found to be successful is "to provide the highest quality services at the least possible cost."

2. *The cash conservation business.* This means that the not-for-profit delivers its desired services in the best manner possible with the least expenditure of cash. This allows for the cash not used to be available for providing other additional services. In effect, the goal of the not-for-profit is to maximize the delivery of desired services with the least possible expenditure of its cash. Although the not-for-profit is not in business to produce profits, it is in business to maximize the delivery of services. If the not-for-profit delivers such services with a minimum expenditure of cash, it may operate so that it increases its cash reserves, which can be used for other necessary purposes. Remember, the organization is a not-for-profit, not a nonprofit. In other words, there is no legal reason why a not-for-profit cannot operate at an excess of revenues over expenditures (in business terms this constitutes a profit), which over time creates financial empowerment.

The correlating philosophy to this goal can be stated as follows: "to achieve desired service results using the most efficient methods so that the not-for-profit can optimize the use of limited resources."

This means that the not-for-profit is in existence to stay for the long term—to serve its customers and clients and grow and prosper.

BUSINESSES A NOT-FOR-PROFIT IS NOT IN

Once short-term thinking is eliminated, not-for-profit management realizes it is not in the following businesses and decision making becomes simpler:

- *Funding business.* Successfully going after funding that does not move the not-for-profit in the direction of its vision and mission results only in inappropriate funding. It may result in additional funding that requires the not-for-profit to provide undesirable services and gear up for services that it may not desire to continue. Funding efforts must be addressed to the right services. Getting the wrong funding may result in the not-for-profit's being in the wrong business. Imbue upon all funding sources that they are purchasing services from the not-for-profit—not providing charity—and paying for those who cannot pay or for a community who cannot afford to maintain the not-for-profit otherwise.

- *Client statistic business.* Logging clients onto a client list where the not-for-profit cannot appropriately provide needed services results only in adding to a statistical base that may only be important to contributors and funding sources. The not-for-profit must know its service limitations and pursue providing the best-quality services to its limited client base. Providing less-than-desirable services to a wider client base is usually a prescription for failure.

- *Accounts receivable business.* Providing services prior to cash collections can result in placing the not-for-profit in a very precarious financial position. While many funding sources and third-party reimbursers (e.g., governmental and social service agencies) prefer to operate in this manner, it is not in the best interests of the not-for-profit. Not-for-profit management must seek to turn this system around—that is, collect the money first and then provide the service. This is not always easy or attainable in the not-for-profit sector.

- *Property and equipment business.* The not-for-profit needs to provide its services with the minimal amount of property and equipment. Typically, expenditures for this purpose provide little in the way of increasing service delivery. This may impress potential funders and contributors, but rarely does excessive property and equipment enhance operations. Such items need to be provided that enable the not-for-profit to be most efficient (e.g., computer systems), but not in excess.

- *Employment business.* The not-for-profit needs to get by with the fewest number of employees possible. It should never hire an additional employee (even where funding sources allow it) unless absolutely necessary. The not-for-profit needs to learn how to cross-train and use good employees across service lines, and to use volunteers most effectively. Not only do employees cost ongoing salaries and fringe benefits, but they also need to be paid attention—which results in organization building.

- *Management and administration business.* The more the not-for-profit has of management and administration, the more difficult it becomes to manage its operations. It is easier to work with less and be able to control operations than to spend time managing the managers. So much of management becomes getting in the way of those it is supposed to manage and meeting with other managers to discuss how to do this. Management becomes the promotion for doing.

If the not-for-profit can do both of these—that is, pay attention to its mission and stay away from the areas it should not be involved in—it will more than likely (outside economic and political factors notwithstanding) grow and prosper through well-satisfied stakeholders and keep itself in a positive cash conservation position, in spite of itself.

Keep in mind that the not-for-profit is a business, not a charitable enter-prise that eases public consciousness. While not-for-profits are not primarily mo-tivated by the concept of profits, there is nothing wrong in operating the not-for-profit most economically, efficiently, and effectively—and to build up re-serves for use in providing additional services in future periods. Understanding that the not-for-profit is a business and can profit from best practices developed in the private (and public) sector will assist the reviewer in assisting the not-for-profit better.

Not-for-profit management must decide which of the above factors it wishes to embrace as goals, which ones it will not include, and which additional criteria it will embrace. These criteria become the overriding conditions on which the not-for-profit conducts its operations and against which the operational re-view team will judge its effectiveness.

BASIC PRINCIPLES OF OPERATIONS

Each not-for-profit, usually through its board of directors and executive director (e.g., chief operating officer) determines the basic principles that guide its opera-tions. These principles become the foundation on which the not-for-profit bases its desirable goals. Examples of such basic principles include:

- Provide the most possible and best-quality services at the least possible cost.
- Set costs to the public (e.g., admissions, copays, tuition, and etc.) realisti-cally so that the public desire for its services can afford to use its ser-vices.
- Build trusting relationships with its stakeholders such as management, employees, volunteers, vendors, clients, and other interested parties.
- The entity is in the customer service and cash conservation businesses.
- Do not spend a dollar that does not need to be spent; a dollar not spent is a dollar to future reserves.
- Control costs effectively as there is more to be gained here than by in-creasing fund-raising efforts
- Manage the not-for-profit—do not let outside funders or interested par-ties manage the managers.
- Provide guidance and direction to the vision and mission of the not-for-profit, not crises.
- Identify the not-for-profit's services and its client base and then develop service programs that meet the needs of this client base. Serve the client—do not sell them undesired services.
- Do not hire employees unless they are absolutely needed.

- Keep facilities and equipment to the minimum necessary to provide desired services.
- Plan for the realistic—both revenues and expenditures—but develop contingency plans for the positive unexpected.

With sensible basic operating principles such as those above as the hallmark for the not-for-profit's operations, the not-for-profit can be clear as to the direction for positive improvements and avoid merely improving poor practices. Clear operating principles that make sense to all levels of the not-for-profit's organization allow the not-for-profit to identify and develop the proper organizational goals. In this manner, everyone in the not-for-profit is moving in the same desired direction. Operational review, with its basic principle of doing the right thing, assists the not-for-profit to build economic, efficient, and effective organizations and maintain them properly at all times using the correct techniques (i.e., best practices) for the situation. Operational review techniques assist the not-for-profit identifying its critical problem areas and then in treating the cause of the problems, not merely the symptoms.

KNOW WHY THE NOT-FOR-PROFIT IS IN EXISTENCE

ECONOMY, EFFICIENCY, AND EFFECTIVENESS

Operational review procedures embrace the concept of conducting operations for economy, efficiency, and effectiveness. The following is a brief description of each of the "three Es of operational reviews."

1. *Economy* (or the cost of operations). Is the organization carrying out its responsibilities in the most economical manner, that is, through due conservation of its resources? In appraising the economy of operations, and related allocation and use of resources, the reviewer may consider whether the organization is:
   - Following sound purchasing practices
   - Overstaffed as related to performing necessary functions
   - Allowing excess materials to be on hand
   - Using equipment that is more expensive than necessary
   - Avoiding the waste of resources
2. *Efficiency* (or methods of operations). Is the organization carrying out its responsibilities with a minimum expenditure of effort? Examples of operational inefficiencies that the reviewer should be aware of include:
   - Improper use of manual and computerized procedures
   - Inefficient paperwork flow

- Inefficient operating systems and procedures
- Cumbersome organizational hierarchy and/or communication patterns
- Duplication of effort
- Unnecessary work steps

Note that *economy* and *efficiency* are both relative terms, and it is not possible to determine whether the area under review has reached the maximum practicable level of either. However, the reviewer and operations personnel are continually looking for best practices in a program of continuous improvements. Economy and efficiency are continually being appraised and improved upon—they are not put in place based on the operational review and then ignored.

Economy and efficiency are concerned with achieving the optimum balance between costs and results. In performing this part of the review, the reviewer evaluates cost minimization, emphasizing reduction of costs, but not to the point where results are not accomplished. In addition, productivity maximization may be analyzed, but not to the point where the costs become excessive. In evaluating economy and efficiency, the reviewer analyzes the use of resources—people, facilities, equipment, supplies, and money. For example, the reviewer might analyze the following:

- Allocation of responsibilities and authority within the organization structure
- Physical deployment of distribution of resources
- Scheduling of resources—when people work, when facilities are used
- Segmentation of tasks into logical groupings
- Match between skill level, capacity, performance capability, and so on, and the way a resource is used
- Prices paid
- Charges levied
- Rate at which tasks are performed
- Number of tasks completed

Within the economy and efficiency concept, the reviewer does not ask whether the function is worthwhile in terms of what it accomplishes. The reviewer accepts that the function exists and asks whether this is the most economical and efficient way to get it done. Results are considered as part of the review of effectiveness.

3. *Effectiveness* (or results of operations). Is the organization achieving results or benefits based on stated goals and objectives or some other measurable criteria? The review of the results of operations includes:
   - Appraisal of the organizational planning system as to its development of realistic goals, objectives, and detail plans

- Assessment of the adequacy of management's system for measuring effectiveness
- Determination of the extent to which results are achieved
- Identification of factors inhibiting satisfactory performance of results

Although it is management's continuing responsibility to assess the results of operations, its objectives and measurement criteria are not always clearly defined. Without such clarification, the reviewer cannot meaningfully evaluate the results of operations. If management has not done so prior to starting the operational review, the reviewer should work with management to (1) state the objectives, (2) establish measurement criteria, and (3) establish methods for accumulating the data necessary to measure achievement of operational results.

Effectiveness is concerned with results and accomplishments achieved and benefits provided. In evaluating the effectiveness of operations, the reviewer asks whether the activity is achieving its ultimate intended purpose.

The relationship of economy and efficiency and their impact on results can be seen as a seesaw; that is, there is an attempt to balance them to achieve just the right amount of each. In a perfectly balanced situation, the cost of operations would be maintained at the lowest possible level without sacrificing efficiency (or the methods of operations) and effectiveness (or the results of operations)—thus effecting economy. At the same time, the methods of operations would be performed at the least possible cost without sacrificing results—thus producing efficiency. It should be clear why economy and efficiency are normally reviewed together as part of the operational review procedure.

It could be said that operational review is a review of operations performed from a management viewpoint to evaluate the economy, efficiency, and effectiveness of any and all operations, limited only by management's desires.

The three Es of an operational review—economy, efficiency, and effectiveness—are shown graphically in Exhibit 1.1. Note the examples shown for each E.

ECONOMY, EFFICIENCY, AND EFFECTIVENESS: THE CORNERSTONES OF THE OPERATIONAL REVIEW

WHY PERFORM AN OPERATIONAL REVIEW?

What are some of the reasons an operational review should be performed for a not-for-profit entity? The focus and scope of many operations in the not-for-profit sector have changed in recent years. Management has increased demands for more relevant information on the conduct of their operations and the related results than can be found solely in financial data. Management seeks more informa-

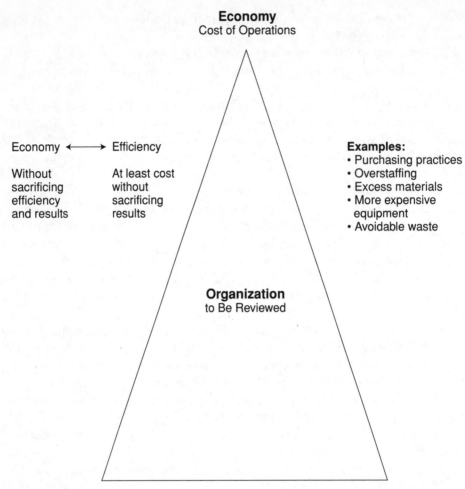

Economy
Cost of Operations

Economy ⟷ Efficiency

Without   At least cost
sacrificing   without
efficiency   sacrificing
and results   results

Examples:
• Purchasing practices
• Overstaffing
• Excess materials
• More expensive
  equipment
• Avoidable waste

Organization
to Be Reviewed

Efficiency
Methods of Operation

Examples:
• Manual vs. EDP
• Paperwork flow
• Systems and procedures
• Organizational hierarchy
  and communication
• Duplication of efforts
• Unnecessary work steps

Effectiveness
Results of Operation

Examples:
• Production/service
  provided
• Planning system:
  goals, objectives
  and detail plans
• Results achieved
• Expectations

Exhibit 1.1   The Operational Review Triangle: The Three Es: Economy, Efficiency, and Effectiveness

tion with which to judge the quality of service delivery operations and results and make operational improvements. That is why operational review techniques are needed to evaluate the effectiveness and efficiency of operations.

Not-for-profit management, with the assistance of others, both internal and external, are being asked more frequently to evaluate the organization's operations. Although this is not a new service for internal management to provide, requests by top management for such specific operational reviews have increased due to the greater emphasis on the economy, efficiency, and effectiveness of operations and related results. Many times, operations management does not possess the specific skills necessary for an objective evaluation of those activities reporting to them—they may be too close to the operations or they may be part of the problem. The technical skills internal and external consultants possess, particularly those of analysis, fact finding, and reporting, make them excellent choices for performing such operational reviews.

An operational review involves a systematic review of an organization's activities in relation to specified objectives. The general purposes of the operational review could be expressed as follows.

Assess Performance

To assess performance is to compare the way an organization conducts its activities with: (1) objectives established by management, such as organizational policies, standards, goals, objectives and detail plans; (2) comparisons to other, similar functions or individuals within the organization (internal benchmarking); and (3) comparisons to other organizations (external benchmarking).

Identify Opportunities for Improvement

Increased economy, efficiency, and effectiveness are the broad categories under which most improvements are classified. The reviewer may identify specific opportunities for improvement (best practices) by analyzing interviews with individuals (within or outside of the organization), observing operations, reviewing past and current operational data, analyzing transactions, making internal and external comparisons, and exercising professional judgment based on experience with the particular organization or others.

Develop Recommendations for Improvement or Further Action

The nature and extent of recommendations developed in the course of operational reviews vary considerably. In many cases, the reviewer may be able to make specific recommendations. In other cases, further study not within the scope of the review may be required. The reviewer should be continually looking for best practices (both internal and external) in a program for continuous improvements.

It may seem that operations personnel would be involved in establishing and implementing recommendations. However, in most instances such procedures are set by management, causing operations personnel to resist them (and often to sabotage them) and work against their being successful. Organization structure tends to evolve over a period of time; with minimal regard to economy, efficiency, and effectiveness.

In most not-for-profit entities, there are built-in incentives to increase organizational levels; such as budget systems that reward larger organizations and politicking to build empires. It is the reviewer's role to identify such organizational inefficiencies and to recommend improvements. However, when the reviewers do this, they do not put themselves in the position of recommending specific individual cuts. Assuming that the entity's personnel are all good employees (and hiring, orientation, training, and promotion policies and procedures are adequate), the reviewer may recommend achieving desired results with fewer overall personnel. However, it is then management's responsibility to decide what to do with extraneous personnel, such as downsizing or eliminating functions, departmental transfers, retraining, lateral moves, and so on. It is usually more desirable to be able to use existing good personnel somewhere else in the organization than to terminate them.

SPECIFIC OBJECTIVES

There are many reasons why not-for-profit management might desire to have an operational review performed. Some of these reasons are listed below. Keep in mind that management may be looking for a single objective (e.g., operational efficiency), a combination of objectives (e.g., least cost but most efficient systems—best practices), or its own specific agenda (e.g., achievement of results on the basis of cost versus benefits).

Financial and Accounting

- Adherence to financial policy
- Performance of accounting procedures
- Procedures performed by individuals with no incompatible functions
- Adequate audit trail exists
- Procedures can be observed

Adequacy of Internal Controls

- Accounting controls:
  - Safeguarding of assets
  - Reliability of financial records
  - System of authorizations and approvals

- Separation of duties
- Physical controls over assets
- Administrative controls:
  - Operational efficiency
  - Adherence to managerial policies
  - Adequacy of management information and reporting
  - Employee competency and training
  - Quality controls

Procedural Compliance

- Laws and regulations—federal, state, and local
- Adherence to administrative policy
- Performance of authorization and approval
- Evidence of action to achieve stated goals and objectives
- Adherence to long-range/short-term plans
- Achievement of management objectives
- Effective recruiting and training
- Evaluation of organizational policies
- Compliance to grants and contracts—from political entities, funding sources, foundations, and so on

Organizational Efficiency

- Clear understanding of responsibilities and authority
- Logical, nonconflicting reporting relationships
- Current job/functional descriptions
- Productivity maximization (internal benchmarking)
- Staffing levels compared with those of similar organizations (external benchmarking)
- Elimination of non–value-added functions and activities
- The right number of people to do the right job

Operational Results

- Organizational planning—goals, objectives, and detail plans
- Detail plan development and implementation—considering alternatives, constraints, cost–benefit, and resource allocation
- Evaluation of operational results:
  - Appropriateness of measurement criteria
  - Feedback on success or failure
  - Adjustment of goals, objectives, strategies
- Doing the right job, the right way, at the right time

**KNOW WHY THE OPERATIONAL REVIEW
IS BEING PERFORMED**

BENEFITS OF OPERATIONAL REVIEWS

Depending on its scope, an operational review can be of significant benefit to top management and staff, in some or all of the following ways:

1. Identifying problem areas, related causes and alternatives for improvement.

This is a major purpose of operational reviews. Although often aware of a problem, management cannot always define exactly its dimensions. The reviewer's third-party objective viewpoint helps to achieve the proper focus on operational problems. To define a problem in some instances, the reviewer need merely talk to operations personnel and then share their viewpoints with management. Keep in mind that people in operations are usually more aware of problems and their causes than management personnel.

The reviewer's role is also to identify the actual causes (not the symptoms or believed causes) of problems, which may be the result of management policy or actions. Finally, the reviewer must formulate realistic, practical solutions to these problems. This is where the reviewer's experience in working with numerous other departments and/or organizations is valuable. Remember, the reviewer is always looking for best practices (internal or external) that can be practically implemented in the specific situation as part of a program of continuous improvement. A good rule for the reviewer to follow is not to recommend any course of corrective action that he or she could not assist in implementing. Often, not-for-profit management will ask the review team or members of the team to come back and implement their recommendations.

2. Locating opportunities for eliminating waste and inefficiency—that is, cost reduction.

Keep in mind that each dollar of cost reduction (without sacrificing efficiency or effectiveness) contributes dollar-for-dollar to not-for-profits reserves— that is, it provides a dollar that can be used for other purposes. Cost reduction is a significant element in operational reviews. However, be wary of short-term cost reductions causing long-term problems (for instance, downsizing of operations and/or personnel when contributions or funding falls off). It is the role of the reviewer to assist the not-for-profit to operate at the lowest possible cost in relationship to adequate plans. Costs should always be at the correct level, and when costs need to be cut, proper decisions are made so as not to adversely affect operations and necessary service delivery. This is in contrast to typical cost cutting across the board, which not only constricts all operations, but also fails to provide for the necessary resources for those operations which actually need increased funds.

3. Locating opportunities to increase revenues—that is, funding improvement.

Increasing revenues also has an effect on the not-for-profit's reserves, yet only to the extent that additional revenues exceed the cost of obtaining them. Increasing revenues may, in fact, be detrimental in terms of operating efficiencies (short term and long term). Often, revenues are increased to present a more favorable budget picture in the short term or to increase service capacity, rather than on the basis of sound planning. In most not-for-profits a greater amount of resources (e.g., fund raising and grantsmanship) and emphasis is devoted to revenue improvement than to cost economies, even though effective cost cutting offers greater rewards.

4. Identifying undefined organizational goals, objectives, policies, and procedures.

It would be nice to think that all not-for-profits are doing effective long-term *perhaps* and short-term planning. However, in reality, this is usually more the exception than the rule. This means that the reviewer will have to assist not-for-profit management in recognizing undefined goals, objectives, and detailed plans and to assist in developing such plans prior to starting the operational review. Without defined plans, there are no yardsticks or milestones against which to measure the organization's effectiveness.

5. Identifying criteria for measuring the achievement of organizational goals.

See also p. 34

As mentioned in item 4, there is great likelihood that plans and related goals and objectives are not in existence. Even when they do exist, there may not be appropriate criteria for measuring their achievement, thus requiring the reviewer to assist management in the development of such criteria. The review team will typically possess the background and experience on which to base the development of sound criteria for the not-for-profit being reviewed.

6. Recommending improvement in policies, procedures, and organizational structure.

The reviewer may find instances in which the cause of the problem lies with existing policies or procedures. Policies should be set by senior management and relate to the rules by which the organization conducts its business (e.g., service to the customer). However, many times either such policies get in the way of operations personnel performing their functions (e.g., excessive controls and paperwork to process a client in-take and program acceptance) or insufficient authority is delegated to allow them to be most effective (e.g., sending a supervisor to investigate a client complaint). In these instances, the policies may be wrong and in need of correction.

Procedures are the ways in which functions are performed based on stated policies. As such procedures refer to operations, it might seem that operations personnel would be involved in establishing and implementing them. However, in most instances, procedures are set by management, causing operations personnel to resist them (and many times sabotage them) and work against their success.

Organization structure tends to evolve over a period of time, with minimal regard to economy, efficiency, or effectiveness. For many not-for-profits, there are never sufficient funds to properly staff some or all operating programs—with either paid employees or volunteers. In effect, the program may be always operating inefficiently. In other not-for-profits in which funds are more than adequate, there may be built-in incentives to increase organizational levels, such as budget systems that reward the growth of organizations and encourage politicking to build empires. It is the reviewer's role to identify such organizational inefficiencies and to recommend improvements. However, when reviewers do this, they do not put themselves in the position of recommending specific individual increases or cuts in staffing levels.

Assuming that the organization's personnel are all good employees (and that hiring, orientation, training, and promotion procedures are adequate), the reviewer may recommend achieving desired results with fewer overall personnel. However, it is then management's responsibility to decide what to do with extraneous personnel, possibly effecting departmental transfers, retraining, lateral moves, and so on. It is usually more desirable to use existing good personnel elsewhere in the organization than to terminate them.

7. Providing checks on performance by individuals and by organizational units.

Assuming that proper results have been defined for individuals and work units, it is the reviewer's responsibility to ensure that adequate checks or measurement criteria have been established to monitor progress toward their achievement. In cases in which such criteria exist but are deficient or do not exist at all, the reviewer must help not-for-profit management to develop appropriate criteria.

8. Reviewing compliance with legal requirements and organizational goals, objectives, policies, and procedures.

The reviewer makes sure that the organization complies with the laws and internal rules under which it performs its functions. If there is a lack of compliance, the reviewer defines the consequences. For instance, the not-for-profit may be receiving public funds from the federal, state, or local governmental entity that requires the not-for-profit to expend its funding for specific purposes. In addition, the not-for-profit may be receiving funding from private foundations that may require similar compliance and reporting.

9. Testing for existence of unauthorized, fraudulent or otherwise irregular acts.
Such testing for unauthorized fraudulent acts is normally a requirement for
operational reviews—particularly where such acts have an adverse effect on operations. Areas that might be considered for review include:

- Reasonableness of compensation—particularly those at the top
- Amount, degree, and type of fringe benefits
- Perquisites afforded to senior management (e.g., use of an automobile)
- Perception that expenditures for program services are a low portion of to-
  tal expenditures
- Including administrative costs (particularly where they are excessive) as
  part of program service costs
- Improper valuation of worthless investments and receivables
- Excessive amount of assets held by the not-for-profit
- Portion of revenues earned from fees for goods and services
- Portion of revenues contributed by key individuals such as the executive
  director (who may also be the founder) and individual board members
- Pressure to maximize investment returns
- The perception that operations are made to appear as efficient as possible

10. Assessing management information and control systems.
The reviewer will address a number of concerns in this area:

- Are reporting systems adequate to provide management and operations
  personnel the information necessary to effectively operate all aspects of
  the organization?
- Is the level of detail commensurate to the level of operations (i.e., more
  detail at lower levels; less detail at higher levels)?
- Is there information lacking that should be present?
- Are all key indicators being considered (e.g., number of clients or atten-
  dants, services provided, and degree of satisfaction)?

11. Identifying possible trouble spots in future operations.
Many times, the reviewer senses a future problem based on troubles in the
past. For instance, problems with past computer conversions may indicate future
troubles with an extensive computer processing upgrade. Computer processing
may be a critical area for most not-for-profits because the not-for-profit typically
does not have such expertise on its staff. Many such computer implementations
are done by an outside consultant either on a "pro bono" basis or for less-than-
normal charges. Even when such computerization is accomplished adequately,
often there is little residual expertise within the not-for-profit.

In addition, as many not-for-profits are continually fighting a budget and
cash crunch, many projects are substantially completed by volunteer or in-kind

assistance. This may result in less-than-desirable results initially, together with a lack of effective backup in properly maintaining the project.

12. Providing an additional channel of communication between operating levels and top management.

In many organizations there is a clear (or unclear) separation between management and operations—that is, management makes the decisions and operations personnel carry them out. One of the most important benefits of the operational review is the reviewer's ability to convey operational concerns to management in those instances in which such concerns are not being communicated on an ongoing basis.

Because many not-for-profits are staffed by personnel who perceive themselves as working for less compensation and fewer benefits than parallel personnel in the private sector, such personnel may not be as committed as they should to identify and correct obvious operational concerns. In addition, there may be less commitment in bringing such matters to the attention of not-for-profit management. Many times, not-for-profit top management are adequately qualified in the delivery of expected services (e.g., counseling services, substance abuse treatment, the arts, etc.), but not as qualified in the business side of operations. Accordingly, other staff may feel that communicating around operational concerns with top management is a futile effort. In addition, top management may be the founders of the not-for-profit and with their egos and pride of authorship getting in the way may not be as objective and forthcoming in listening.

13. Providing an independent, objective evaluation of operations.

Both management and operations personnel are often too close to what is going on within their own operations to effectively evaluate their results. The independent operational reviewer can do this objectively, pointing out those areas in need of improvement as well as those that are being performed well. Top management, as described above, is more likely to listen to those from the outside who really know something than to not-for-profit employees and volunteers who would not be working there if they really knew anything.

**SELL THE BENEFITS OF OPERATIONAL REVIEWS
AND THEY WILL SELL THEMSELVES**

WHAT FUNCTIONS TO REVIEW

The most critical question for the not-for-profit to answer is what function or functions to include in the operational review. Where should it review? Does it perform the operational review for all functions of the not-for-profit or for only selected areas? A good starting point is to list the not-for-profit's major functions, to check off those in which operational review would be most helpful, and then to prioritize each function as to its criticalness and/or the desired order of review. Exhibit 1.2. is a sample checklist of a representative not-for-profit's major organizational functions.

One way to decide which functions to review is to determine how critical each function is to overall not-for-profit operations. For instance, for a counseling-type not-for-profit, the most critical areas might be the client intake, service delivery, and support functions. For a service-oriented not-for-profit such as a rape crisis center, where personnel costs are approximately 70 percent of total expenditures, the personnel function might be more critical. For an arts organization, the most critical functions could be talent, production, and quality delivery. Normally, reviewers work with a limited budget in terms of hours allocated to the operational review, so they are greatly concerned to use these hours on functional areas that offer the greatest potential for operational improvements in return for their effort. Criteria for determining a company's critical areas include:

- Areas with large numbers in relationship to other functions; such as percentage of revenues and costs, client contact hours, number of productions/events, percentage of total budget, number of outcomes, and levels of personnel.
- Areas in which controls are weak; for example, a lack of effective service delivery scheduling and production, management reporting, or organizational planning and control systems.
- Areas subject to abuse or laxity; for example, there may be client scheduling and contact controls that allow service delivery transactions to go unreported and undetected, uncontrollable time and cost reporting, and ineffective personnel evaluation procedures.
- Areas that are difficult to control; for example, there may be ineffective printing and copying, material and supplies, or time recording procedures. In many not-for-profits, the concept of control may be an unpopular concept—emanating from the desire not to be like the business sector or a lack of understanding by management and operations. Such controls need to be strengthened for operational efficiency as well as to provide for reliable and accurate reporting.
- Areas where functions are not performed efficiently or economically; e.g., there may be ineffective procedures, duplication of efforts, unnecessary work steps, inefficient use of resources such as computer processing equipment and volunteers, under-or overstaffing, and excess purchases.
- Areas indicated by ratio, change, or trend analysis, such as characterized by wide swings up or down when compared over a number of periods. Examples include client contact changes by type of service, costs by major

BOARD OF DIRECTORS

❏ Members—number and who are they?
❏ Selection policy
❏ Purpose and function
❏ Policy setting
❏ Areas of control
❏ Advisory or operational

MANAGEMENT

❏ Organizational
❏ Departmental or program
❏ Operational responsibilities
❏ Reporting and control

PLANNING SYSTEMS

❏ Organizational—strategic, long term, and short term
❏ Departmental and program planning
❏ Detail planning and budgeting

PERSONNEL

❏ Number and type—by department, program, and in total
❏ Hiring procedures
❏ Orientation and training procedures
❏ Evaluation procedures
❏ Staffing levels—employees and volunteers, full time and part time
❏ Promotion and firing procedures
❏ Payroll procedures—time reporting and control and payroll processing

ACCOUNTING

❏ Assets—reporting and control (e.g., accounts receivable, furniture, and equipment)
❏ Liabilities—reporting and control (e.g., accounts payable, long- and short-term debt)
❏ Budget procedures—planning integration, fixed versus variable, analysis and control
❏ Payroll processing—inside/outside, procedures, controls, reporting
❏ Billing and collections (if applicable)—client/third party, procedures, follow-up
❏ Financial reporting—overall NPO, programs/projects, funds, grants
❏ General ledger—chart of accounts, financial statements, financial/operational reporting

COST ACCOUNTING PROCEDURES

❏ Program/project costing—accumulation, reporting, and analysis
❏ Revenue versus cost analysis
❏ Cost versus benefit analysis
❏ Cost allocation procedures

Exhibit 1.2   Checklist of Major Not-for-Profit Organizational Functions

---

COMPUTER PROCESSING

❑ Systems design and analysis
❑ Programming and software development
❑ Computer equipment and networks
❑ Computer operating procedures
❑ Data control—input, processing, and output
❑ Reporting—what is there (significance) and what is missing

OPERATIONS

❑ Service delivery operations—intake, service providing, close out
❑ Event/production planning—planning, development, execution, follow-up, promotion
❑ Administration—management, control, reporting
❑ Personnel—use, control, and reporting
❑ Fund raising—grants and contracts, events, drives
❑ Facilities—building, office/service delivery space, furniture and equipment

---

Exhibit 1.2 *(Continued)*

category, number of personnel (employees and volunteers), types of revenues (e.g., client fees, event attendance, and grants), and so forth.

- Areas in which not-for-profit management has identified specific weaknesses or needs for improvement such as personnel functions, service delivery procedures, computer processing operations, and management reporting. The reviewer will receive greater cooperation in addressing these areas as management is already responsive to the need for improvement.

Although not-for-profit management has identified critical areas for review, another factor to consider when choosing these critical operational areas is the willingness of the personnel in the area to cooperate in the performance of the review. First, those management and operating personnel in these areas should want to have their operations reviewed and be willing to work with the reviewers in the improvement of their operations. Without such top management and operations commitment, the operational review is not likely to succeed. Second, staff and operating personnel must be willing to work with the reviewers both in performing the operational review and in the subsequent implementation of operational improvements. Cooperation at all levels of the organization is essential to a successful operational review.

The reviewer must enlist the cooperation of all personnel—members of management to ensure top commitment to the review, and operations personnel to help in identifying areas to review and proposed improvements. Normally, in most not-for-profit operations, the staff or operating personnel know precisely what is going on day-by-day, and with firsthand knowledge of operations, can help the reviewer to identify the most critical areas to review.

**CHASE THE ELEPHANTS
DO NOT MILK THE MICE**

THE BUDGET

In addressing the number of critical areas to be covered in the operational review, it is important to understand the relationship between budgeted review time and the scope of operational review work desired to be accomplished. In many situations, the budget hours are established first and then the scope of the operational review is made to fit within the budget. While this procedure may work from an internal standpoint in regard to budget and staffing, it does not fully take into account the aspect of such reviews that require flexibility and expandability of formulated operational review work programs. In addition, it is important for the reviewer and not-for-profit management to consider the cost against the expected benefits of the specific operational review. This is a significant concept in helping to determine how much time to allocate to the operational review. In many cases, the not-for-profit has limited funds to allocate to the operational review, and therefore, the review team must be careful to maximize their effectiveness in conducting the review.

Remember: In performing an internal- or external-type financial audit, the audit group is budgeting staff time and related costs. In effect, the financial audit becomes a cost center. In an operational review, however, operational benefits and dollar savings should greatly surpass the cost of the review (savings should be at least five times its cost). In effect, the operational review becomes a profit center. Theoretically, the more operational reviews are done, the greater the savings realized by the organization. In reality, however, some guidelines are needed to establish the extent of an operational review in a given functional area, once the critical areas for review have been identified.

There are a number of factors to consider in establishing the operational review budget:

- *The scope of the operational review.* For example, are all significant operational areas to be reviewed, or only the major ones identified? Is this to be an operational review of the entire not-for-profit's operations, a functional review, a program or project review, or a review of an area across functional lines (e.g., use of volunteers).
- *The frequency of the operational review.* Is the operational review of major scope to be done on a one-time basis, which requires more up-front planning and research; or is it to be performed for an area that is reviewed on a regular basis and requires minimal up-front efforts?
- *The nature of the not-for-profit's operations.* For example, service delivery operations dealing primarily with the use of staff time, such as a counseling, cri-

sis intervention, substance abuse treatment, and AIDS-related services which normally requires more time for an operational review than a referral and information operation such as a day care or medical referral service.

- *The degree of management effectiveness.* Functional areas that are ineffectively managed will normally require more operational review time than those that are more effectively managed. The not-for-profit executive director may be quite effective, but operational management and staff may not be effective or vice versa. The board of directors may be overcontrolling and really operating the not-for-profit resulting in ineffective management and operations. Whatever the situation, these factors of management effectiveness need to be considered.
- *The expectation of benefits.* Those areas that afford the greatest expected benefits, in terms of the number of potential recommendations or savings, should be the areas reviewed first. However, these areas may take more time to review than those with lesser expectations. The budget time to be allocated to any function and activity must be considered in terms of the benefits to be derived from the use of that time. Minimize the time—maximize the benefits.

Operational reviews, to be most successful, require a large amount of preplanning, fact gathering, and research. This can make the costs of conducting an operational review considerable. However, when compared with the potential benefits and savings, costs become less significant. That is why, when determining how much time to spend on the operational review, it is best to use a cost-versus-benefit approach—tempered, of course, with the reality of available staff and hours. In effect, an effort should be made to cover competently as many of the major critical areas as possible within the limited staffing constraints.

THE INITIAL SURVEY

To achieve the greatest results from limited operational review resources, the reviewer identifies those areas of major importance and those offering the greatest potential savings or benefits. The identification of these areas is done as part of an initial survey, either prior to or as part of the planning phase of the operational review. If performed before the planning phase, either because the client requests it, because of the relatively small scope or budget, or for some other reason, the survey usually consists of some type of management and operational questionnaire. The purpose of the questionnaire is to determine what functions are performed, who performs each function, why each is performed, and how each is performed.

Answers to these questions should provide insight into the organization's objectives, activities, work performance, systems and procedures, limits of authority, and so on. The reviewer uses the questionnaire as a guideline and does not rely solely on yes or no responses. This is a quick review tool to help identify critical areas for further review. However, for large operational reviews a survey of this kind should not be used in lieu of the planning phase, as it is still the reviewer's responsibility to substantiate, with adequate evidence, the identification of critical operational areas to be reviewed.

Exhibit 1.3. is a sample operational review initial survey form. The purpose of the initial survey is to identify areas of major importance in the total organization or specific operations to be reviewed. Improper identification results in expending unnecessary effort on less significant activities and insufficient effort in more important areas. The survey should provide for more detailed answers, rather than simple yes or no responses. The same questions are reviewed with various personnel; such as departmental management, functional supervision, and operations and support personnel. The reviewer thus isolates patterns of agreement and disagreement, as well as various interpretations and perceptions, that lead to the correct conclusions. Where necessary, each question is supported by available documentation. This form can also be used as part of the more formal planning phase, but should be more specific to a departmental or functional area.

The initial survey should be developed specifically for the not-for-profit being reviewed, individualized by the way it is organized, the services that it provides, and the manner in which it operates. The survey form can be completed by top management (e.g., the board of directors and the executive director), operations management, staff and operations personnel, or a combination of these parties. The reviewer is attempting to get a quick fix of not-for-profit operations, particularly looking for strengths and weaknesses and agreed on patterns by those completing the survey form. The review and analysis of the survey form becomes the starting point for the operational review and many times provides direct assistance in identifying critical operational areas for inclusion in the operational review.

A model survey is included on the accompanying website.

**KNOW YOUR OBJECTIVES
BEFORE YOU START**

ENGAGEMENT DEVELOPMENT

An operational review could be conducted by an external consulting firm, an internal review group, an independent in-house unit, departmental personnel, volunteers, or a combination of staff from these entities. Whichever organization has primary responsibility for conducting the operational review, the major steps in

PLANNING AND BUDGETING

1. How does the not-for-profit plan? Describe the system of planning.
2. Does a strategic and long-range plan exist? If so, attach copy.
3. Do current short-term plans exist? If so, attach copy.
4. What are plans for expansion or improvement?
5. What are plans for facilities or operations development?
6. What are plans for future financing? Grants, contracts, fund raising, or borrowing?
7. What are personnel plans? Additions, deletions, changes?
8. How does the organization budget? Describe the system.
9. Does a current budget exist? Does it include revenues and expenditures? Obtain or prepare copy.
10. Do budget versus actual statistics exist for the last two full years of operations? Obtain or prepare copy.

PERSONNEL AND STAFFING

1. Does an organizational chart exist? Obtain or prepare copy.
2. Do functional job descriptions exist for each block on the organization chart? Obtain or prepare copies.
3. Do staffing statistics (employees and volunteers) by functional area exist? Obtain or prepare copy.
4. Is there a system of employee evaluations? Describe.
5. How are employees recruited, hired, evaluated, promoted, and fired? Describe procedures.
6. How are employees oriented and trained? Describe.
7. What are promotional policies? Describe.
8. How are raises and promotions determined? Describe.
9. Is there a grievance mechanism? Describe.
10. What type of personnel records are maintained? Obtain copies.

MANAGEMENT

1. Does a board of directors exist? Attach list of names and credentials.
2. Is there a criteria for selecting members of the board of directors? Describe.
3. What are the expectations of the board of directors? Describe.
4. What is the major function of the board? Policy setting, governing, advisory, operational, legal only?
5. Who is considered top management (e.g., executive director)? Attach list of names and credentials.
6. Who is considered middle management? Attach list of names and credentials.
7. How adequate are existing reports in furnishing information for making management decisions? Describe.
8. Are there tools for internal downward communication to the staff? Attach copies.
9. Is authority effectively delegated to management and operational levels? Describe.
10. Are there effective internal upward communication tools to the management levels? Describe and provide copies of examples.

(Continued)

Exhibit 1.3 Sample Operational Review Initial Survey Form

POLICIES AND PROCEDURES

1. Who is responsible for setting policies for the not-for-profit? (e.g., board, executive director, operations management)?
2. Do written policies exist? Obtain copies.
3. Are written policies current?
4. Who is responsible for establishing operating systems and procedures?
5. Are systems and procedures documented? Obtain or prepare copy.

COMPUTER PROCESSING

1. What computer equipment is used? Obtain or prepare copy of equipment list and locations.
2. What major applications are computerized? Obtain or prepare copy of list of applications with general systems narratives.
3. Are management, operational, control, and exception reports provided? Describe.
4. What is total cost of equipment rental or purchase price if owned?
5. Is the computer system networked throughout the organization? Describe.
6. What operating system is used? (e.g., Windows).

SERVICE DELIVERY SYSTEMS

1. Is a computerized service delivery control system being used? Describe.
2. What type of service delivery processes are being used? Describe.
3. How are clients, events, projects, and so on controlled? Describe.
4. Is a cost system used, by program, project, client, event, and so on? Describe.
5. Are operational and management reports provided to control service delivery operations? Obtain or prepare copies.
6. Is a program, project, or event control system being used? Computerized? Describe.
7. What type of staff control procedures are being used? Describe.

ACCOUNTING SYSTEM

1. What is the chart of accounts used? Obtain or prepare copy.
2. Is the accounting system computerized? Obtain documentation.
3. What financial (and operational) reports are produced? Obtain documentation.
4. Is there an internal audit function? By and to whom?
5. Are there internal operating reports produced? Obtain copies and determine uses.

REVENUES

1. What are the sources of revenue for the last five years? Obtain or prepare statistics.
2. Have there been any substantial changes in revenues during this period? Document.
3. Are actual versus budgeted revenue data available? Obtain or prepare copy.

Exhibit 1.3   *(Continued)*

EXPENSES

1. What are the major expense accounts used? Obtain or prepare copy.
2. What are actual expenses for these accounts for the last five years? Obtain or prepare copy.
3. Have there been any substantial changes in expenses during this period? Document.
4. Are actual versus budgeted expense data available? Obtain or prepare copy.

PURCHASING

1. What is purchasing authority? Obtain or prepare copy of policies.
2. Is purchasing centralized or decentralized? Describe operations.
3. How are purchases processed? Describe operating procedures and practices.

RESPONSIBILITY AND AUTHORITY

1. Are responsibilities clearly defined and understood by managers and staff personnel?
2. Has authority been delegated effectively to managers and lower levels within the organization?

Exhibit 1.3 *(Continued)*

its development and performance should be similar. These steps are graphically summarized in Exhibit 1.4.

Recognize and Define the Problem

The first step is to recognize and define the problem. Normally, it is management's prerogative to identify the major problem area or areas to be addressed in an operational review. However, if requested by management, the reviewer can assist in such problem definition as described previously, or the reviewer may perform a preliminary survey to identify significant operational areas to be reviewed.

Gather Appropriate Data

The second step is to gather the appropriate supporting data and is usually accomplished by the operational reviewer. The purpose of this data gathering is to provide background information relative to the problem areas defined in the first step, so as to substantiate the problem situation.

Evaluate the Situation

The next step is to evaluate the situation within the not-for-profit to determine such things as the organizational structure and resources available. These are the

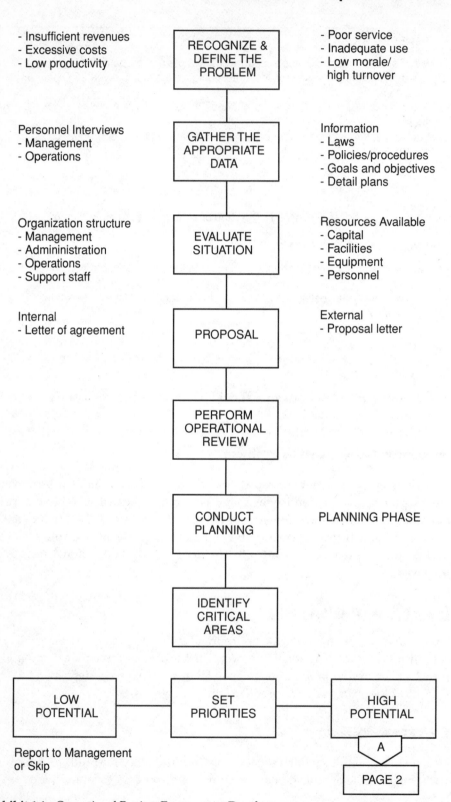

- Insufficient revenues
- Excessive costs
- Low productivity

RECOGNIZE & DEFINE THE PROBLEM

- Poor service
- Inadequate use
- Low morale/ high turnover

Personnel Interviews
- Management
- Operations

GATHER THE APPROPRIATE DATA

Information
- Laws
- Policies/procedures
- Goals and objectives
- Detail plans

Organization structure
- Management
- Admininistration
- Operations
- Support staff

EVALUATE SITUATION

Resources Available
- Capital
- Facilities
- Equipment
- Personnel

Internal
- Letter of agreement

PROPOSAL

External
- Proposal letter

PERFORM OPERATIONAL REVIEW

CONDUCT PLANNING

PLANNING PHASE

IDENTIFY CRITICAL AREAS

LOW POTENTIAL   SET PRIORITIES   HIGH POTENTIAL

Report to Management or Skip

A

PAGE 2

Exhibit 1.4   Operational Review Engagement Development

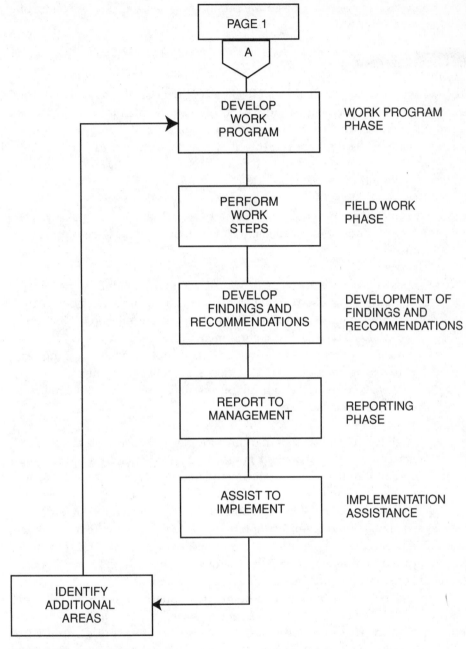

Exhibit 1.4 *(Continued)*

factors on which the reviewer bases the proposal to management for conducting the operational review.

Proposal Letter

The reviewer has gathered sufficient background data on the operational problem areas identified for review, and has decided on the plan for conducting the operational review. Now the reviewer needs to submit a written proposal or engagement letter to clarify for not-for-profit management such considerations as:

- Background of the situation describing the need for the operational review
- Operational review engagement objectives
- Scope of the review engagement or which operational areas are to be included
- The reviewer's approach to conducting the operational review
- Proposed general work steps to be included in the conduct of the review
- Operational review staff and client personnel who are expected to participate in the operational review; including each one's responsibilities and expectations as well as time commitments
- Reporting requirements to management, such as progress meetings and final reporting, including a description of all deliverable output
- Benefits to be provided as a result of conducting the operational review
- Estimates of time and cost

Although it is usually an external consulting firm that submits the proposal letter to management, it is also good practice for an internal group to submit a similar proposal prior to the start of the operational review engagement. The major purpose of such an internal proposal letter is to ensure clear communication, as to the purpose and scope of the operational review, between the review group and management. In this context, the internal proposal becomes a letter of understanding between the internal review group and management. The contents of the internal proposal letter would differ somewhat from an external proposal, and would only include those areas necessary to the situation.

Exhibit 1.5 provides an example of an operational review proposal (or engagement) letter for the Counseling Agency, as well as sample time and cost budget estimates. These cost estimates are for the reviewer's use and are not given to not-for-profit management. Note that an external consulting firm proposing to perform an operational review for a client may have to estimate time and costs before starting an engagement. To enable the reviewer to estimate accurately requires sufficient initial survey work and adequate prior experience on similar engagements. Although it is obviously advantageous to estimate the amount of field work required after completion of the planning phase, the client normally wants to know these amounts up front. The sample budget provided is

The Counseling Agency

December 10, 20XX

Ms. Carmen Counselor, Executive Director
The Counseling Agency
XXXX Avenue
Anywhere, USA XXXXX

Dear Ms.Counselor:

Reider Associates is pleased to submit this proposal to The Counseling Agency relative to technical assistance in the conducting of an operational review relative to the analysis of documents processing, workload analysis and compliance with accounting practices and appropriate training.

This proposal letter outlines our approach to providing such consultative services as well as our proposed budget for providing these services. We believe the best results will be obtained by our designing our consultative efforts to meet the specific needs of your agency and other concerned parties.

We should be able to complete the entire scope of work by your desired ending project date of March 31, 20XX should we be able to begin this engagement by the third week of January, 20XX.

We appreciate the opportunity to submit this proposal and are prepared to discuss any aspects with you, should you so desire. Moreover, we welcome the opportunity to work with you on this important project.

BACKGROUND

The Counseling Agency (TCA) is interested in analyzing their operations as to the flow of documents, the workload of individual employees and departments, the determination of whether general internal accounting practices are applicable to their responsibilities and are in accordance with general accounting principles. In addition, The Counseling Agency management is interested in providing necessary individual and group training relative to present requirements as well as any areas recommended for improvement.

Against this background, TCA management is concerned as to the effectiveness of their operations and whether they are functioning most economically in producing the maximum results. Accordingly, TCA requested Reider Associates to submit this proposal as to how they would assess such operational effectiveness and provide technical assistance that would enable TCA employees to become more effective in providing required services.

PERSONNEL

Dr. Rob Reider, CPA, MBA, PhD, President of Reider Associates, would be personally responsible for the technical conduct and successful completion of this important project. Colleen Kelley and Robert Ott, associates of the firm, would be assigned to work with Dr. Reider in the conduct of this engagement. Dr. Barbara Reider, PhD, Principal of the firm, would act as a consultant to the engagement. All of the above personnel have

(Continued)

Exhibit 1.5   Sample Operational Review Proposal Confirming Letter

extensive experience in developing and conducting similar consulting engagements for other clients in both the public and private sectors. The resumés for these individuals are attached to this proposal. Reider Associates qualifications are also included as an attachment to this proposal.

METHOD OF IMPLEMENTATION—OUR APPROACH

We believe that the consultative assistance to be provided by us will ensure a positive and effective method of evaluating present operational effectiveness and provide support to TCA and its employees to enable them to become more effective. The scope of our assistance focuses on providing for the design and implementation of effective operational review techniques which will encompass present service delivery procedures as well as provide for flexibility for growth and adaptation for operational continuity. Accordingly, we plan to provide our consultative assistance to address your requested scope of work in the following manner:

1. General Review

General review of existing methods and procedures related to TCA operations and expected results. This review will provide us with a clear understanding of present TCA goals and objectives (desired results), accomplishments to date, and a clear understanding of present systems and procedures. This will allow us to provide the most effective assistance in performing reviews of individual performance, transaction processing, record maintenance, and developing recommendations for improvement, and providing technical assistance.

As part of this general review, we would plan to include at least the following activities:

- Meeting and interview with Ms. Carmen Counselor, TCA Executive Director to provide us with an overview of TCA operations and expectations as well as desired results from our consultative assistance in performing this operational review.
- Meeting and interview with Mr. Jason Adams, TCA Assistant Director to provide us with his insight as to TCA operations, potential areas for improvement, specific concerns to be addressed, and expected results of our participation.
- Development and design of pre-interview forms for all TCA personnel included in this study to provide us with overall concerns as to TCA operations and specific job responsibilities of each TCA employee to be included in this study. Examples of such forms include:
  - Operational Initial Survey Form
  - Job Responsibilities Questionnaire Form
- Entrance conference to introduce our personnel to TCA employees, explain fully the purpose for the study, communicate TCA management commitment, and establish effective rapport between Reider Associates and TCA personnel.

2. Review of Operations

We will develop appropriate operational review tools and procedures based on our general review as outlined above. Our operational review of TCA activities would encompass at least the following areas of operation:

Exhibit 1.5 *(Continued)*

- Program administration and management
- Program planning and evaluation
- Internal operating procedures
- Organization and use of people
- Effective use of resources
- Scope of TCA activities and related transactions
- Relevance to TCA and funding sources goals and objectives
- Integration of TCA activities to other related entities
- Population served: TCA users and others
- Measurement systems: services provided and effectiveness, relationship to desired results, impact on relevant activities, and so on

The focus of our operational review would be to identify internal processes and activities, areas of responsibility, organizational considerations, understandings of job responsibilities, accounting principles, and internal controls. As a result of our operational review we would expect to develop recommendations as streamlining internal processes, maximizing organizational efficiencies, eliminating such things as unnecessary activities and duplications, and strengthening employee understanding of organizational purpose, individual and group responsibilities, accounting principles, and internal controls.

We would plan to interview TCA employees in all areas of operations—service delivery as well as administrative functions. The focus of such TCA personnel interviews would be to:

- Identify job responsibilities and the manner in which each individual carries out such responsibilities.
- Identify TCA staff members involved in similar activities (e.g., counseling services, intake procedures, and processing documents).
- Analyze and review document flow as to processing operational and financial transactions including:
  - Identification of types of documents processed
  - Determination of the purpose of each document
  - Identification of the procedures followed in processing each document
- Determine the appropriateness and efficiency of each process and the meaningfulness of TCA employees (and others) involved.
- Develop recommendations as to more efficient, economical, and effective systems and methods.

3. Analysis of Work Distribution

Based on our personnel interviews, observations, review and analysis of work practices, we would analyze the distribution of the work involved in the processes identified above. Included in this work step would be the following activities:

- Document the process for approving each type of operational and financial transaction and develop recommendations as to more efficient (and time saving) procedures and the reduction or elimination of the number of approvals.
- Identify the relevant tasks and approximate monthly volume of transactions

(Continued)

Exhibit 1.5   *(Continued)*

processed by TCA individual staff member—or by program, project, work unit, or department.

- Identify the average amount of time (and document steps in calculating) needed to complete each task and transaction.
- Prepare a report of each TCA staff workload (and/or program, project, work unit, or department).

4. Internal Control Review

Review relevant internal operating and accounting controls (manual off-line and computer on-line) on operational and financial transaction processing as they relate to acceptable administrative and accounting practices.

As part of this review, we would:

a. Identify any controls that are missing or inadequate
b. Provide a written report as to the operation of TCA's internal controls which would include a description of present controls as well as recommendations for improvement

5. Engagement Reporting

We would plan to meet with appropriate TCA management and operations personnel as necessary during the course of this engagement. We expect that Mr. Jason Adams, TCA Assistant Director would be our liaison and coordinator during the course of this engagement. Should any interim progress reporting be necessary, we would plan to coordinate such reporting with Mr. Adams.

We would plan to have an end of engagement oral reporting session with TCA management and operations personnel to review the results of the engagement and clarify engagement findings and develop an agreement as to those areas for operational improvement that are desired to be pursued.

We will submit a final report to TCA management relative to our performance under this contract enumerating the scope of our work, our findings (both general and specific to a department, work unit, program, project or individual), our recommendations, and accomplishments. All recommendations will be documented so as to enable TCA management and operations personnel to implement them easily and effectively. We would, of course, be available to assist TCA in such implementation efforts.

6. Training Sessions

We would develop and conduct any necessary individual and group training sessions related to any operational areas for improvement or areas recommended for improvement. For each such training session, we would be responsible for developing the training materials and contents such as outlines, text, flowcharts, overheads, case studies, and references. In addition, we would be responsible for the on-site conducting of any such training sessions. It is our understanding that TCA would be responsible for providing the training location and duplicating any participant training materials.

COST FOR SERVICES

The fees for our services are determined by the amount of time actually spent on the consulting project. For this engagement, we would use an hourly composite rate of $150 which would include all personnel involved. Based on our experience on similar

Exhibit 1.5   *(Continued)*

engagements, we estimate that our time participation for this engagement (excluding training sessions) would be approximately 120 hours or a total cost not to exceed $18,000. In addition, we would expect to be reimbursed for all out-of-pocket expenses such as meals, lodging, transportation and the like. The cost for any necessary training sessions would be at the rate of $250 per hour which would include development and providing of all training materials, and the conducting of training sessions (at least two presenters). We estimate twelve hours of training at a cost not to exceed $3,000. Any additional technical assistance that you might require would be billed at the $150 per hour rate. Based upon our experience on similar work of this nature, our proposed budget as to time expended by work unit and related costs is as follows:

PROPOSED BUDGET

Activity	Cost For Services	Estimated Hours
1. General Review hours	$ 3,600	24 hours
2. Review of Operations	5,400	36
3. Analysis of Work Distribution	2,400	16
4. Internal Control Review	2,400	16
5. Engagement Reporting	4,200	28
	$18,000	120
6. Training Estimate	3,000	12
Total Fees	$21,000	132

The above includes our total fees to provide services under this engagement. We are not planning to use any subcontractors. We expect that each of our participants on this engagement will be spending approximately equal time. We cannot estimate the completion date of each work element as it is based on the starting date. However, should this engagement start by the third week in January 20XX, it should be completed by your requested end date of March 31, 20XX.

We appreciate the opportunity to submit this proposal and are prepared to discuss any aspects with you, should you so desire. Moreover, we welcome the opportunity to work with you on this important project.

Should you have any further questions, please let me know.

Rob Reider, President

REIDER ASSOCIATES

Exhibit 1.5 *(Continued)*

for a relatively small operational review. In a situation in which potential operational review engagements may be larger in scope, the two phases may be budgeted separately.

Although it is usually an external consulting firm that submits the proposal letter to management, it is also good practice for an internal group to submit a similar proposal prior to the start of the operational review engagement. The major purpose of such an internal proposal letter is to ensure clear communication, as to the purpose and scope of the operational review, between the review group and management. In this context, the internal proposal becomes a letter of understanding between the internal review group and management. The contents of the internal proposal letter would differ somewhat from an external proposal, and would include only those areas necessary to the situation.

THE OPERATIONAL REVIEW PROPOSAL
COMMUNICATES WHAT WILL BE DONE

Perform the Operational Review

The proposal letter has been submitted and accepted by management. Now what? Now begins the actual operational review, using the proposed phase approach of planning, work program, field work, development of findings and recommendations, and reporting. Should management request it, the reviewer might also help to implement the recommended operational improvements. Or client personnel may feel confident that they can implement the agreed-upon recommendations on their own.

As part of the reporting process, it is also important to identify other significant operational areas in which the operational review approach could offer specific improvements and quantifiable benefits. This could lead to a follow-up operational review engagement for the external consulting firm, particularly if it has proven its worth in the current operational review. For the internal review team, it could result in management's asking for additional operational reviews. Not only is such an approach productive in selling the entire operational review concept, but it reinforces the concept of the internal review group existing as a "profit center" in the conducting of operational reviews. The "profit center" concept is based on convincing management that the benefits to be derived from operational reviews far exceed the costs involved. This is where the quantification of findings is extremely important.

Another aspect to consider is that if the operational review is performed properly with the help of departmental personnel, the department retains the residual ability to perform operational review procedures in other areas.

As the operational review team cannot normally cover every operational area that could be improved within the scope of the original operational review, the team should identify those additional areas for further review and, possibly, for review by the department. Management then decides whether to pursue these areas on their own or with the operational reviewer's help. One of the goals in acquainting an organization with the operational review approach is to multiply the effectiveness of operational reviewers. In other words, while performing the operational review, reviewers are also training client personnel. In this way, operational review procedures and results are multiplied throughout the organization, and the reviewers can then spend their time on the most significant areas and tasks.

PERFORM THE OPERATIONAL REVIEW
WITH ECONOMY, EFFICIENCY, AND EFFECTIVENESS

OPERATIONAL REVIEW PHASES

Operational reviews consist basically of gathering information, making evaluations, and developing recommendations where appropriate. An operational review is essentially the evaluation of an activity for potential improvement. Management has the primary responsibility for proper planning, conduct, and control of activities. Thus, review and evaluation of the way management itself plans, conducts, and controls the activities become a major consideration and focal point in the conduct of the review. In addition, the review includes analyzing results and being alert to problems. These also provide insights into the effectiveness of management and the potential for improvements.

The phases through which an operational review progresses are:

- Planning
- Work Programs
- Field Work
- Development of Findings and Recommendations
- Reporting

The operational reviewer may perform two types of reviews, preliminary and in-depth, each having all five phases. The difference between the two is the degree of emphasis, the specific techniques chosen, and the objectives of a particular phase. In a preliminary review, field work might consist of limited transaction testing and interviewing, and the report may be a briefing to management. In an in-depth review, field work might consist of detailed examination using techniques such as work measurement, workload analysis, cost–benefit analysis, and so on, and the report may be formally written, with wider distribution. The operational review phases can be described as follows.

Planning

The reviewer obtains general information about the kinds of activities performed, the general nature of those activities and their relative importance, and other general information to help plan the early portions of the review.

Work Programs

The reviewer prepares the operational review work program for the preliminary review of those activities selected for review in the planning phase. Well-constructed work programs are essential for conducting operational reviews in an efficient and effective manner. Such programs must be individualized for each situation, and each work step must state clearly the work to be done and why.

Field Work

The reviewer analyzes operations to determine the effectiveness of management and related controls. Such functions and controls are tested in actual operation, with particular emphasis on areas difficult to control and having high potential for weakness. The purpose of this phase is to determine whether a situation needs improvement, whether it is significant, and what should be done about it.

Development of Findings and Recommendations

Based on the significant areas identified during the field work phase, specific findings are developed according to the following attributes:

- Condition: What did you find?
- Criteria: What should it be?
- Effect: What is the impact on operations?
- Cause: Why did it happen?
- Recommendation: What needs to be done to correct the situation?
  (Based on present best practices, and always subject to change)

Reporting

The reviewer prepares the report relative to the results of the review. The purpose of the report is to bring these results to the attention of those having an interest in or responsibility for the findings. In reality, the majority of findings, if not all, should have been reported to management with remedial action already being taken or completed prior to the formal report. The report becomes a summary of the results of the review.

DO NOT BE PHASED BY THE OPERATIONAL REVIEW PHASES

CONCLUSION

Not-for-profits are going through some rough times at present, creating increased pressure on management to operate their entities more economically, efficiently, and effectively. Not-for-profit management must adjust to the present realities and continue to search for more effective ways in which to operate with less resources (revenues and contributions) while still providing the desired level of services. This requires that not-for-profit management pay more attention to the manner that their entity operates and institute differential systems that meet current demands from their organizations. Only in this manner will they be able to turn the current downward spiral around. The operational review team can play a key role in this turnaround through the providing of their knowledge of the not-for-profit's operations and their special expertise as to revenue enhancement, expenditure reduction, and results increases.

The succeeding chapters will further discuss the five phases of the operational review—planning, review program, field work, development of findings and recommendations, and reporting—as they relate to the systematic approach to conducting an operational review of a not-for-profit.

OPERATIONAL REVIEW SITUATION VEHICLE INSURANCE COSTS

During the course of an operational review at the Senior Citizens Adult Day Care Center (SCADCC), the review team found that SCADCC had a fleet of vans and automobiles used for agency business—primarily for transporting clients to and from the center and for field trips. The review team found that SCADCC was paying for liability and property damage insurance as part of their lease agreement on 14 vans and 9 automobiles. The cost of the insurance was hidden in the fixed weekly/mileage rates billed by the lessor.

SCADCC's policy is to self-insure or assume certain risks (such as auto collision and certain other property losses, and the front end of unknown claims such as liability claims) and to purchase protection for any other risks under a blanket policy.

Question and Solutions for Consideration

What steps would you take to follow through on this operational practice?

   a. Compare annual hidden insurance costs paid to the lessor as part of fixed weekly/mileage rates, with what insurance would cost under the company's self-insurance and blanket insurance for major losses.
   b. Request insurance charges from lessor for preceding year.
   c. Determine insurance costs under company's blanket policy.
   d. Based on amount of savings (if any), decide what to recommend:

- If substantial savings, recommend insurance provided by the lessor be dropped, and insurance to be provided under company's blanket policy.
- If no savings or if savings are not substantial, recommend continuing present practice of lessor providing insurance. (May also look into lessor's reducing coverage and/or insurance premiums presently being carried).
- If practice of obtaining insurance as part of the lease agreement is more economical than the policy of self-insurance, consider changing the self-insurance policy.
- If the policy of self-insurance is the most economical route, review operations to determine to what extent the policy is being ignored and resultant cost.

Note: In a "real life" version of this particular situation, it was found that lessor insurance costs totaled $39,000 for the year, and that the costs under SCADCC self-insurance and blanket policy would have been $6,000. Accordingly, an annual savings of $33,000 was realized by reverting back to the self-insurance policy. This situation would be reviewed periodically in the future to ensure that conditions had not changed or that other best practices had not come into existence.

CHAPTER TWO

The Planning Phase

*Planning provides the focus for the future—
not the guarantee of results.*

*Progress requires change;
if you never change, you will never progress.*

*The budget does not dictate the plan,
circumstances and need do.*

*Funding sources are not your plan,
funding sources are part of your plan.*

INTRODUCTION

This chapter discusses the planning phase of an operational review for a not-for-profit. The planning phase is where the reviewer first learns about the not-for-profit's operations through various techniques such as review of planning and budget systems, interviewing, review of organizational structure and management, gathering and analyzing information, analysis of financial data and statements, physical inspection of facilities and work procedures, and so forth. Through the performance of these work steps, the reviewer identifies possible critical operational problem areas to be analyzed in more depth in the field work phase, through the development of an operational review work program. In addition, the proper steps to be taken in the planning phase to ensure successful results from an operational review are fully discussed in this chapter.

This chapter will:

- Increase understanding of the purpose of the planning phase in an operational review of a not-for-profit.
- Introduce information that must be obtained during the planning phase and related sources of information.
- Increase knowledge of how to use planning phase information in the identification of critical operational areas.

- Increase understanding of planning and budget concepts and their expansion into operational areas and related principles of good operational controls.
- Introduce a sample operational review planning phase work program.

PLANNING PHASE OVERVIEW

The starting point for the operational review is not-for-profit management's decision as to which operational area or areas are to be reviewed, and whether the operational review is to be preliminary or in-depth. Based on management's decision, the operational reviewer then starts the planning phase of the operational review. The primary purposes of the planning phase are to gather information about the operational area, identify possible operational problem areas, and start to develop the basis for the operational review work program.

In the planning phase, general working information on all important aspects of the not-for-profit's operations is obtained in a relatively short time. This is usually accomplished on site at the not-for-profit's facilities. However, if this is a first-time review of this not-for-profit or a new area of review, the reviewer may need to do some additional on-site research and learning, such as reviewing the not-for-profit's planning and budget systems, its organizational structure and management, financial data over a period of years including revenues and expenditures, management information, and so on.

It is important to get this information quickly. The information gathering need not be a long drawn-out process, with laborious readings of manuals and other materials. Time-consuming efforts to show the existence of significant deficiencies should not be undertaken. However, if any indications of serious deficiencies are found, the reviewer should document them so that they will be considered in deciding on areas for additional work. This procedure provides for an orderly approach to the planning phase and directs operational review effort to those areas with the greatest payout in terms of significant improvement.

Remember the 80/20 rule. Its application in this case states that 20 percent of the problems in the not-for-profit's operations cause 80 percent of the critical impact, and 80 percent of the problems cause only 20 percent of the impact. The reviewer is advised to chase the elephants, the 20 percent, and not the mice, the 80 percent. The difficulty is in identifying and prioritizing the real elephants.

**IF YOU CHOOSE TO STOP THE PLAN
BEFORE IT IS FINISHED,
KNOW THAT THE PROBLEM WILL RETURN AT ANOTHER TIME**

To expedite the collection of information in the planning phase it is a good practice to maximize the use of user provided data, where the reviewer can quickly analyze such information to identify areas of deficiency as well as patterns of agreement with such deficiencies. Exhibit 2.1, Violations of Principles of Good Practices, shows such a form.

At the end of the planning phase, the reviewer should have adequate working knowledge of the objectives and controls of the reviewed area. The reviewer should be familiar with the organization: its objectives, its problems, its physical layout, and the relative significance of the various responsibilities it has been assigned or has assumed. This enables the reviewer to determine at the outset how much time is required to perform the remaining phases of the review.

THE REVIEW TEAM

In the operational review of the not-for-profit, the review team analyzes and reviews those activities that make up the critical operational areas for improvement. The review team can consist of all not-for-profit employees and volunteers—from management and operations from the areas under review and/or from areas of the not-for-profit—or a combination of internal personnel and outside consultants. It is extremely important that the not-for-profit consider who is included in the review team as the review of operations and resultant best practice recommendations are a direct correlation to the background, experience, and expertise of the members of the review team. Typically, the review team will address two major areas of the not-for-profit's operations: people and operating procedures. Some questions that the study team should ask as part of the planning phase of the operational review relative to people and operating procedures are shown in Exhibit 2.2.

**THE OPERATIONAL REVIEW
IS ONLY AS GOOD AS
THE REVIEW TEAM**

IDENTIFICATION OF CRITICAL AREAS

The operational review process really starts with the identification of critical areas in which positive improvements can provide maximum results. Often, such critical areas are identified in the not-for-profit's process of strategic, long-term, and short-term planning (assuming the not-for-profit goes through such a process). In addition, during this planning process, a number of functions and activities may be identified that can be resolved without inclusion in a more formal

Please review the following items representing violations of good administrative and program operation practices. Place a check mark next to those items which you believe the organization or your area to be guilty of doing.

A. Planning
_____ 1. Not setting or updating organizational standards or goals.
_____ 2. Not establishing clear long-term or short-term objectives
_____ 3. Not developing detail plans as to how plans are to be carried out.
_____ 4. Not developing budgets that relate to short-term plans.
_____ 5. Not prescribing a system of review and replanning.

B. Organizing
_____ 1. Not hiring the right people for the job.
_____ 2. Not orienting, training, or instructing employees and volunteers.
_____ 3. Not assigning work on an even distribution.
_____ 4. Not having the right number of personnel—more or less.
_____ 5. Not providing adequate resources, facilities, or equipment.

C. Scheduling
_____ 1. Not providing schedules and budgets for each job.
_____ 2. Not highlighting oldest, off schedule, or over budget jobs.
_____ 3. Not setting priorities for incoming work.
_____ 4. Not readjusting schedules when changes are necessary.
_____ 5. Not requiring approval for nonscheduled work.

D. Coordinating
_____ 1. Not providing for coordination of organization goals and objectives with those of each program, project, or functional area.
_____ 2. Not periodically reviewing the needs of all work units.
_____ 3. Not communicating organization policies and procedures to personnel.
_____ 4. Not effectively communicating downward.
_____ 5. Not coordinating information related to various areas.

E. Directing
_____ 1. Not providing clear expectations and instructions.
_____ 2. Not reviewing work and providing positive feedback so as to provide correction rather than ongoing criticism.
_____ 3. Not fixing the situation rather than fixing the blame.
_____ 4. Not providing a coaching or facilitative environment.
_____ 5. Not periodically reviewing work loads and priorities.

F. Obtaining Feedback
_____ 1. Not providing feedback on the quality of work, so as to build on work done well and remediate work not done well.
_____ 2. Not comparing results with communicated expectations and investigating variances—both positive and negative.
_____ 3. Not effectively communicating to the worker where a job does not meet standards.
_____ 4. Not effectively inspecting ongoing processes at strategic points in the system (that is, adequate quality control procedures).
_____ 5. Not acting on client or other complaints.

G. Achieving Improvement
_____ 1. Not replacing ineffective standards, procedures, or systems.
_____ 2. Not establishing a program of continuous positive improvements.
_____ 3. Not reviewing operations so as to be most economical, efficient, and effective.
_____ 4. Not encouraging (or coaching or facilitating) employees and volunteers to upgrade their capabilities.
_____ 5. Not correcting or reporting variances promptly.

Exhibit 2.1   Violations of Principles of Good Practices

PEOPLE

1. Who is involved and why?
   - Number of people
   - Number of positions
   - How organized and managed
   - Current personnel resource demands

2. Are all personnel needed?
   - Reasons for involvement
   - What are they doing?
   - Value-added or non–value-added (contribution to service delivery)
   - Vital operation or task
   - Special expertise

3. Responsibility for outcomes?
   - Hierarchical pyramid: power and control
   - Management oriented: review and redo
   - Employee self-motivated disciplined behavior
   - Delegation of authority to lowest operational levels
   - Empire building: work continues—reason no longer valid

OPERATING PROCEDURES

1. Why is task performed? (It's always been done this way)
2. Necessary or unnecessary? (That's the way we do it)
3. Adding value to client or service recipient? (Internal versus external viewpoint)
4. Unnecessary bureaucracy? (Unwieldy hierarchy)
5. Ineffective, inefficient, or redundant procedures? (We need to keep busy)
6. What does each one do and why does the employee do it? (Foundation for internal improvements)
7. What are the bundles or groups of value-added and non-value-added procedures and activities? (Separating the wheat from the chaff)

Exhibit 2.2 Operational Review Planning Phase Questions: People and Operating Procedures

operational review. In most organizations, the 80/20 rule applies; that is, 20 percent of all activities result in 80 percent of the organization's ineconomies, inefficiencies, and ineffectiveness; and 80 percent of the activities result in 20 percent of their problems. Therefore, the review team focuses its efforts on the 20 percent most critical areas—chasing the elephants and not the mice. The remaining 80 percent of activities should be handled by internal operations staff as part of the not-for-profit's program of continuous improvement.

Not-for-profit management may be able to identify a number of these critical areas on their own or through the process of developing organizational mission, goals, and objectives; detail plans; and basic operational principles. The process itself forces management to analyze all aspects of not-for-profit operations. As they compare each operation, function, or activity, they need to look at its strengths and weaknesses and determine what is working well and what is not. Through this process, management identifies those critical areas they believe should be analyzed in greater depth in the operational review. It is good practice to include lower levels of management as well as operations personnel in this process, because these personnel typically have greater insight into operational concerns and what needs to be done to correct any faulty practices than those management personnel at the top of the not-for-profit.

Many times, organizational or operations management can assist in identifying which critical areas to start with. Other times, they can provide guidance as to which areas they believe are most critical for the review team to consider. It is usually a joint effort between management and the review team in making the decision as to which operational areas to include in the study.

Prior to the formal operational review, not-for-profit management and operations personnel should strive to have all of its operating activities in the best shape possible based solely on their knowledge of the not-for-profit's operations. These personnel can make identified changes themselves or work with the review team to make such changes. These areas may also be included in the operational review for further best practices and improvements. Keep in mind that it is the ongoing responsibility of all not-for-profit personnel—management and operations—to continually improve their area of responsibility and operation. The operational review, then, is not just a one-time study but an ongoing process. The review may provide the not-for-profit with a proper starting point as to best practices relative to economical, efficient, and effective operations. However, it is the responsibility of all not-for-profit personnel to do the right thing at all times— and keep it that way.

**DO THE RIGHT THING AT ALL TIMES
AND KEEP IT THAT WAY**

OPERATIONAL REVIEW PROCESS

While there is no precise way in which to conduct the operational review for all not-for-profit's, as each one is different as to its focus and services, there are certain guidelines as to how to conduct the review. It is incumbent on the review team to decide which work steps to include in their specific work program based on the not-for-profit and the functional areas to be reviewed. The time allotted to the review would be a factor of the scope of services provided by the not-for-profit and the functions to be reviewed, as well as the size of operations.

An overview of some of the areas to be reviewed in the planning phase of the operational review, as well as in the field work phase, is shown in Exhibit 2.3.

---

1. **Review of physical conditions**
   - Service delivery and administrative layout—ineffective working conditions
   - Overcrowding conditions
   - Too much space for limit of activities
   - Inadequate or improper equipment or materials
   - Under or over capacity
   - Poor work distribution and routing
   - Overextravagant for functions being performed

2. **Review of functional activities**
   - Who is involved? Number, levels, organization, type, functions
   - Why are they involved? Responsibility, authority, function, value-added or non–value-added, redundant, multiply effectiveness, special expertise, necessary for action
   - What are they doing? Material and supplies needed, activities performed, reformatting, enhancing, value-added activities, communicating
   - Why are they doing it? That's the way we do it , always done this way, directed by supervision or management, control purposes, necessary value added

3. **Identify value and nonvalue activities**
   - Is function or activity necessary for the providing of the service?
   - Does the service benefit from the activity being performed?
   - Can the cost of the activity justifiably be charged back to the grantor or client as part of the service delivery process?
   - Is the activity considered part of non–service delivery overhead costs?
   - Can the function or activity be eliminated? In its entirety? Internally with external provision of the same service at less cost?

4. **Compare and contrast activities**
   - Which activities are necessary and unnecessary in the providing of the service?
   - Which activities are performed efficiently and inefficiently?
   - Which activities can be eliminated or reduced in scope immediately?
   - Which activities can be improved immediately or in the short term?
   - Which activities can be compared to other activities as best practices?
   - Which activities are not present which should be?

5. **Identify for operational review**
   - Identification of not-for-profit mental models, belief systems, basic operational principles, and performance drivers
   - Selection of operational goals and performance measures
   - Identification of operational targets—by not-for-profit, department, function, activities, and processes
   - Identification of type of study—entire not-for-profit, specific programs or projects, specific functions or activities

Exhibit 2.3   Overview of Operational Review Areas

INFORMATION TO BE OBTAINED

All of the documents gathered during the planning phase are used to start the permanent files for the operational review. The planning phase can be performed efficiently and systematically if the reviewer has a clear idea of what is needed. The records and information that could be required may include:

- Laws and regulations, including grants and contracts, that apply to the activities being reviewed
- Material on the organization
- Financial information
- Operating methods and procedures
- Management information and reports
- Problem areas

Laws and Regulations that Apply to the Activities Being Reviewed

An understanding of the basic legal authorities governing the area and its activities is needed. The satisfactory performance of an operational review requires that the reviewer ascertain the purpose, scope, and objectives of the activities being reviewed, the way those objectives are to be achieved, and the extent of authority and responsibility conferred. In addition to the basic legislation relating to the area, the reviewer needs to obtain information on all important laws that specifically apply to the area or activity, including related regulations and legal decisions. As to each law, the reviewer should find out:

- Its history and background
- The objectives sought
- The authority vested to achieve the objectives
- The responsibilities imposed
- The nature of any restrictions imposed
- Any other significant requirements

In operational reviews in which related legislation is a major consideration, the reviewer should be aware of the following two factors:

1. Management may justify certain activities on the basis of general authority contained in basic laws. Whenever general authority is relied on for conducting an activity, the reviewer obtains complete and clear explanations as to such reliance. The reviewer determines and reports on the extent to which such general authority has been used, and makes full disclosure of unused authority, if significant.
2. Legislation, and related grants and contracts, may impose various restrictions on a not-for-profit in carrying out an activity. Compliance with

these restrictions is a basic responsibility of management. The reviewer should be familiar with the nature of these restrictions and determine specifically how management provides for ensuring compliance.

Material on the Organization

The second area from which the reviewer needs to gather information involves the not-for-profit and its activities. Primary emphasis should be on the activities that are within the scope of the operational review. This information should include:

- Division of duties and responsibilities
- Principal delegations of authority
- Nature, size, and location of each operational entity (i.e., a not-for-profit headquarters location and any field offices)
- Number of employees by program and project segment and location
- Nature and location of physical assets and accounting records

Among the reviewer's primary concerns is to determine how the not-for-profit is organized to carry out its functions and how duties and responsibilities are assigned. In addition, the reviewer must determine where the area being reviewed fits into the organizational pattern of the entire not-for-profit and its relationship to other areas. This knowledge is necessary for a full understanding of the not-for-profit's operations.

Financial Information

The third area of interest to the reviewer is all pertinent financial information, such as:

- Cost of operations (by not-for-profit and program and projects) by periods
- Year-by-year record of revenue by funding source
- Budget versus actual data for the present and past periods
- Cash flow analysis
- Cost accounting data

Operating Methods and Procedures

Normally, the reviewer is more concerned with operating data than with the data typical in a financial statement. A fourth area is investigated to obtain a general description of the not-for-profit's operating methods and procedures. The reviewer analyzes and documents the operating methods and procedures by which activities being reviewed are performed. In the planning phase, the reviewer should obtain information as to the general methods and procedures top management prescribes for operating in the area under consideration. In this phase, the review of methods and procedures should not extend below the management level. If it is necessary to get accurate information on which to base a conclusion of how certain systems and procedures actually work, the reviewer may want to talk with a limited number of operations personnel. However, the information obtained may be generalized and may require further development later in the review to determine the precise methods and procedures at the operating level.

Management Information and Reports

A fifth category of interest is management information and reports. The reviewer should identify all available management information as well as the nature, content, and timing of all reporting. The reviewer should also look for management information that should be present but is not. It is extremely important to identify the key operating indicators that management has singled out for reporting purposes and those items subject to exception reporting.

Problem Areas

Finally, the reviewer gathers information regarding any problem areas. The reviewer identifies and documents all important problem areas relative to the activities to be reviewed. Areas of major deficiency and those that lend themselves to the greatest improvements are to be emphasized. Remember, these are the items to be pursued in the work program and field work phases. To spend review time most efficiently, it is important to analyze those operational areas with the largest potential pay out in terms of improvements. Again, the not-for-profit "elephants" should be identified in terms of present problem areas, and the "mice" considered only for in-house correction. Some method of prioritization is usually recommended so that the areas of criticalness can be addressed in the order of their need.

Prior to the end of the planning phase, the review team should reach agreement with not-for-profit management as to which critical areas are to be considered in the operational review.

IF IT IS NOT INCLUDED IN THE REVIEW
IT WILL NOT BE IMPROVED

SOURCES OF INFORMATION

What are the sources of the information to be gathered in the planning phase? Such information could come from various sources; however, the following are the most usual sources:

- Organizational review questionnaire
- Effective interviewing
- Organizational data
- Financial data
- Policies and procedures
- Operating and management reports
- Physical inspection

Organizational Review Questionnaire

One of the best, and most efficient, methods for acquiring information about the not-for-profit's operations is the providing of user provided data through a well-designed and inclusive organizational review questionnaire. Such a questionnaire can be submitted to not-for-profit management and operations personnel for their completion or used by the review team as a basis of data collection during planning phase interviews. The purpose of the questionnaire is to quickly collect as much pertinent data relative to not-for-profit operations as possible in a relatively short time—and to help identify those critical areas for further review.

An example of such an organizational review questionnaire for a private school not-for-profit is shown in Exhibit 2.4.

Effective Interviewing

One of the major sources of information about the not-for-profit's activities, procedures, and systems is an effective interview. The purpose of the interview is to find out what is going on and why. Interviews in the planning phase should normally be limited to management, to obtain an overview of the operations without becoming involved in the time-consuming details of interviewing the technical personnel more directly engaged in the operation. In practice, however, limited interviews with operations personnel are usually conducted to ensure that a full and accurate picture is obtained.

Organizational Data

Organizational data may include such things as copies of organization charts, functional job descriptions, and position charts. The reviewer should be sure to ascertain actual duties, responsibilities, and levels of authority for each individual; written job descriptions should not be automatically accepted at face value. This could entail talking to selected management and operations personnel and/or having them prepare a description of their perceived job duties and responsibilities .

We use various operational review tools to assist in gathering and analyzing information about the organization. One tool that could be considered is a

I.   Executive Director/Headmaster
  1. What are plans for expansion or improvement?
     • New programs
     • Enrollment
     • Faculty/student ratios
     • Strengthening faculty
     • Research
     • Other
  2. What are plans for future financing?
     • Tuition changes
     • Fund raising
     • Other sources (what kind?)
     • School related service income (e.g., bookstore, snack bar, student fees)
     • Program contribution (e.g., cash and in-kind)
     • Others
  3. What are plans for physical plant development?
     • Land acquisition
     • New structure
     • Remodeling or rehabilitation of existing structures
  4. How are the schools accredited?
  5. Are non-academic salaries high, average, or low in relation to local hiring market?
  6. What are plans regarding professional salaries?
  7. Is there an organization chart for the organization? (Prepare or obtain copy)
  8. Have formal and/or functional job descriptions been prepared? (Obtain copies)
  9. Has a strategic plan or other long range projection been prepared? (Obtain copy)
  10. How adequate are reports received in furnishing information necessary for making management decisions?
  11. What is the date of original appointment and expiration date of present contract for the executive director/headmaster?
  12. Executive director/headmaster meetings:
     • With principals and program directors
       • How often are meetings held?
       • Is there a regular schedule? (Obtain copy)
       • Is a formal agenda prepared? (Obtain copy)
     • With administrators and operating personnel
       • Who attends?
       • How often are meetings held?
       • Is there a regular schedule? (Obtain copy)
       • Is a formal agenda prepared? (Obtain copy)
     • Other meetings
       • With whom?
       • How often? (Obtain schedule)
       • Purpose?
  13. Is there an advisory council of professional staff members?
     • What is its composition?
     • How are members chosen?
     • Does executive director/headmaster participate?
     • What powers does the advisory council have?
     • How often does it meet? (Obtain schedule and agenda)
     • How effective is it? (Provide examples)

Exhibit 2.4   Organizational Review Questionnaire: A Not-for-Profit Private School

14. Is there an internal written communication instrument for the staff?
    - To whom is it distributed? (Obtain list)
    - How often is it distributed? (Obtain schedule)
    - Does it meet the needs of the non-professional as well as the professional staff?

II. Board Members
    1. Number of members authorized by not-for-profit by-laws?
    2. Present membership? (Obtain list showing names, addresses, gender, age, outside profession, date of appointment, length of service, expiration date and so on)
    3. Method of selection—elected by board or appointed
       - If elected by board—how nominated, elected, and how many for and against?
       - If appointed - by whom, how recommended (e.g., an advisory committee), and process?
    4. What are the standing committees of the board? (Obtain list of committees and members of each committee). How often does each committee meet? Possible committees include audit, budget, buildings and grounds, curriculum, finance, human relations, and personnel policies.
    5. Are there any special or ad hoc committees of the board? (Obtain list with members)
    6. Meetings of the board:
       - Regular meetings
       - Special meetings
       - Executive sessions
       Show number of meetings, formal agenda, staff members required to attend, open to others or closed, and minutes. Obtain copies where relevant.
    7. What reports does the board receive regularly? How often?
       - Budget—both revenues and expenditures
       - Annual report—showing financial condition
       - Revenues and expenditures—with comparison with budget
       - Audit report—internal and external (if applicable)
       - Other reports (Specify and obtain copies)
    8. Minutes of meetings: (Obtain list and copies where applicable)
       - Who prepares?
       - Where are they kept?
       - Who gets copies?
       - How soon are copies available after each meeting?
    9. Policies:
       - Is a written policy manual currently maintained? (Obtain copy)
       - How does the board adopt policies?
    10. Administrative regulations:
       - Is there a written body of administrative regulations, based on policy manual, that is currently maintained?
       - How are such administrative regulations adopted?

III. General Information
    1. Enrollment statistics:
       - By school or program (e.g., pre-school, kindergarten, elementary, middle school, high school, special education, arts, math and science, integrated curriculum, mixed ages, commercial, vocational, and so on)
       - By grades

(Continued)

Exhibit 2.4   *(Continued)*

Prepare or obtain list of schools and programs showing type, grades, professional and non-professional staff, number of pupils, number of classrooms, special rooms, equipment, condition of facilities and equipment, and so on.

2. Is the school or program fiscally dependent or independent? (If dependent, name of other entity)
3. Is there a tuition limitation?
   - What is the limitation by school or program?
   - Can any of these limitations be increased? (Explain how this is done)
   - What is present tuition to cost margin - by school or program?
4. Is there a debt limitation—is it static or can it be increased? (Document what it is)
5. Class size:
   - Is there a board policy on class size? (Obtain copy)
   - What are the actual sizes of classes by school or program?
6. Does entity provide services to other private and public schools? (Describe)
7. Describe type of students (e.g., race, ethnics, geography, income levels and so on)
8. Revenues—current and prior five years:
   Indicate source of revenue and amounts (budget and actual) for the current and prior five year operating periods.
   - Tuitions
   - Academic fees
   - Non-academic revenues (e.g., bookstore, snack bars, concessions)
   - Contributions (e.g., federal, state, and local grants, private grants and contributions)
   - Interest and earnings from investments
   - Balance from previous year
   - Other sources of revenues
9. Expenditures—current and prior five years
   Indicate major functional expenditure categories and amounts (budget and actual) for the current and prior five year operating periods.
   - Total actual expenditures per classification
   - Total as budgeted
   - Difference actual to budget—amount and percent

IV. Staffing Statistics—list faculty or non-faculty, professional or non-professional, type of contract (e.g., full-time, part-time, student, or volunteer), length of service, gender, age, turnover statistics and so on.
Obtain list of all personnel together with professional and non-professional salary schedules.
1. Central administration—list names, titles, and number of positions
   - Executive Director/Headmaster's office
   - Instruction/curriculum director
   - Business manager
2. School wide services
   - Personnel administrator
   - Director of pupil personnel
   - Health services
   - Student statistics (e.g., attendance, grades, special concerns, and so on)
   - Counseling (e.g., guidance, psychology, counseling, and social work)
   - Central services (e.g., telephone, printing, duplicating, computer processing, purchasing, accounting, instructional media center, and so on)

Exhibit 2.4   *(Continued)*

3. Instructional
   - Instructional administration
   - Teaching faculty—by school and program
   - Library and research
4. Physical plant
   - Building and grounds administration
   - Operations (e.g., custodial)
   - Plant maintenance
5. Support services
   - Transportation—administration and staff
   - Food service—administration and staff
   - Bookstore and student stores

V. Budget and Budget Control
   1. Are proposed program changes or changes in level of operations approved in principal by the board prior to budget preparation? (Describe the process)
   2. Is the budget process part of an overall planning process or a stand-alone system based on last year's amounts? (Describe the process)
   3. How are the following determined? (Describe)
      - Academic program changes
      - Academic staff requirements
      - Non-academic staff requirements
      - Equipment and supply needs
      - Travel and other expenses
   4. Who is responsible for?
      - Assembling the budget—revenues and expenditures
      - Compiling revenue and expenditure estimates
      - Assuring mathematical accuracy and reasonableness of revenue and expenditure estimates
   5. What is budgetary screening process? (Describe)
   6. Is a function and object basis used for budget preparation? (Obtain copy of revenue and expenditure chart of accounts)
   7. Is budget prepared on an overall basis as well as by school and program? (Obtain copies of current and last five years budgets)
   8. Budget versus actual comparisons—revenues and expenditures:
      - Is present year's budget shown—as adopted, as amended to date, with expected results for period?
      - Is actual dollar results shown with comparisons and differences to budget?
      - Are prior years budget and actual results shown and for how many years?
   9. Does explanatory narrative material accompany the budget information reported?
   10. Are the projected costs of requested program or operational changes shown beyond coming year when budget is submitted? How many years?
   11. What is the budget approval process? (Describe the process)
   12. Are school, program, and department heads given copies of approved budgets for their respective operations?
   13. Are comparative reports of actual revenues and expenditures versus budget prepared?
       - How often?
       - Who gets copies?

(Continued)

Exhibit 2.4 *(Continued)*

- Hard copy or computer available?
- How detailed (e.g., are encumbrances or commitments included)?
14. Are sophisticated planning and budget processes used? (e.g., strategic and long-term planning, short-term planning (goals, objectives, and detail plans), program planning and budgeting, flexible budgeting, zero-based budgeting and so on). If so, describe how such processes are being used.

VI. Accounting
   1. Accounting system
      - Does the state or some other entity mandate or recommend the accounting system to be used and to what extent?
      - Are the principles of school fund accounting followed? Any deviations?
      - What funds are being used? (e.g., general operating, capital, debt, fixed assets, enterprise and so on)
      - Are there charts of accounts? (Obtain copies)
      - General ledgers
      - Revenues
      - Expenditures
      Is the entity on a cash or accrual basis for revenues and expenditures?
   2. Processing—manual or computerized
      - What is extent of computer processing? (Describe hardware and software used)
      - What accounting applications are computerized? (Provide list of software applications and software with systems narratives)
      - What are computer processing practices? (Describe)
      - What are basic computer control techniques? (Describe, input, processing, and output control procedures)
      - What procedures are still maintained manually? (Describe)
   3. Accounting applications
      - Payroll
         - How many payrolls are there annually?
         - How is payroll handled - in-house or outside payroll processor?
         - How is payroll data accumulated and compiled? (Describe)
         - How is payroll disbursed? (Describe)
         - How are payroll costs distributed?
         - What reports are produced? (Obtain copies)
      - Revenues
         - How are tuition and other charges determined and recorded?
         - What records are maintained relative to revenues?
         - What is the billing procedure? (Describe)
         - Who is responsible for collections and what is the process?
      - Expenditures
         - What is the approval process for expenditures? (Describe)
         - How often are expenditures posted?
         - Are encumbrances or commitments posted to the accounting records?
         - At what point in the process is the budget availability check made? Is the budget amount posted to the expenditure accounts?
         - Are all disbursements made by check supported by approved vouchers, vendor invoices, delivery receipts, and so on?
         - How often are vendors paid? (Obtain statistics as to vendors and number of payments)

Exhibit 2.4   *(Continued)*

- General ledger
  - How often are trial balances taken?
  - How often are financial statements issued? (Obtain copies)
  - Are revenue and expenditures versus budget reports issued? (Obtain copies)
  - Are profit and loss statements of enterprise funds such as bookstore, cafeteria, and other activities issued? (Obtain copies)
  - How long does statement preparation take? In number of days and days after the end of an accounting period.
4. Cash considerations
   - Is temporarily idle cash invested as a regular procedure?
   - Are cash flow projections made? How often are they analyzed and revised? (Obtain copy)
   - What are controls over cash collections? (Describe procedures)
     - Is all cash received through a central cashier function?
     - Are receipts prepared for all cash received?
     - Is all cash deposited daily intact?
     - How soon after receipt is cash deposited?
     - How many checking accounts are maintained? (Obtain list)
     - How often are cash balances reported?
   - How many petty cash funds are there? (Obtain list with amounts and location of each one)
     - Are they operated on an imprest basis?
     - Are personal checks cashed for employees?
     - How often are funds replenished?
   - What are cash balances in each checking account? (Obtain list and reconcile)
5. Audit concerns
   - Is there an internal audit function? By and to whom? (Obtain copies of any such reports)
   - Is there an annual independent audit? (Obtain copies for last five years)
     - Are any exceptions taken?
     - Is the audit performed at least annually or more often?

VII. Purchasing
1. How is purchase request initiated?
   - Is a purchase requisition used? (Obtain blank and filled-in copy)
   - Who is authorized to initiate and approve purchase requisitions?
   - Are there any purchase limits? (Document)
2. Is availability of funds against the budget checked before purchase is undertaken?
3. Is availability of materials being purchased checked before purchase is made?
4. Is standardization of items being purchased considered?
5. Who determines quality and quantity considerations?
6. Are all purchases initiated by purchase order or contract?
7. Bidding procedures
   - When is formal, advertised, competitive bidding required? (Describe process)
   - Are bid bonds and/or performance bonds required?

(Continued)

Exhibit 2.4 *(Continued)*

- Are there regulations or policies relative to competitive bidding? (Obtain copy)
- Without competitive bidding procedures, how are competitive prices obtained?
8. To what extent is purchasing function centralized? (Describe any decentralized procedures)
9. Has a system been established for emergency purchasing? (Describe)
10. Is there a policy favoring local vendors? (Obtain copy)
11. How are goods received and purchasing notified of receipt? (Describe process)
12. How is current status of purchase requisition and purchase order known? (Describe)
13. Purchasing statistics
    - Source and number of requisitions
    - Source and number of purchase orders
    - Vendors used—number of transactions and dollar volume and returns

VIII. Personnel Administration
1. Are there separate personnel offices for professional and non-professional staff?
2. How are staff (full time, part time, and volunteers) recruited? (Describe)
3. Is there a policy to promote from within?
4. Are in-service training sessions held?
5. Who is authorized to hire?
6. Is there a regular established employment and indoctrination procedure? (Obtain copy)
7. How are wages and salaries, promotions, raises and so on determined?
    - Are descriptive position titles used?
    - Are job descriptions prepared for each position title?
    - Are pay grades and scales established and known?
8. Is there a grievance mechanism?
9. What type of personnel records are kept? (Obtain copies)
10. What fringe benefits are available?
11. Is tenure granted to employees? Any exceptions?
12. Are there any unions? What are they and who do they cover?
13. How are employees terminated? (Describe process)
14. How are daily substitute teachers contacted? (Describe procedure)
15. What is application and job offer procedure? (Describe)
    - How many applications are received annually - professional and non-professional?
    - How many job offers are made?
    - How many job offers are refused?
    - What is the time lag between filing of applications and offering of employment?
16. What is the annual rate of turnover for professional and non-professional staff? (Provide statistics)

Exhibit 2.4 *(Continued)*

Job Responsibilities Questionnaire to be filled in by each employee, as shown in Exhibit 2.5. This tool is an example of user or client provided data, which is to be encouraged as this minimizes the data gathering time of the operational review team.

Financial Data

Another source of planning phase information is financial data, such as financial statements by fund over a number of years; budget-versus-actual reports (present and past); cost of operations by period; revenues year by year by source; cash flow analysis; cost accounting data; and ratio, change, and trend analysis. Normally, such financial data are produced as a matter of course in ongoing not-for-profit operations. Many not-for-profits are required also to have an audit or review of their financial records resulting in a set of financial statements. Such audits or reviews may be required by a funding source (e.g., governmental entity or private foundation) or by the board of directors as directed in the not-for-profit's corporate bylaws.

Policies and Procedures

Existing policies and procedures, which should be documented in procedures manuals, policy pronouncements, directives, and regulations are yet another source of information. For many small not-for-profits, such materials will probably not exist, except in the heads of management personnel. In this case, the reviewer would then interview these persons to determine what they believe to be existing policies and procedures, and then test them to determine whether they are actually being followed.

Operating and Management Reports

A further source of information are operations and management reports submitted either internally or externally, prior and related review and audit reports and workpapers, and, if available, internal audit and review reports. The reviewer would also determine whether management has responded to any findings identified in these reports and whether any action has been taken. If the not-for-profit requires a single report due to its receiving sufficient dollars of federal dollars, either directly or through pass-through dollars received from a state or local governmental entity, the reviewer should analyze all such reporting particularly any findings reported, corrective action plans, and remedial actions taken.

Physical Inspection

Finally, the reviewer makes a physical inspection of the not-for-profit operation— headquarters, administrative, and service delivery programs and projects—in-

INSTRUCTIONS

The purpose of this form is to help you describe the duties and responsibilities of your job and the jobs of your supervisees. A separate questionnaire is to be completed for each employee or volunteer under your supervision, as well as one for your own job. In the event that two or more employees perform identical duties, only one questionnaire need be completed. However, the names of all employees covered by the questionnaire should be included in the identification section. Please read the entire questionnaire carefully before answering any questions; type or print your answers clearly.

PLEASE RETURN THIS QUESTIONNAIRE TO:
Mr. Rob Reider
By April 30, XXXX

IDENTIFICATION

Employee Name _____ Title _____

Division _____ Department _____

Name of Immediate Supervisor _____

Title of Immediate Supervisor _____

Your Name _____ Date _____

A. Description of Regular Duties and Tasks

Describe each of the duties and responsibilities in the employee's regular routine, in two or three sentences. The first sentence in each case might tell what the employee is supposed to do, and the next sentence might tell how it is done. Do not refer to previous job descriptions or attempt to describe what you think the job should be. Write what is actually done. In addition, enter the number of hours usually spent on each duty or responsibility under either the "Daily," "Weekly," or "Monthly" column. If you do not have enough room to describe the job duties and responsibilities, you can complete them on the back of Page 2 or on a blank piece of paper, and then attach.

	Time		
Duties and/or Responsibilities	Daily	Weekly	Monthly
1._____	_____	_____	_____
_____	_____	_____	_____
2._____	_____	_____	_____
_____	_____	_____	_____
3._____	_____	_____	_____
_____	_____	_____	_____
4._____	_____	_____	_____
_____	_____	_____	_____
5._____	_____	_____	_____
_____	_____	_____	_____

Exhibit 2.5   Job Responsibilities Questionnaire

B. Difficulty of the Job

What, in your opinion, is the most difficult feature of the job, and why is this so?

_____

_____

_____

_____

_____

C. Description of Contacts

List the persons (by general job title, not name) with whom the employee comes in contact in the performance of normal job duties. Contacts may be either 1) within the employee's own area or 2) within other areas of the organization. Under the heading of "Frequency," indicate whether these contacts (conversations, correspondence, meetings, etc.) are made "not often," "moderately often," "very often," or "constantly."

Contacts Within Your Own Area of Discipline	Reason for Contact	Frequency

Contacts with Other Areas of the Organization	Reason for Contact	Frequency

(Continued)

Exhibit 2.5   _(Continued)_

D. Work Flow

The purpose of this question is to determine where the employee's work originates and where the results of employee's contributions to the work terminate; i.e., where do the data for completing a form originate, and where copies of the form are sent.

Form Title	Data Source	Frequency (No. Forms/Week)

	Form Destination					
Form Title	Copy A	Copy B	Copy C	Copy D	Copy E	Copy F

E. Additional Remarks

State here additional information that you believe would help in describing or understanding the duties of this job.

F. Types of Employees' Jobs Supervised

List the job titles of employees supervised and the number in each classification.

Exhibit 2.5   *(Continued)*

cluding a tour of all pertinent operational areas and the observation of significant activities being performed. A physical review of the operations area, whenever appropriate, should be made relative to the nature of the activities to be examined. The purpose of this physical review is to improve understanding of the activity in physical terms, and to provide support for information about the activity obtained during interviews.

YOU CANNOT IMPROVE WHAT
YOU HAVE NOT CONSIDERED

REVIEW OF NOT-FOR-PROFIT PLANNING AND BUDGET SYSTEMS

A good starting point for the reviewer in the planning phase is to understand the not-for-profit, why it is in existence, and what it is trying to accomplish—that is, its goals and objectives. To accomplish this, the reviewer needs to understand the not-for-profit's strategic, long- and short-term planning methods and related budgeting and control processes. The reviewer should focus on the not-for-profit's approach to planning and its integration with the budgeting process. The not-for-profit's planning and budgeting techniques should be a means of achieving improved organizational effectiveness. The reviewer should also be aware of the elements of an effective planning and budgeting system to compare to the practices of the not-for-profit under review.

There should be interaction and interdependence of the strategic, long-term, short-term, and detail planning systems with the budgeting and monitoring processes. The planning process should be an essential first step in the preparation of an effective budget for the not-for-profit. By learning effective planning and budgeting procedures, the reviewer will be able to more effectively review and analyze such procedures as part of the not-for-profit's organization-wide, departmental, or specific program or project operational review.

Although not-for-profits may plan and budget, particularly in support of specific public and private foundation grants and contracts, many not-for-profits consider the planning and budget processes as separate. In reality, they should be one process. Planning comes first until the organization defines its goals and objectives and the detail plans as to how it plans to achieve its objectives. Knowing where to allocate scarce resources to such detail plans constitutes the budget process. All not-for-profits plan to some extent, as well as budget. Some do it formally with weighty documentation approved by its board of directors, others informally (or even furtively) with minimal documentation if any. Some are quite effective planners and budgeters, others ineffective or even counterproductive in their methods. The advantages of formalizing and throwing open the planning and budgeting process provides an open, integrated, and reasonably structured process that significantly benefits the long-term visibility of the not-for-profit. It is for these benefits that the not-for-profit's planning and budgeting procedures are considered a critical function to include in the planning phase of its operational review.

The not-for-profit must plan for its future direction if it desires to achieve its goals and objectives. The not-for-profit organizational plan is an agreed-upon course of action to be implemented in the future (short and long term) and directed toward moving the not-for-profit closer to its stated goals and objectives. The planning process, if exercised effectively, forces the not-for-profit to:

- Review and analyze past accomplishments—successes and failures
- Determine present and future needs
- Recognize strengths and weaknesses—and its uniqueness (Exhibit 2.6. shows some examples of such not-for-profit strengths and weaknesses.)
- Identify future opportunities
- Define constraints or threats that may get in its way (Exhibit 2.7 shows some tips on how to beat out not-for-profit competition.)
- Establish organizational, department, program, or project goals, objectives, detail plans, and budgets
- Develop action plans based on the evaluation of alternatives and the needs of your clients (Exhibit 2.8 shows some principles of the client-driven not-for-profit.)
- Prioritize the selection of action plans for implementation based on the most effective use of limited resources

---

**IF YOU DO WHAT YOU HAVE ALWAYS DONE,
YOU WILL ALWAYS GET THE SAME RESULTS**

MENTAL MODELS AND BELIEF SYSTEMS

Many not-for-profits operate on the basis of prevalent mental models or belief systems—usually emanating from past and present management and sometimes from the perpetuation of not-for-profit stereotyped attitudes. These mental models and belief systems have an overriding effect on the condition with which operations within the not-for-profit are carried out. They can help to produce a helpful working environment or atmosphere—or a hindering one as many of these mental models, real or perceived, become negative performance drivers for employees and volunteers in the achievement of desired results. In effect, such mental models become performance drivers—those elements within the not-for-profit that shape the direction of how employees and volunteers will perform their functions. These mental models and belief systems need to be identified so as to develop an effective plan for remediation or elimination.

STRENGTHS

❏ Competent people—employees and volunteers
❏ High technical capabilities
❏ Reputation high in area
❏ Variety of clients: able to serve different sectors
❏ Quality of services delivered
❏ Consistency among services provided
❏ Positive attitude
❏ Rapport between employees and volunteers
❏ Qualified in areas of services delivered
❏ Well established
❏ Diversity of services provided
❏ Specialized skills
❏ Location

WEAKNESSES

❏ Timeliness of providing services
❏ Lack of internal organization
❏ Indecisiveness—too much time getting too little done
❏ Fear of growth and success
❏ Lack of technical skills in specific areas of areas of service delivery
❏ Lack of business expertise
❏ People, people, people
❏ Lack of knowledge in areas of services delivered
❏ Identifying opportunities for additional funding and services
❏ Not knowing how to develop not-for-profit business
❏ Lack of major commitment
❏ Pricing structure—too high or too low

Exhibit 2.6 Analyzing Your Not-For-Profit: Strengths and Weaknesses

---

1. Get a reputation for providing quality services.
2. Treat your clients to good service—always give 125%.
3. Get your name out in your community—be visible.
4. Manage your not-for-profit well.
5. Keep your costs down.
6. Build financial strength—increase your net assets and reserves.
7. Build a solid list of happy clients.
8. Make your services unique.
9. Get a large share of the market for your services.
10. Increase your knowledge of the business end.
11. Get effective and efficient employees and volunteers.
12. Be flexible—know what you can and cannot do.
13 Build a powerful image.
14. Develop good relations with all of your stakeholders.

Exhibit 2.7 Tips on Beating Your Not-For-Profit Competition

- An entity that understands the client and
  - Stays in touch with the client
  - Knows what the client is looking for
  - Understands important elements of the client's choice
  - Listens to client and works on solving problems
  - Responds to the client's unmet needs
- Knowing how the client perceives your not-for-profit
  - Knows how the not-for-profit is perceived
  - Knows why the not-for-profit is perceived
- Delivers quality and value
  - Cares about the quality and value the client receives
  - Measures client satisfaction often
  - Responds to the client's input and feedback

Exhibit 2.8   What is a Client-Driven Not-For-Profit Business?

Examples of such mental models and belief systems as they might relate to not-for-profits include:

- Doing what you are told, and not asking questions, are the keys to success for the individual and the not-for-profit.
- The obedient child in the not-for-profit survives and is promoted, while the rebellious child is let go or leaves the not-for-profit.
- The individual who mirrors management best gets the promotion—whether qualified or not.
- The individual who challenges ideas and strives to improve operations creates discomfort and is discounted by management.
- Efficient and productive employees should not be recognized or promoted because no one else would be left to do the work.
- Employees and especially volunteers need to be closely watched and controlled to ensure that they do their jobs.
- Male managers may have personality and job-related quirks that are tolerated, while female managers must be perfect without any flaws.
- Not-for-profit employees and volunteers never keep busy; to get anything done requires at least three people—two to supervise and one to do the work.
- Not-for-profit management is the art of going to meetings for the purpose of deciding when to meet again. And, when you call the meeting, you not only fill your time, but that of other managers at the meeting.
- Not-for-profit employees are paid much less than their counterparts in the private sector and therefore you cannot expect much from them.
- Those who work hard, efficiently, and professionally in the not-for-profit are looked at strangely by others in the not-for-profit.

- Managers are necessary in the not-for-profit to ensure that employees and volunteers are doing their jobs—concern with putting in the hours not necessarily what they put into the hours.
- There may be no minimum of not-for-profit operational and financial acumen and savvy for board members and top management.
- Management needs to spell out in minute detail the tasks to be performed to ensure that they get done correctly.
- Employees and volunteers cannot be trusted on their own—they need to be policed and controlled.
- Only management can make decisions—employees and volunteers are there to do the work under close supervision.

The accurate identification of organizational mental models, belief systems, and performance drivers is extremely important in the review team's strategy. If these things are not changed, reviewing best practice recommendations will change only the system and not not-for-profit results.

For example, a not-for-profit that believes employees and volunteers need close supervision to ensure that the work gets done may result in spiraling upward costs of management where salaries are higher. Working with scarce total resources, this results in less funding for lower levels and the increased need to use more volunteers—requiring even more close supervision. To turn this detrimental and inefficient system around and turn a vicious cycle into a virtuous cycle, the not-for-profit could consider a system of individual employee and volunteer expectations and results. The employee and volunteer would be recognized and rewarded based on the achievement of actual results and not the subjective evaluation of management. The goal would be to eliminate the present inefficient belief system and replace it with a best practice that meets management's desired and stated organizational goal of a more economical, efficient, and effective organizational structure. This best practice recommendation places the burden of productivity on the employee or volunteer and eliminates the need for management to police and control—the employees and volunteers control themselves. This creates a best practice of working together and cooperation, eliminating the negative mental model of necessary close supervision by management to achieve any results. These mental models, belief systems, and performance drivers need to be watched diligently so that they do not spring up again; they are difficult to diffuse, particularly when dealing with long-serving belief systems.

**WE FORM OUR BELIEFS WHEN WE ARE VERY YOUNG
AND WE SPEND THE REST OF OUR LIVES
CREATING EXPERIENCES TO MATCH**

ORGANIZATIONAL STRUCTURE AND THE ROLE OF MANAGEMENT

Theoretically, not-for-profit organizations are put together so that the not-for-profit can deliver its services more efficiently, and so that the board members and/or management can multiply their effectiveness, that is, maximize their desired results. Organizing is intended to be a helping process to enable the not-for-profit to conduct its business and deliver its services better.

However, for many not-for-profits it has become a costly getting in the way process. As part of the planning phase, the operational reviewer must ascertain whether the organization is properly organized or whether improper organization is the cause of its problems. As just discussed, there are many mental models, belief systems, and negative performance drivers related to not-for-profit organizational structures and the use of employees and volunteers and the role of management. The review team must consider all of these elements in its effective review of organizational and personnel concerns.

The organization chart for the Santa Fe Chamber Music Festival is shown in Exhibit 2.9. which graphically displays the reporting relationships from the board of directors down through program levels. This not-for-profit is of relatively large size for a typical performing arts organization, with revenues of over $2 million and expenditures of over $1.7 million, resulting in an annual addition to reserves of over $400,00 (Net differences between revenues & expenses for the year). We will discuss this not-for-profit further as a case study in the field work phase.

This typical structure would fit most not-for-profits. It is based on hierarchical pyramid concepts wherein the ultimate power starts at the top and is delegated down through the pyramid. This model originates from the military, specifically from Napoleon's time. Its purpose is to maintain control within the organization through a chain of command that demands obedience from each level of the organization to a higher level. To this day, many not-for-profits, as well as businesses in the private sector, still function in this manner, where the purpose for the organizational hierarchy is to police and control those reporting to them to make sure they do their jobs. The structure is also set up with the intrinsic message that those in a higher position on the chart know more. Hence, much of their time is spent on reviewing the work of those under them and then having those under them redo it so it looks more like what the manager would do.

It is these policing and control, review and redo processes that make many supervisors and managers superfluous (non–value-added) organizational overhead, and often more hindrance than help. If these non–value-added processes are eliminated, management is strictly limited to necessities, and the not-for-profit creates an atmosphere that encourages the motivation of self-disciplined employee behavior, we can eliminate many of these layers of unnecessary organization. For many not-for-profits, they must achieve more results with fewer personnel resources than desired or necessary. The reviewer must consider these concerns when reviewing organizational and personnel concerns.

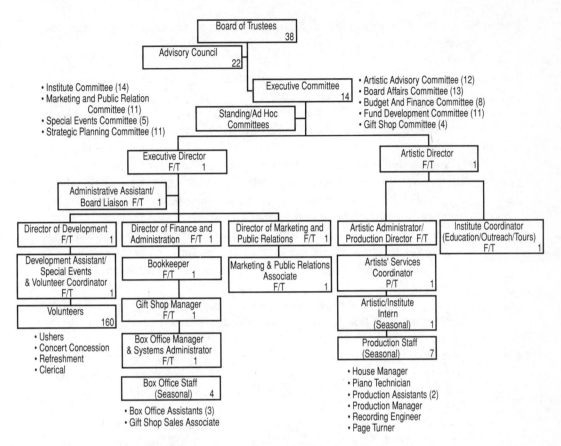

Exhibit 2.9 Santa Fe Chamber Music Festival Organizational Chart

Adequate organizational control requires that each employee know clearly what his or her role and function is in the not-for-profit, and exactly what authority and responsibility have been assigned. It also requires proper separation of duties so that the same individual is not charged with the responsibility for recording and reporting on how a particular task has been accomplished. Most not-for-profits do not have the luxury that private-sector businesses have of continually adding employees rather than operating most economically and efficiently. Not-for-profits in most cases are forced to use more part-time assistance or volunteers (e.g., board members and others) or sacrifice needed functions. There is also a tendency to have full-time employees' time split among a number of functions in which separate individuals would be more efficient and desirable, as well as have these employees spend additional time at no additional pay.

As the review team looks at the organizational chart in Exhibit 2.9, they may have many questions and see areas for review related to making this organization more effective and efficient and, as a result, more economical. Some of the areas that the review team might identify in the planning phase for further review and analysis are:

- Role and function of the board of trustees—organizational authority and their purpose in overseeing and managing operations.
- The large number (38) of members of the board of trustees. Does this result in effectiveness or the creation of unwieldy and cumbersome decision making?
- The underlying reasons for accepting an individual onto the board. Is it anyone who is interested or can make a contribution (monetary or otherwise) or does each position on the board have a specific purpose (i.e., fund raising, financial expertise, operational advice, etc.)?
- What is the purpose of an additional 22-member advisory council? Does it support the board and the executive director, is it superfluous, is it mainly to acquire additional contributions, or is it an additional effective asset?
- What are the special expectations of the 14-board-member executive committee? Does it really manage the board and operations, are there too many members, or is there an effective role for this body?
- Standing ad hoc committees of the board—are there too many of them, are they effective in carrying out operations, are they just a means of making board members feel needed and useful, are they really necessary, and so on?
- Executive director—what are the roles and expectations of this position? Does this individual have sufficient authority to achieve these results and expectations or is there too much board involvement in the same areas?
- Artistic director—what are the roles and expectations of this position? How does this individual coordinate with the executive director and the board?
- Administrative assistant/board liaison—what does this individual do? Is the position really necessary or is it make work due to the organizational structure?
- Director's level—Development, Finance and Administration, Marketing and Public Relations, Artistic Administrator/Production Director, and Institute Coordinator. What are the functions of these individuals? Does each position require someone at the Director's level? Are there too many of these positions or not enough?
- Other full-time positions (designated on the organization chart as F/T)—Development Assistant/Special Events & Volunteer Coordinator, Bookkeeper, Marketing and Public Relations Associate, Gift Shop Manager, and Box Office Manager and Systems Administrator. Are these the best use of full-time positions—are the right ones using the not-for-profit's scarce resources most effectively? Do all of these functions need to be performed by a full-time employee? For instance, why are these positions full

time while the Artists' Services Coordinator is part time? Can any of these full-time positions be done on a part-time or outsource basis?

- Seasonal staff (e.g., production and box office)—this is typical for a performing arts not-for-profit in which such staff are needed only during the performance season? Are there too many of these individuals or not enough? How are they used and controlled by permanent employees during this period as opposed to a slower pace during nonperformance times?
- Volunteers—for purposes such as ushers, concert concessions, refreshments, and clerical. Are volunteers used only during the performance season? Can they be used effectively during other times of the year? How are 160 volunteers used and controlled? (It appears that there is only one volunteer coordinator.)
- Gift shop operations—this is possibly a non–business-related activity. What is its purpose? Does it enhance the overall purpose of the organization? Is its contribution (monetary and promotion) worth the effort of managing and conducting such an operation?

The above questions are only examples. The review team could consider all of these concerns, some of them, or others that they find to be more significant. The purpose of the planning phase is to question these areas as to their criticalness. If the review team decides to include such personnel and organizational issues in the field work phase of the operational review, it is then that the review team will discover whether such concerns are detrimental or helpful to the not-for-profit's operations.

**THE ART OF ORGANIZATION
IS NOT TO CREATE ORGANIZATIONS
BUT TO MULTIPLY OUR EFFECTIVENESS**

SAMPLE PLANNING PHASE WORK PROGRAM—ORGANIZATION

Work steps that might be included in a planning phase operational review work program related to organizational structure issues for the above not-for-profit might include:

- Secure or prepare an organization chart with descriptions of each department's and work units' specific functions.
- Determine formal and informal reporting relationships from top to bottom, bottom to top, and across functional lines.
- Analyze actual operations to determine if such reporting is proper as to how the organization functions and whether it results in operational concerns and problems.

- Analyze each work unit's functions to determine whether they are appropriate.
- Document the duties and responsibilities of each employee. Obtain copies of existing job descriptions or prepare them through the use of user provided data such as a Job Responsibilities Questionnaire.
- Interview members of the board, executive director, managers and supervisors, and each employee, to validate their functions.
- Observe actual work being performed to determine the necessity of all duties and responsibilities.
- Obtain or prepare policies and procedures relating to each function under review.
- Determine that authority and responsibility relationships are clearly defined and understood by all personnel.
- Ascertain that all employees know their delegated authority and responsibilities; ensure that the responsibilities are proper and do not overlap or duplicate another area.
- Look for functions and individuals that either are not providing value-added services or are not being cost effective. Examples may be isolates, dispatchers, controllers, unwieldy hierarchies typified by policing and control, and management and supervision that gets in the way.
- Review hiring, orientation, training, evaluation, promotion, and layoff/firing practices.

IDENTIFICATION OF CRITICAL PROBLEM AREAS

Now that needed information has been obtained, how should it be used? The planning data gathered provide the background and general working information for the operational review staff. It should also be used to help decide which specific areas of activity to examine in the field work phase. In most operational reviews, the review staff decides which specific areas to review. The general objective is to direct attention to those matters that most urgently need it. Identifying these critical areas is an important component of each operational review.

Techniques for preliminary identification of critical areas vary with the type of engagement and the nature of the not-for-profit (i.e., is it a social service, arts—visual and performing, museum, educational, etc.). They require a reviewer's ingenuity and judgment. Such techniques include the following.

Identification of Key Activities

The information obtained may disclose key activities or aspects of an activity that appear to be difficult to control or susceptible to abuse or laxity. For instance, in a purchasing operation, the key critical areas might well be:

- Determinations of quantities and qualities to be purchased
- Methods used in obtaining the most advantageous price
- Methods of determining whether the correct quantities and qualities are actually received and are used properly.

Use of Management Reports

Examining the reports management uses to assure itself that work is progressing within established time and cost goals and that results are being achieved should provide valuable information in selecting areas of inquiry. Examples of such reporting are operational exception reporting and actual versus plan reporting, which would compare actual results with goals and objectives. The reviewer should look closely at those items management has selected as critical for exception reporting, such as staffing levels (number and use), service delivery measures (number, timeliness, and quality), revenue analysis (sources and amounts), expenditure analysis (amount, relationship to budget, needed or not), and so on. Indications of critical areas to look at will surface if major deviance's are found between the plan and actual results. Keep in mind that the plan could be all right and the operational results critical, or the operational results may be all right but the planning process may be deficient.

Examination of Past Review and Audit Reports

Past review and audit reports (internal and external) may be a valuable source of information in determining direction of effort. There should be an examination not only of reports prepared by the internal or external review or audit groups, but also of those of other internal review organizations, as well as supervisory groups, where applicable, such as licensing agencies (e.g., substance abuse treatment, boarding homes, senior facilities). The reviewer should determine whether management agrees with specific review or audit findings, particularly if mentioned by more than one review or audit group, and whether any action has been taken to correct the situation.

As mentioned previously, not-for-profits can receive funding and contributions from many sources, including private donations and contributions (individuals and foundations) as well as public political entity grants. Sometimes an individual may make a large donation for a restricted or specified purpose. The not-for-profit must then have systems in effect to ensure that these moneys are used only for that specific purpose. Private foundations providing grant money to a not-for-profit may also require that their moneys be spent only for the purposes requested in the grant proposal and usually require a reporting of such. Public grants and contracts from the federal, state, or local political entities, also require such reporting. The reviewer should review the original grant applications and such subsequent reporting.

A not-for-profit may also be receiving substantial funding from federal government agencies that require a Single Audit or a Program Specific Audit. The reviewer must analyze the situation to determine whether the not-for-profit under review is subject to such audit. Specifically, if the not-for-profit receives over $100,000 in federal funds (either directly from federal programs or from pass-through federal money from a state or local government or another not-for-profit), it is subject to audit—either single audit or program-specific audit. If over $250,000 is received in federal funds, the not-for-profit is subject to a single audit. In addition, if the not-for-profit is receiving pass-through federal moneys, the pass-through agency may require the not-for-profit to be part of its single audit or require other examination under its subrecipient monitoring requirements. Should the review team determine that the not-for-profit under review is subject to such an audit, they should be aware of the level of reporting required to include in their operational review.

- Report on an examination of the general purpose or basic financial statements, together with the General Purpose Financial Statements.
- Report on internal accounting control based solely on a study and evaluation of accounting and administrative controls as related to the financial statements.
- Report on compliance with laws and regulations that may have a material effect on the financial statements.
- Report on a supplementary schedule of Federal Financial Assistance showing the total receipts and expenditures for each federal assistance program.
- Report on the study and evaluation of internal control systems identifying the not-for-profit's significant internal accounting controls, and those controls designed to provide reasonable assurance that federal programs are being managed in compliance with program laws and regulations.
- Reports on compliance applicable to federal financial assistance programs:
  - Compliance with specific requirements applicable to major programs (over $300,000 in receipts), including types of services allowed or unallowed; eligibility for services provided; matching, level of effort, or earmarking requirements; required reporting; cost allocation criteria; claims for advances and reimbursements; monitoring subrecipients; and specific individual program requirements.
  - Compliance with general requirements applicable to major programs such as political activity, civil rights, cash management, and so on.
  - Compliance with specific requirements for selected nonmajor program (less than $300,000) transactions.
- Schedule of all findings and questioned costs, with each finding documented separately for not-for-profit management response and action.
- The not-for-profit's response to the audit groups findings and recommendations, together with the not-for-profit's plan for corrective action.

Should the not-for-profit under review be subject to some part of a Single Audit, the review team should be aware of what is required and available for review. In many instances, such Single Audit reporting can be quite helpful in assisting the review team to identify areas of operational deficiencies. However, the review team may find that the not-for-profit has allowed such federal requirements to impact on its nonfederal program activities, making the not-for-profit less economical, efficient, and effective as possible. The review must also determine if the receipt of such federal funds is worth the possible negative impact on the not-for-profit's operations.

Physical Inspection of the Activities

A physical inspection of activities requires alertness for signs of ineffectiveness or inefficiency such as bottlenecks, excess accumulations of equipment or material, and idleness of personnel. Such inspections may disclose serious weaknesses warranting inquiry, or they may depict a pattern prevalent throughout the organization.

Discussions with Responsible Personnel

Finally, discussions with responsible officials and personnel directly concerned with the activity may assist in the identification of critical areas. Sometimes valuable leads can be obtained through discussions with responsible officials and others directly concerned with the activities performed. These individuals can often identify troublesome areas or request that the reviewer look into specific matters that they are concerned about, but for which they lack information regarding the actual conditions.

**CRITICALNESS IS BASED ON EFFECT—
IT IS NOT MERELY IN THE EYE OF THE BEHOLDER**

FINANCIAL STATEMENT ANALYSIS

Because members of the operational review team usually have some financial expertise, a good place to start in determining critical operational areas is to analyze the not-for-profit's financial data and statements as follows:

- Statement of Financial Position (e.g., the balance sheet for a private entity)
- Statement of Activities (e.g., the income statement for a private entity)
- Statement of Cash Flows

Keep in mind that financial statements, produced from a financial accounting standpoint, are essentially historical documents that present the organization's assets, liabilities, and equity (net assets or reserves for future periods) in a Statement of Financial Position and its revenues (restricted and unrestricted) and expenses in a Statement of Activities. These financial statements tell what has happened within the organization during a particular period or series of periods.

These same financial statements can be used from an operational review standpoint to help identify present and future critical areas for review. The use of certain analytical tools can effectively help to analyze the financial statements, determine how the organization is doing, and zero in on critical areas that need attention and improvement. These tools are summarized as follows.

Comparisons

Financial statements are static historical documents showing data related only to a specific period of time. Operational reviewers are concerned with the period being reported, and what the trend of events has been and will be over longer periods of time. Comparing financial statement data with the results of other periods, or of other organizations, provides a better understanding of trends and helps in making proper decisions as to their relative significance. Comparisons can be made with the historical performance of the not-for-profit, a competitor's performance, performance of other not-for-profits providing the same services, and organizational goals, objectives, and detail plans.

Comparison within the same not-for-profit is also known as *internal benchmarking*, which looks for best results and related best practices. Comparison outside of the not-for-profit (competing not-for-profits, similar not-for-profits as a group, and best in class as to functions within various types of not-for-profits) is also known as *external benchmarking*, which looks for best practices that can be embedded in the not-for-profit's operations in a program of continuous improvement.

Trend Percentages

Financial statement analysis can also be accomplished through the use of trend percentages, which are used to state a number of years' financial data in terms of a base year. The rule in using trend percentages is that at least three data points need to be examined before a trend can be identified.

Consider the ABC not-for-profit:

	XXX9	XXX8	XXX7
Revenues (all sources)	$12,500	$11,000	$10,500
Increase in net assets	$1,200	$900	$900

Analyzing the dollar data alone, it could be concluded that both revenues and net asset increases have increased over the three-year period. However, it cannot readily be concluded how fast revenues have increased and whether these increases have kept pace with net asset increases. Using dollar data alone may make it difficult to conclude adequately. Now assume that the base year XXX7 is equal to 100 percent; the other years can be stated as a percentage of the base year:

	XXX9		XXX8		XXX7	
	Dollars	%	Dollars	%	Dollars	%
Revenues	$12,500	119%	$11,000	105%	$10,500	100%
Net assets	$1,200	133%	$900	100%	$900	100%

By using these trend percentages as well as the differences in real dollars (or numbers), the increase in revenues and net assets can be put into proper perspective. It can now be clearly seen that the relative growth in revenues has been surpassed by the growth in net assets; revenues in XXX9 are 19 percent greater than the base year, but net asset increase is 33 percent greater. Note also that revenues growth was better than net assets growth in XXX8, and that the growth in revenues in XXX9 over XXX8 was considerably below the growth in net assets for the same year. Such an analysis could indicate major operational areas for review, such as source of revenue analysis, expenditure analysis, funding source analysis and procedures, and cost analysis.

Common-Size Statements

A common-size financial statement shows the line items as percentages in addition to absolute dollars. Each line item on the financial statements is shown as a percentage of some total, such as assets or revenues. The preparation and presentation of common-size statements is known as *vertical analysis*, revealing changes in the relative significance of each line item. An analysis of financial statements on a common-size basis could disclose such areas as shown in the following:

Statement of Financial Position:

	% of Total Assets		
	XXX7	XXX9	Change
Current assets	58.8%	39.3%	−19.5%
Fixed assets	32.4	55.1	+22.7
Current liabilities	20.6	18.7	−1.9
Long-term debt	16.2	28.0	+11.8
Net assets	63.2	53.3	−9.9

Comments: There has been a major shift into fixed assets (e.g., that is facilities and equipment) financed by reduction of current assets and additional long-term debt. The reason for this major investment needs to be investigated.

Statement of Activities:

	% of Total Revenues		
	XXX7	XXX9	Change
Program expenses	64.8%	57.4%	−7.4%
Fund raising expenses	8.6	10.8	+2.2
General and administrative expenses	11.4	14.6	+3.2
Total expenses	84.8	82.8	−2.0
Net asset increase	15.2	17.2	+2.0
Totals	100.0%	100.0%	—

Comments: The switch between program expenses and fund raising and general and administrative expenses indicates a major change from direct program expenses to some other significant change in emphasis. The increases in fund raising and general and administrative expenses is also significant, and needs to be investigated.

Financial and Operational Ratios

Proper financial analysis of a not-for-profit's results provides for the measurement and evaluation of its progress toward accomplishment of program and financial goals and objectives, for example, increase in the delivery of services or the maintenance of a satisfactory financial position. The organization's financial position usually involves two fundamental considerations:

1. *Potential for survival*: measured by short-term liquidity (ability to meet short-term financial obligations) and long-term solvency (ability to meet long-term financial obligations)
2. *Performance* (toward meeting financial and operational goals): measured by net asset growth and service delivery results

Ratios, both financial and operational, represent a mathematical relationship between two quantitative conditions, and are the primary method used for such financial and operational analysis. Measured over a period of time, these ratios can be used to identify changes or trends in operations. They can also be used to provide information for identifying operational trouble spots. By analyzing changes and trends using ratios and comparisons between time periods of various performance measures (such as clients served, services provided, changes in revenue sources and total revenues, expenses incurred, etc.), they can also provide advice and insight into the not-for-profit's operations as well as indicate where the most critical problems might lie. These ratios should be analyzed in combination as well as related to specific operations.

**FINANCIAL STATEMENTS ARE MORE
THAN JUST NUMBERS—
THEY CAN BE A GUIDE TO IMPROVEMENTS**

IDENTIFYING CRITICAL AREAS

As a result of the initial survey and analysis of financial and operational data of the not-for-profit, the operational review team should be able to help management identify its critical operational areas in which operational review procedures would provide the most benefits. This step is not always required, as quite often management has already decided which areas would provide the biggest payout by an operational review. However, based on the reviewer's analysis of the not-for-profit, a list of potential areas for operational review were developed as follows:

- Cash management—short term and long term
- Services provided—the right mix, others to add, some to change or delete
- Fund-raising procedures—including donations, contributions, grants, and contracts
- General and administrative expenses—necessary and unnecessary
- Capital expenditures (property, plant, and equipment)
- Financing/borrowing
- Program expenses
- Net asset reserves
- Cost accounting—program, project, functional, and service
- Marketing and promotion
- Administrative operations
- Computer processing procedures
- Management information and reporting
- Personnel—board members, management, full- and part-time staff, volunteers

Although all of the operational areas recommended for operational review should produce beneficial results and adequate payout, the review team and not-for-profit management must decide on which areas to review first. For instance, they may decide that marketing and promotion must be addressed initially so that the not-for-profit can grow in the direction desired. Or they may decide that services provided must be initially addressed as the demand for certain services has greatly decreased which has placed the not-for-profit in a tenable position for survival.

PRIORITIZING CRITICAL AREAS FOR THE OPERATIONAL REVIEW

Once the critical operational areas have been identified for possible inclusion in the operational review, it is good practice to prioritize which areas to include in the present review, which ones to review in the future, and which items can be substantially improved immediately or in the short term without a formal operational review. For instance, the review team might schedule the not-for-profit's critical areas as shown in Exhibit 2.10.

Prioritization of which areas to include in the present operational review is usually done by brainstorming with the review team and others. Criteria to be considered should include which areas could be most improved through the identification of best practices, which offer the greatest potential for improvement, and which ones impact the stakeholders most favorably. Remember, the 80/20 rule; that is 20 percent of the not-for-profit's activities cause 80 percent of its problems. Concentrate on the elephants, not the mice.

In addition, the review team must consider the resources of time, personnel, and costs. Normally, this helps to determine the number of areas to benchmark at one time. Based on the summary shown in Exhibit 2.10, the review team would consider the areas of fund-raising procedures, services provided, program expenses, cash management, and cost accounting as identified and agreed on in the planning phase.

Critical Area	Cost	Improvement Impact	Improvement Potential	Rank	*P/F/I
1. Cash management	$ 80,000	High	60	4	P
2. Services provided	$ 50,000	High	80	2	P
3. Fund-raising procedures	$300,000	High	100	1	P
4. General and administrative	$ 30,000	Low	40	10	F
5. Capital expenditures	$120,000	Medium	20	12	I
6. Financing/borrowing	$ 30,000	Medium	20	8	I
7. Program expenses	$160,000	High	90	3	P
8. Net asset reserves	—	Low	80	9	I
9. Cost accounting	—	High	100	6	P
10. Marketing and promotion	$200,000	High	75	5	I
11. Administrative operations	$60,000	Medium	60	7	I
12. Computer processing	$40,000	Medium	20	13	I
13. Management information	—	Low	20	14	F
14. Personnel	$80,000	Medium	60	11	F

* P/F/I = Present Study, Future, And Immediate.

Exhibit 2.10   Prioritizing Areas for the Operational Review

PRIORITIZING THE CRITICAL AREAS
RESULTS IN IMPROVING THE CRITICAL AREAS

FINAL PLANNING REVIEW

Once these critical areas are identified as a result of the planning phase, a final planning review may be performed to obtain data on the activities such as:

- Who is involved and how they relate to the activity and its desired results and each other. Document the number of individuals, their relative positions, the method of organization and management, and so on.
- Why each individual is involved and his or her value-added or non–value-added activities. Is each one performing necessary operations, do they have special expertise, or bear necessary responsibility—or are they merely excess structure?
- What activities are being done, and whether each one needs to be done, can be done more efficiently, or is being done well (a best practice).
- Why each activity is being done—do each of the activities relate to desired goals and objectives, and is each one being performed most effectively?
- What resources are allocated to each activity—is the allocation most economical, or are allocated resources excessive or are they deficient to achieve desired results?

The focus of the final planning review is to provide understanding and clearly document existing practices and procedures by:

- Identifying key aspects of the entire not-for-profit, department, or work unit's activities and performance results
- Identifying inherent, structural, and performance drivers
- Identifying critical operational areas and opportunities for improvement (one part learning from another)
- Establishing channels of communication within the company
- Identifying pockets of good, desirable practices (best practices and areas of excellence)
- Establishing standards for good practices to reflect the adoption of best practices

Defining the elements of each activity and determining its value-added or non–value-added contributions and what each individual does in the process and why he or she does it is the basis for analysis as to positive improvements.

This final planning groundwork is the initial input into the development of the operational review work program, which will be discussed in Chapter 3.

AREAS NOT SELECTED FOR REVIEW

The other operational areas for which it is determined that additional operational review work will not be performed at this time are not to be merely put aside. They should all be mentioned to not-for-profit management in an oral and/or written report, recommending further action, such as:

- *Immediate action.* For example, facility changes can be made so that program operations personnel have adequate space in which to accomplish their tasks. At present, all personnel from various programs are working in the same space and very little is getting effectively accomplished.
- *Further analysis and review by not-for-profit and program management.* For example, management might consider changing the structure and personnel of the various functional areas. Are they needed, and at what level?
- *Future operational review by the review team or internal not-for-profit personnel.* For example, the review of special approval procedures such as capital expenditures, overbudget limitations, and special projects.

AREAS NOT SELECTED FOR REVIEW
ARE NOT IGNORED
BUT ARE PART OF THE IMPROVEMENT PROGRAM

CONCLUSION

As a result of the work steps conducted in the planning phase as described above, a properly indexed and organized planning phase workpaper file should have been developed for all the materials gathered and work steps performed. The workpaper file is then used as a resource in developing the in-depth work program and the corresponding field work. A number of critical operating areas should also have been developed where more in-depth review procedures need to be performed in the work program phase leading toward development of a significant operational review finding.

For example, the following areas may have been identified for more in-depth analysis from the planning phase as described in this section.

- Inadequate planning procedures, resulting in no identification of goals, objectives, and detail plans

- Revenue and service delivery trends on a downward spiral in certain programs
- Overall expenditures increasing, particularly:
  - Program expenses
  - Fund-raising costs
  - General and administrative
  - Marketing and promotion
- Increased facilities and equipment
- Increase in the number of administrative positions
- Increase in employee turnover
- Inefficient use of computer processing equipment
- Crowded working conditions, in both program and office areas

The in-depth operational review work program should also have been started. Based on the identification of possible critical operational areas, each member on the review team should have begun thinking about and have documented suggested work steps to be incorporated into the in-depth work program. This is the starting point for developing the operational review work program. The steps required for its finalization are discussed in Chapter 3.

OPERATIONAL REVIEW SITUATION: SERVICE DELIVERY TIME REPORTING TOLERANCES

During the planning phase of an operational review of The Counseling Agency (TCA), the review team found in reviewing the counseling program's methods and procedures that counselors were allowed to charge client time spent to the nearest half-hour increment. Because most of this time was reimbursed through a subrecipient contract with the local county government, TCA management was not concerned as long as they maximized their revenues. These funds were federal pass-through moneys subject to a single audit. The county had performed subrecipient monitoring but had never identified this practice or mentioned it as a finding, questioned cost, or fraudulent or illegal act.

Questions and Solutions for Consideration

1. What additional steps might the reviewer want to perform in the planning phase relative to this situation?

Response

Time-consuming efforts to show the existence of significant deficiencies should not be undertaken. Accordingly, this situation should only be documented at this point, for consideration when deciding on areas for additional work.

2. What could the reviewer suggest, if anything, to the not-for-profit and counseling program management to correct the situation at this point?

Response
Written instructions should be prepared for each counselor stating the specific service delivery procedures and reporting requirements.

Note that the institution of such written instructions, and exercise of such instructions by the counselors resulted in an increase of total real client contact hours served and resultant increases of approximately $80,000 in reimburseable billings as well as the acquisition of three additional counseling contracts in the amount of $280,000.

A Social Service Agency

New Mexico Suicide Intervention Project, Inc.

BACKGROUND

Dr. Kathryn Klassen, a professional psychotherapist in the field of suicide prevention, had a vision to start a social service agency to deal with and ultimately reduce youth suicide risk in northern New Mexico. She was quite concerned with the increasing number of youth suicides and wanted to do something meaningful about it. Dr. Klassen, with a group of community volunteers, established the New Mexico Suicide Intervention Project (NMSIP) in 1990 to provide a continuum of suicide prevention strategies aimed at preventing youth suicidal behavior. In 1994, NMSIP incorporated as a 501(c)(3) not-for-profit.

In 1994, private funds were raised to introduce Natural Helpers, a peer helping program in the local schools aimed at preventing youth suicide. The State Department of Health provided a grant to allow for the training of school suicide crisis teams in each local middle school and high school. In 1996, a local funding organization that provides grants to social service agencies focusing on at-risk children and youth granted NMSIP sufficient funds to establish a teen suicide hot-line. As a result of this grant, in 1997, 20 hot-line volunteers were trained in suicide crisis response skills. At the same time, NMSIP became a collaborator with the University of Washington in its national research project, "Measuring Adolescent Potential For Suicide," which assesses high school students at risk for suicide and depression in New Mexico high schools.

In 1998, NMSIP transferred the teen suicide hot-line to another social service agency provider as they received sufficient funds from a local family foundation to establish a counseling center (SKY Center) for seriously depressed and suicidal youth. In 1999, Natural Helpers formally became part of NMSIP and an Executive Director was hired to coordinate all NMSIP programs.

NMSIP CHALLENGES

NMSIP has been able to keep the agency and its mission—to reduce youth suicide risk in northern New Mexico—alive during these very difficult years. It has been almost a continual struggle from Dr. Klassen's initial vision to find sufficient funding and personnel (paid and volunteer) to provide the necessary services. There has always been a greater need for the services than could be provided.

In 1998, only one year after opening the teen crisis hot-line, NMSIP was forced to give up this service. Competition from another local crisis line initiative and lack of new funding led to this unpleasant decision. In the same year, Dr. Klassen, the founder and executive director (unpaid) became seriously ill and died. However, the board and staff continued their dedication to NMSIP's mission and were able to secure additional funding for youth suicide crisis counseling services.

NMSIP GOALS

NMSIP's overall goal is to stop youth suicide, with supporting goals as follows:

- To promote community awareness that youth suicide is a community-wide health problem and make facts about suicide and its prevention widely available.
- To provide an effective education and training program that helps students, family members, human service professionals, and others who work with youth to recognize, respond to, and refer youth showing signs of suicide risk.
- To provide prevention and crisis intervention counseling services designed to reduce risks associated with youth suicide and increase each individual's protective resources.

NMSIP PROGRAMS

NMSIP is the only social service agency in northern New Mexico that provides services specifically aimed at stopping youth suicide. It strives to reconnect young people to their schools, families, and communities by providing accessible and affordable services. There are no fees for services, no insurance requirements, and no extensive intake interviews.

Services For Kounseling Youth (SKY Center)

The SKY Center is a suicide prevention counseling center that offers free services for young people, referred primarily by local school personnel, who are experiencing school failure, depression, involvement with drug or alcohol use, or other related behaviors that may lead to suicide. The SKY Center focuses on reconnecting these children and teens to their schools, families, and communities in order to reduce their risk and increase their supportive network.

The initial start-up of the SKY Center resulted from a collaborative effort between NMSIP and the College of Santa Fe (CSF). CSF provides space to house the counseling center and other in-kind support, and the SKY Center serves as a teaching and training field site for CSF students of the Masters of Arts in Education counseling track. The SKY Center offers opportunities for such graduate students to complete counseling internships under the supervision of SKY Center licensed professionals in a setting that focuses exclusively on working directly with highly vulnerable youth.

Natural Helpers Program

Natural Helpers is a peer helping program in Santa Fe schools aimed at preventing youth suicide. The program provides intensive training to students, who have been identified as listeners by peers and school staff, and teaches them to respond effectively when their fellow students experience a wide range of difficulties. The program is designed to meet the following goals:

- To lower the adolescent suicide rate in Santa Fe county
- To address the root causes of adolescent suicide
- To train and support student helpers
- To educate teens in the use of existing resources in the schools and larger community
- To create a caring and supportive community within each school

The program exists in all four Santa Fe middle schools, the two high schools, and the New Mexico School for the Deaf. Over 3,500 students come in contact with a "natural helper" during each school year.

NMSIP ORGANIZATIONAL OBJECTIVES

NMSIP board of directors has adopted a two-part approach in accomplishing the above goals:

1. Expand and enhance services in the Santa Fe area.
2. Extend services to other northern New Mexico counties.

NMSIP's priority objectives for achieving its goals include:

- To conduct an education campaign about NMSIP and suicide prevention for the community at large
- To develop and implement a suicide prevention training and education component
- To maintain, enhance, and expand SKY Center and Natural Helpers programs
- To fund raise for operating support
- To reestablish a youth crisis line
- To further develop the board of directors to support NMSIP programs

Three action plans related to these objectives are shown in Exhibit CS1.1.

NMSIP ORGANIZATION

NMSIP is governed by a five-member board of directors who are all dedicated to the mission of the organization from a service delivery viewpoint. NMSIP employs seven part-time employees as shown on the organization chart in Exhibit CS1.2, as follows:

- Executive director, recently hired in 1999, devotes 20 hours per week to the job
- SKY Center program director, since 1997, 20 hours per week
- Natural Helpers program director, since 1995, 20 hours per week
- SKY Center clinical coordinator, 25 hours per week
- Three (3) SKY Center clinical supervisors, 8 hours per week each

GOAL 1. To promote community awareness that youth suicide is a community-wide health problem and make facts about suicide and its prevention widely available.

Priorities	Action Steps	Responsible Parties	Needed Resources	Potential Barriers
Conduct an education campaign about NMSIP and suicide prevention for the community at large	Develop NMSIP pr materials (brochure, suicide prevention information, etc.)	ED with help from program directors	None	Time and Cost
	Present education information to schools, tribal leaders, parent groups, civic groups, etc.	ED and NH program director	Education materials, contacts	Time, cooperation, and funding for travel
	Develop annual fundraising letter	ED, board, and maybe consultant	Mailing list contacts	Time
	Provide information to media: local newspapers and radio stations	ED	List of media contacts	Time to develop press releases and cooperation from media
	Develop NMSIP newsletter	ED with help from program directors	Stories/articles	Time and cost to print
	Explore Web site idea for NMSIP	ED	Volunteer help to develop and maintain	Time, computer software and equipment cost
Further develop board of directors to support NMSIP prorams	Determine board needs; identify potential nominees; meet with nominees to determine interest and time; nominate to serve on Board	Board of directors with assistance from ED	Community volunteers	Lack of time or interest

Exhibit CS1.1   Action Plan for Year 2000 Priorities

GOAL 2. To provide an effective education and training program that trains students, family members, human service professionals, and others who work with youth to recognize, respond to, and refer youth showing signs of suicide risk.

Priorities	Action Steps	Responsible Parties	Needed Resources	Potential Barriers
Develop and implement a suicide prevention training and education component	Identify organizations, schools, activity centers, gatekeepers, etc., who might benefit from training and send letter about training.	ED with help from program directors and board	Informational materials, letter of introduction	Time
	Pilot a suicide prevention education program in a local elementary school for students and staff	ED sets up and NH program director con- ducts training with school personnel and students	Informational materials cooperation	Time and school
	Explore local and federal funding for this effort and write grants	ED	List of foundations and Federal Register publications	Time
To maintain, enhance and expand NH programming in Santa Fe	Explore local and federal funding for expansion and enhancement of NH and write grants	ED	Funding sources	Time
	Expand NH program to other SF schools	ED and NH program director	Funding and contacts	Time, funding, and school cooperation
Fund raise for operating support	Research and write grants, conduct annual mail campaign and solicit business donations	ED	Funding sources, mailing list, and busi- ness contacts	Time
Further develop board of directors to support NMSIP programs	Determine board needs; identify potential nominees; meet with nominees to determine interest and time; nominate to serve on board	Board of directors with assistance from ED	Community volunteers	Lack of time or interest

(Continues)

Exhibit CS1.1   *(Continued)*

GOAL 3. To provide prevention and crisis intervention counseling services designed to reduce risks associated with youth suicide and increase each individual's protective resources.

Priorities	Action Steps	Responsible Parties	Needed Resources	Potential Barriers
To maintain, enhance, and expand SKY Center programming in Santa Fe	Increase counseling service hours for clients from 3 to 4 evenings/days per week	SKY Program director and coordinator ED— grant writing	Staff	Lack of funding
	Increase school-based group counseling to 9 groups per week at various sites	Clinical supervisors and coordinator ED— grant writing	Staff	Lack of funding and cooperation from schools
	Find new and expanded counseling space at College of SF	SKY Program Director and Education Chair, College of SF	New facility and additional support from College of SF	Lack of space on campus; funds to support expanded space
Fund raise for operating support of SKY Center	Research and write grants, conduct annual mail campaign and solicit business donations	ED	Funding sources, mailing list, business contacts	Time
Reestablish crisis line	Gather data on youth crisis calls from Crisis Response and City of Santa Fe	ED	Information from City of SF and Crisis Response	Cooperation from City and Crisis Response
	Meet with funders and President of P.M.S.	Board and ED	Data on youth crisis calls	None
	Research funding opportunities	ED	Federal and private funding sources	Time
Further develop board of directors to support NMSIP programs	Determine board needs; identify potential nominees; meet with nominees to determine interest and time; nominate to serve on board	Board of directors with assistance from ED	Community volunteers	Lack of time or interest

Exhibit CS1.1   *(Continued)*

NMSIP also tries to make effective use of volunteers such as the following:

- Student interns: Five to seven CSF masters students provide counseling at the SKY Center during each school semester.
- School sponsors: Seventeen public school teachers and counselors work as school sponsors in the Natural Helpers Program each school year.
- Parent volunteers: Approximately 175 parents of Natural Helpers provide in-kind services during the school year.

NMSIP FINANCIAL DATA

NMSIP's financial data is presented in Exhibits CS1.3. and CS1.4. for the most recent 12-month period ending December 31.

- Budget versus actual data for both revenues and expenditures
- Statement of Financial Position
- Statement of Activities
- Statement of Functional Activities

It can be seen that NMSIP is managing its operations well within the expected budget amounts (approximately $7,000 in additional revenues and $12,000 less in expenses) and has accumulated over $57,000 in total net assets with $58,500 in cash.

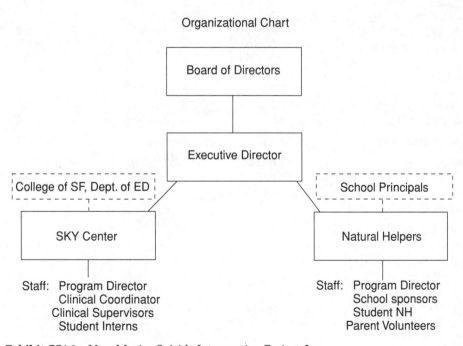

Organizational Chart

Exhibit CS1.2   New Mexico Suicide Intervention Project, Inc.

Income	Projected	Actual	Variance
Contributions	$ 2,000.00	$ 2,000.00	$
Donations	$ 175.00	$ 200.00	$ (25.00)
Grants	$118,074.20	$124,557.23	$ (6,483.03)
Interest income	$ 244.00	$ 426.34	$ (182.34)
Reimbursed expenses	$ 71.00	$ 70.95	$0.05
Total Income	**$120,564.20**	**$127,254.52**	**$ (6,690.32)**

Expenses	Projected	Actual	Variance
Advertising	$ 360.00	$ 379.03	$ (19.03)
Dues and subscriptions	$ 250.00	$ 229.40	$ 20.60
Education and training—NH	$ 10,000.00	$ 5,245.26	$ 4,754.74
Equipment maintenance	$ 200.00	$ 72.29	$ 127.71
Equipment—office	$ —	$ 379.97	$ (379.97)
Equipment telephone	$ —	$ 42.49	$ (42.49)
Equipment rental	$ 14.00	$ 13.90	$ 0.10
Fees	$ 50.00	$ 49.69	$ 0.31
Insurance	$ 500.00	$ 432.60	$ 67.40
Intern stipends	$ 1,500.00	$ 1,500.00	$ —
Payroll	$ 56,725.00	$ 56,129.26	$ 595.74
Payroll taxes	$ 6,200.00	$ 5,814.28	$ 385.72
Postage	$ 300.00	$ 224.74	$ 75.26
Printing and copying	$ 1,000.00	$ 433.46	$ 566.54
Professional fees	$ 3,500.00	$ —	$ 3,500.00
Program expense	$ 800.00	$ 703.09	$ 96.91
Repairs—building/equipment	$ 350.00	$ 208.91	$ 66.09
Services—contractual	$ 3,000.00	$ 2,494.73	$ 505.27
Sponsor stipends	$ 5,000.00	$ 5,500.00	$ (500.00)
Staff development and Training	$ 350.00	$ 385.00	$ (35.00)
Supplies	$ 3,000.00	$ 1,941.56	$ 1,058.44
Telephone	$ 2,800.00	$ 2,663.17	$ 136.83
Travel and promotions	$ 2,600.00	$ 2,249.63	$ 350.37
Capital Outlay**	$ 3,000.00	$ 2,853.99	$ 146.01
Total Expenses	**$101,499.00**	**$ 90,021.45**	**$ 11,857.52**
Net Income	**$ 19,065.20**	**$ 37,233.07**	**$(18,547.84)**

Exhibit CS1.3   NM Suicide Intervention Project, Inc. Budget Comparison
12 months ending

Statement of Financial Position
December 31

Assets	
Cash	$58,503
Property and equipment, net	3,427
Total assets	$61,930

Liabilities and Net Assets	
Accounts payable	$ 4,352
Net assets:	
Unrestricted	3,427
Temporarily restricted	54,151
Total net assets	$57,578
Total liabilities and net assets	$61,930

Statement of Activities
Year Ended December 31

	Unrestricted	Temporarily Restricted	Permanently Restricted	Total
Revenues, gains, and other support:				
Foundation grants and gifts	$ —	$115,819	$ —	$115,819
Government grants	—	8,740	—	8,740
Contributions	—	2,200	—	2,200
Interest income	426	—	—	426
Other operating revenues	232	—		232
Net assets released from restrictions:				
Satisfaction of program restrictions	91,063	(91,063)	—	—
Total revenues, gains, and				
other support	91,721	35,696	—	127,417
Expenses:				
Program Expenses:				
Natural Helpers	24,210	—	—	24,210
SKY Center	41,428	—	—	41,428
Support Services:				
General and administrative	14,367	—	—	14,367
Fundraising	9,124	—	—	9,124
Total expenses	89,129	—	—	89,129
Change in net assets	2,592	35,696	—	38,288
Net assets, beginning of year	835	18,455	—	19,290
Net assets, end of year	$ 3,427	$54,151	$ —	$57,578

(Continued)

Exhibit CS1.4 New Mexico Suicide Intervention Project Statement of Financial Position

Statement of Functional Expenses
Year Ended December 31

	Natural Helpers	Sky Center	General and Administrative	Fund Raising	Total
Wages and payroll taxes	$10,771	$37,092	$6,658	$9,124	$63,645
Intern stipends	—	1,500	—	—	1,500
Sponsor stipends	5,500	—	—	—	5,500
Office supplies	—	200	180	—	380
Program supplies	825	531	586	—	1,942
Postage	10	52	163	—	225
Staff development and training	5,395	100	135	—	5,630
Travel and promotion	1,456	410	383	—	2,249
Insurance	—	82	351	—	433
Printing and copying	22	188	224	—	434
Dues and subscriptions	—	140	137	—	277
Telephone	231	265	2,209	—	2,705
Equipment rentals	—	14	—	—	14
Maintenance and repairs	—	326	30	—	356
Advertising	—	—	379	—	379
Depreciation	—	—	262	—	262
Program expense	—	503	200	—	703
Bookkeeping services	—	25	2,470	—	2,495
Total expenses	$24,210	$41,428	$14,367	$9,124	$89,129

Exhibit CS1.4   *(Continued)*

OPERATIONAL REVIEW—AREAS TO CONSIDER

Based on the materials presented above in the case situation, the review team might want to consider the following areas in developing their plan for conducting an operational review of NMSIP.

- The vision of the founder of NMSIP was to ultimately prevent youth suicidal behavior. This vision was one of altruistic service delivery—that is, to provide such services as a community service with minimal regard as to building NMSIP as a business. Accordingly, the emphasis has remained on maximizing services with the expectation that NMSIP would be able to always find funding. This philosophy and its effectiveness should be indluced as part of the operational review.
- Since its inception, NMSIP has faced a continuous struggle to find sufficient funding and personnel—both paid and volunteer—to provide the necessary services. With such an all-encompassing vision and mission, there has been (and probably always will be) a greater need for the services than could be provided with existing funding. NMSIP management needs to decide what its long-term mission should be—that is, to provide as much services as possible (possibly with no end point) and to seek the funds to do that or to define spe-

cific levels of services that it can provide efficiently and effectively and then develop reliable ongoing sources of funding at that level.

- NMSIP goals and related objectives are mostly geared to improving and increasing services rather than stabilizing present services within existing funding constraints, building NMSIP to service a practical and defined population base, and developing a community reputation for quality and effective services that would promote increased contributions.

- Fund-raising activities are primarily geared toward grants from outside sources such as federal, state, and private entities. Such grants require an amount of time for the grant writing and approval process, which many times makes effective planning difficult. In addition, such funding sources provide no guarantee of continued support and many times will fund such agencies as NMSIP only for a stated time period (e.g., three years). This results in continual grantsmanship activities, which tend to consume a major part of the executive director's time and efforts.

- NMSIP receives minimal support from sources other than grants (approximately $2,500 of total revenues of $120,564). The revenue side of NMSIP's operations must be strongly considered to ensure continued growth and survival. It is too dependent on outside grants. Its planning should be focused more on making NMSIP a unique and desired service provider within the community, which would enhance its image to prospective board members (those who can guide its growth and attract greater participation and contributions) as well as to potential volunteers and contributors.

- While NMSIP may currently enjoy a competitive edge in their community for the providing of such teen suicide prevention services, success usually creates followers. In today's environment of high competition for contributors' dollars (both public and private), NMSIP must work to make itself more visible within the community so that community residents will come forward voluntarily to offer assistance of their time, expertise, and money. NMSIP needs to focus more emphasis on its public relations and marketing efforts.

- NMSIP's two operating programs—the SKY Center and Natural Helpers—appear to be quite successful in the limited time that they have been in existence. Increased efforts should be taken to make these programs as successful as possible before embarking on any plans for expansion.

- The SKY Center operates with part-time professional help—program director, clinical coordinator, and three clinical supervisors—and student interns. It needs to be determined whether such a personnel commitment is sufficient to provide needed services at this time. Emphasis should be on building on the center's successes and matching services provided to desired services. At this point in its growth, NMSIP should be emphasizing the ultimate level of quality services to its population. It appears that NMSIP should be able to build quite easily on its SKY Center success from both a marketing and fund-raising standpoint.

- Presently, NMSIP charges no fees for services, has no insurance requirements, and requires no extensive intake interviews. The emphasis is on the providing of accessible services to an at-risk population. From a social service standpoint, this is certainly commendable. However, from a business survival standpoint, this policy may need to be revisited. NMSIP management should consider as part of its revenue planning the ability to become more self-sufficient and less vulnerable to the whims of funding sources and contributors.

- The Natural Helpers program, a peer-helping program in the schools aimed at preventing youth suicide, has a part-time program director but is mainly dependent on volunteers (17 teachers and counselors and 175 parents) for the direct providing of services. While this program has enjoyed success, this model for providing service should be reviewed as to ways to increase such successes.

- With an increased awareness of a defined universe of services to be provided, the manner in which to provide such services, and the expected results to be achieved, NMSIP should be in a better position to develop plans that result in finite detail plans as to how to make the agency more economical, efficient, and effective. In developing such plans, NMSIP should include all of those involved in its operations, such as management, staff, and volunteers, as well as look at best practices from other similar (and dissimilar) agencies.

- Such detail action plans should result in more flexible program budgets that would reflect the amount of revenues required and the allocation of expenditures based on program activities and results. The projection of necessary revenues establishes a target for each revenue category—that is, grants, contributions and donations, service fees, third-party reimbursements, and so on—with a corresponding detail plan as to how to achieve such revenues. Based on actual revenues, expected service levels would be defined with their corresponding costs, thus creating program expenditure budgets. The level of expenditures would also determine the level of services that could be provided. To increase its services, NMSIP would need to develop plans to increase its revenues. Such an approach provides a specific focus for board members, executive director, program directors, other staff, and volunteers as to revenue efforts as well as correlation to expenditures and related service providing.

Based on the above comments relative to the analysis of NMSIP case materials, the operational review team should consider the following seven critical areas for inclusion in the operational review:

1. *Vision and mission*—maximize suicide prevention services versus balancing such service delivery within revenue constraints.
2. *Services to be provided*—concentration on present programs (SKY Center and Natural Helpers) to be the best they can or continued expansion.
3. *Service delivery versus business model*—that is, provide the services and look for the money, or have the money and then provide the services.
4. *Organization and personnel*—to continue with part-timers and volunteers or pursue a more desirable (and possibly necessary) organizational structure.
5. *Revenue enhancement*—less reliance on outside grants with greater reliance on ongoing contributions and donations as well as the possibility of service fees.

6. *Planning and budget*—the development of organizational and program planning (goals, objectives, and detail plans) directed toward flexible program budgets based on service delivery activity levels.
7. *Internal operations*—analyzing the manner in which activities and services are carried out so as to identify best practices (most efficient at the least cost) in all areas of program operations in an ongoing program of continuous improvements.

CHAPTER THREE

Work Program Phase

INTRODUCTION

This chapter discusses the work program phase of the operational review. It is in the work program phase that the operational reviewer focuses on the significant operational areas identified in the planning phase and develops specific work steps for further review and analysis. Through the performance of these work steps, in the field work phase, the reviewer determines the extent of any operational deficiencies and begins to develop operational review findings. In effect, the work program phase is the bridge between the planning phase and the field work phase. The operational review work program is, therefore, the plan of action for conducting the operational review. However, it is initially written for the preliminary review of those selected activities as determined in the planning phase. Accordingly, it is subject to change based on actual findings during the field work phase. The work program is as important to the operational reviewer as a map is to a navigator.

For instance, the work program would be developed for those areas described in the previous chapter in Exhibit 2.10, prioritizing areas for the operational review in the planning phase as follows:

- Fund-raising procedures
- Services provided
- Program expenses
- Cash management
- Cost accounting

These are the areas identified in the planning phase that show the highest impact on operations and the greatest potential for improvement.

BENEFITS OF THE OPERATIONAL REVIEW WORK PROGRAM

A well-constructed operational review work program is essential to conducting the operational review in an efficient and effective manner. Operational review work programs are the key to successful operational reviews as they provide benefits such as:

- A systematic plan for the work to be performed in the operational review that can be communicated to all operational review staff
- A systematic basis for assigning work to review staff members, according to their specialized skills, technical competencies, and type of task
- A means by which operational review supervisors and other reviewers can compare performance with approved plans, review standards, and requirements
- Assistance in training inexperienced staff members and acquainting them with the scope, objectives, and work steps of the operational review
- The basis for a summary record of work actually performed in the operational review
- Aid in familiarizing successive review groups with the nature of the work performed on this operational review

While these written work programs are essential to efficient and effective management of an operational review assignment, they should never be used simply as a checklist of work steps to perform in a way that stifles individual reviewer initiative, imagination, and resourcefulness in achieving the desired objectives. Remember that the operational review work program is written for the preliminary review of selected activities as determined in the planning phase, but is subject to change based on what is actually found in the field work phase of the review.

**THE WORK PROGRAM
GUIDES THE WORK**

OPERATIONAL REVIEW WORK PROGRAM STANDARDS

The operational review work program is really a plan for the review work steps that the reviewer believes will achieve the best results. Once the actual results are determined, the reviewer may want to change the plan. For instance, in conducting a review work step it may be determined that the perceived deficiency is not really significant. In this case, the reviewer would curtail this work step and any others associated with it. If it is determined that a particular area is really more significant than expected, however, then the work program should be increased by additional work steps.

The review work program is developed for the specific circumstances of the not-for-profit or area under review. Therefore, each review work program is a unique entity. This being the case, the operational review work program is normally developed for one-time use. Unlike financial audits, operational reviews do not have last year's workpapers to refer to. Although there may be previous operational reviews available for reference, keep in mind that each situation is unique and the use of "borrowed" work steps should be minimized and used only in those cases in which they are appropriate.

In preparing the operational review work program, the reviewer should consider certain standards, such as:

- The operational review work program should be tailor-made to fit the specific operational review assignment as to type of organization, personnel involved, systems and procedures in effect, degree of sophistication, and so on.
- Each work step should clearly set forth the work to be done and the reason for doing it. Including a clear explanation of the reasons for each work step is helpful because:
  - The staff member carrying out the work must know why the work step is being done. With this information, the reviewer can be expected to do a much better job than if he or she is asked to perform a work step without sufficient background.
  - It minimizes the inclusion of unnecessary work steps. Sometimes the inability to cite a good reason for doing something leads the work program writer to the conclusion that the work step is not really needed.
  - It makes possible a more intelligent review of the work program for advance approval and post review of work performed.
- The work program should be flexible and permit application of initiative in deviating from prescribed procedures. Because the work program is really a plan based on the work steps that the operational review team believes will achieve the best results, once the actual results are determined, the reviewers may want to change the plan.
- The work program should specifically provide for the development of individual findings. In this respect, it should help to:
  - Determine why the results and conditions found are as they are, not just how they are. In effect, performance is analyzed, not simply reported.
  - Direct attention to evidential matter in support of conclusions.
  - Evaluate performance and evidence in comparison with relevant standards and norms of performance. Note that relevance is a judgment factor dependent on the experience, imagination, and common sense of the operational reviewer.

THE WORK PROGRAM
BENEFITS THE OPERATIONAL REVIEW

WHO DEVELOPS THE WORK PROGRAM

There is no good reason that the review manager has to be solely responsible for the development of the work program. In fact, the more input into work program development, the better the finished product. As a general rule, all members of the operational review team should be involved in developing the work program, particularly those staff members who were involved in the planning phase. In addition, others may be considered to provide input into the work program development process, such as:

- Operational review staff members who have some expertise in the area under review or have participated in a similar review in the past
- Not-for-profit personnel who work in the area being reviewed, who have some special input to provide (take care that such client personnel maintain their objectivity)
- Outside consultants or experts who have special expertise in the area being reviewed or in the operational review process
- Personnel from other similar organizations or functions who may be able to offer another perspective

The same personnel can also be used in the field work phase, development of findings and recommendations, and reporting phase of the operational review. In fact, normally, the greater the mix of personnel involved in the operational review, the greater the potential for positive results. Involving not-for-profit user personnel to the extent possible usually ensures a greater likelihood of the acceptance of recommendations. Often, the use of outside assistance enhances the quality of the operational review, while allowing for the use of operational review personnel in the areas where they are most familiar. However, be aware that outside consultants can be costly—so use them judiciously.

Although the use of the team approach is recommended for the optimum development of the operational review work program, it can be more costly and time-consuming than having one or two operational review team members develop the program. Moreover, it is not always cost effective to use the team approach, particularly when a number of different areas or locations are involved. The approach to be taken often depends on the size of the review and the total of budgeted review hours.

**THE MORE INVOLVED,
THE BETTER THE WORK PROGRAM**

WORK PROGRAM WORK STEPS

After deciding on the makeup of the operational review program team, the next step is to develop the work steps to be performed for each area identified as significant in the planning phase. Although, as previously mentioned, each operational review work program and not-for-profit is unique, this does not prevent the reviewers from using specific work steps from previously completed operational reviews of other not-for-profits. However., they must be careful to use them only if they meet the requirements of the present operational review. Otherwise, entirely new work steps need to be developed. To help in developing these work steps, the reviewer must be aware of some of the more common techniques that can be used in the performance of the operational review in the field work phase, such as:

- Review of existing documentation, such as policy and procedures manuals
- Preparation of organization charts and related functional job descriptions
- Analysis of personnel policies and procedures related to hiring, orientation, training, evaluation, promotion, and firing
- Analysis of organizational policies and related systems and procedures, both administrative and operational
- Interviews with management and operations personnel
- Flowchart preparation:
  - Systems flowcharts, showing the processes of a functional area
  - Layout flow diagrams, showing the physical layout of a work area and its related work flow
- Ratio, change, and trend analysis
- Questionnaires, for use by the reviewer or client's personnel
- Surveys, by phone or in written form, for customers or clients, vendors, and so on to respond to
- Questions within the review work program
- Review of transactions, in which the different types of normal and abnormal transactions are considered
- Review of operations, by techniques such as observation, work measurement, time studies, work performance forms or logs, and so on
- Forms analysis.
- Analysis of results.
- Review and analysis of management information system and related reports
- Compliance reviews; as to compliance with laws, regulations, grants and contracts, policies, procedures, goals, objectives, and so forth
- Use of computer processing; using "through-the-computer" techniques or review and analysis of computer-produced information

These field work techniques should be used, of course, only where they are appropriate. Relative to the determination of which techniques to use in operational reviews is this rule: Whatever work step works best in the situation, use it. There is no reason a reviewer cannot use specific review techniques that he or she or others used in different operational reviews in the past. In fact, this should be encouraged, as it is usually easier and ensures a greater degree of success to use tried-and-true techniques rather than untried approaches. However, this is not meant to discourage creative and innovative approaches to operational review work steps, because quite often such approaches are necessary to fit a specific situation and yield the greatest results in improved operations. Remember, in establishing which operational review work steps to use, the goal is to identify those specific review techniques that most closely fit the situation and have the best possibility of providing operational benefits.

THE BEST WORK STEP
IS THE ONE THAT WORKS

WORK PROGRAM DEVELOPMENT PROCEDURES

In the development of the operational review work program, the review team needs to keep in mind the following procedural steps:

1. Identification of the critical operational areas and their related control and risk areas. These risk areas usually relate to the inability to achieve the operational areas' goals and objectives.
2. Development of key questions and work steps to validate and quantify the perceived risk areas. For instance, for the service delivery function, the reviewer might question procedures relative to client intake, service changes, service providing, case recordkeeping and reporting, client relations, and analysis.
3. Identification of the work steps needed to provide answers to the perceived risk areas and key questions. This entails the matching of the aforementioned field work tasks and others appropriate to the risk area in question. Work steps include observations, flowcharts, interviews, and so on.
4. Development of review work plans for each area to be reviewed, including personnel assignments, time schedules, and review budgets.

As an example of using these steps to develop the review program, consider the fund-raising procedure. The identified control and risk areas include the possibility of not contacting identified contributors, contacting potential donors that should not have been contacted, or contacting more donors at excessive costs than may be necessary. The objective of the work steps might then be to ascertain that only those potential donors and contributors be contacted that are aware of and supportive of the not-for profit at the least possible costs. The work steps that can help the reviewer meet the objective may include:

1. Selecting a number of operating departments or work units where the reviewers will interview and review with department management and operations personnel the way their fund-raising activities are controlled and processed
2. Identifying the need for selected procedures, materials, equipment, or services for approved purposes, plans, or programs of fund-raising activities
3. Determining authority for fund-raising activity approvals, including purpose budgetary requirements within the operating department
4. Analyzing the establishment of fund-raising procedures and their integration with not-for-profit plans and activities
5. Flowcharting the fund-raising process to determine whether there are adequate controls and processing procedures to ensure the effectiveness of fund-raising activities and the subsequent processing of contributions received
6. Reviewing and analyzing fund-raising procedures to ensure that such activities are being conducted in the most economical manner

SAMPLE WORK PROGRAM

A more complete sample operational review work program for not-for-profit fund-raising activities that provides examples of many of these work step techniques is shown in Exhibit 3.1. Note that the sections of the work program and the corresponding areas within each section should relate back to the areas for further review as identified in the planning phase. For demonstration purposes, a number of different areas are presented for review, each of which could have been identified as significant in the planning phase. However, in the conduct of a typical operational review, the number of areas to be reviewed would be based on the establishment of priorities as related to their significance and criticalness to overall operations and the amount of review budget time allocated to this particular operational review.

In Exhibit 3.1, four operational areas were selected for review:

1. Not-for-profit policy and organization, including organizational status of the fund-raising or development activity, responsibility for fund raising, authorization for fund raising, and decentralized fund raising

FIELD WORK PHASE: FUND RAISING ACTIVITIES

	Hours	Dates	Staff
I. NOT-FOR-PROFIT POLICY AND ORGANIZATION			
A. Organizational Status of Fund-Raising Activities			
1. Organization chart and analysis	20	3-25/30	Ted
2. Descriptions: work unit's/individual's specific functions.	30	3-26/4-7	Ted
3. Determine: fund-raising activity reporting	4	3-25	Ted
4. Analyze: individual's/work unit's functions	16	4-1/4-7	Ted
5. Document duties and responsibilities	24	4-1/4-7	Sue
6. Obtain copies of existing job descriptions	2	4-1	Sue
7. Interview each employee, volunteer, supervisor.	30	4-1/4-7	Ted/Sue
8. Observe actual work being performed.	8	4-2/4-3	Ted/Sue
9. Determine necessity of all duties and responsibilities.	4	4-7	Ted/Sue
	138		
B. Responsibility for Fund Raising			
1. Not-for-profit policy on fund-raising activities	4	3-25	Meg
2. Responsibility of the fund-raising activity	4	3-25	Meg
3. Ascertain knowledge of conflicting responsibility	4	3-26	Meg
4. Document other fund raising activities	4	3-26	Meg
5. Policy covering other's relations	4	3-27	Meg
6. Analyze such activities	4	3-27	Meg
7. Heavy contributors and critical donors	8	3-28	Meg
	32		
C. Authorization for Purchasing			
1. Obtain copy or document policies as to:	16	3-25	Joe
• Approval of fund-raising plan and detail procedures			
• Approval limits of solicitation efforts.			
• Expenditure efforts related to fund-raising activities			
• Budget approval of fund-raising activities			
2. Analyze procedures—review of selected transactions:	24	3-26/3-27	Joe
Where the final cost of a fund raising activity exceeds the amount of the funds contributed	40		

Exhibit 3.1   Sample Operational Review Budget

Where changes are made in the amount
of the contribution from expected plan:

D. Decentralized Fund-Raising Activities
   1. Not-for-profit policies and procedures—
      decentralized   8   4-4   Ellen
   2. Select and analyze transactions—
      decentralized   16   4-5/4-7   Ellen
                            24

II. FUND-RAISING ACTIVITY OPERATIONS
  A. Fund Raising Activity Procedures
    1. Fund-raising activity operating procedures.   12   3-28/4-4   John
    2. Flowcharts: major fund-raising operations   32   4-4/4-12   John
    3. Review procedures related to fund-raising
      solicitations   24   4-13/4-17 John
                            68

  B. Fund-Raising Activity Forms
    1. Obtain a copy of each form   4   3-28   Ellen
    2. Analyze purpose of each form   4   3-28   Ellen
                            8

  C. Physical Facilities
    1. Prepare a layout flow diagram   4   3-26   John
    2. Analyze layout flow diagram   4   3-26   John
                            8

  D. Collateral Operations
    1. Determine and describe collateral
      operations   4   3-27   John
    2. Analyze purpose and necessity   4   3-27   John
                            8

III. REVIEW OF FUND-RAISING ACTIVITY TRANSACTIONS
    1. Examine files and select transactions   8   4-1   Evie
    2. Examine each type of transaction selected   24   4-1/4-5   Evie
                            32

IV. RECORDS AND REPORTS
    1. Collect records and reports   16   3-28/4-4   Joe
    2. Analyze purpose and need for all reports   24   4-5/4-12   Joe
                            40

V. REVIEW MANAGEMENT FUNCTIONS
    1. Review of field work results   32   4-20/4-24 Edie/Phil
    2. Development of findings   24   4-25/4-26 Edie/Phil
    3. Oral reporting   16   5-1   Edie/Phil
    4. Written report   32   5-2/5-6   Edie/Phil
    5. Ongoing review management   60   Ongoing   Edie/Phil
                           164

  Total Field Work Budget   562

Exhibit 3.1 *(Continued)*

2. Fund-raising operations, including work area procedures, fund-raising forms and brochures, physical facilities, systems in use, and collateral operations.
3. Review of fund-raising transactions, including selection of transactions to include various types of transactions that the reviewer identified as possible areas of deficiency (e.g., past donors not followed up, current pledges not followed up, and so on), and examination of transactions selected
4. Records and reports—management information and controls being reported, as well as those that should be but are not being reported.

Operational Review Work Program: Fund-Raising Activities

Not-for-Profit Policy and Organization

Organizational Status of Fund-Raising Activities

1. Secure or prepare an organization chart of the fund-raising activity (in some not-for-profits this activity is known as *development*) with descriptions of each work unit's and/or individuals (both employees and volunteers) specific functions. Determine to whom the head of the fund-raising activity reports. Perform analytical work to determine whether such reporting is proper or whether it results in operational concerns and problems. Analyze each individual's and work unit's functions to determine whether they are appropriate and proper fund-raising activity functions.
2. Document the duties and responsibilities of each fund-raising activity employee and volunteer. Obtain copies of existing job descriptions showing authority and responsibilities, and validate through interviewing each employee, volunteer, and related supervisor. Observe actual work being performed. Determine necessity of all duties and responsibilities.

Responsibility for Fund Raising

1. Obtain or prepare not-for-profit policy on fund-raising activities. Determine that the responsibility of the fund-raising activity is clearly defined and understood by fund-raising activity personnel and other non–fund-raising personnel. Ascertain whether the fund-raising activity staff has knowledge of conflicting fund-raising responsibility assumed by other areas or individuals (e.g., specific board or management members). Document any principal fund-raising activities for which the fund-raising activity has no responsibility or limited responsibility.
2. Obtain or prepare policy covering others' relations with present or potential donors as to contacts or discussions or correspondence. Analyze such activities within selected areas or individuals to determine the ex-

tent of such fund-raising and donor relations. Select a number of heavy contributors and critical donors (and grantors) to survey as to their relations with the not-for-profit fund-raising activity and other non–fund-raising not-for-profit personnel. Use both telephone survey and written response survey techniques.

Authorization for Purchasing

1. Obtain copy or document policies as to:
   - Approval of fund-raising plan and detail procedures
   - Approval limits as to type and amount of solicitation efforts
   - Expenditure efforts related to fund-raising activities—time and dollars
   - Budget approval of fund-raising activities prior to commitment, including strategic, long-term, short-term and detail plans
2. Analyze procedures through the review of selected transactions in which the final cost of a fund-raising activity exceeds the amount of the funds contributed (or no funds contributed):
   - Where expected contribution of original plan is not exceeded by final cost
   - Where expected contribution is exceeded, but final cost is still more than the contribution
   - Where there is no contribution made
3. Analyze procedures through the review of selected transactions in which changes are made in the amount of the contribution from expected plan:
   - Contribution exceeds plan
   - Contribution is less than plan
   - There is no contribution made
   - Contribution is made, but expected contribution not in plan

Decentralized Fund-Raising Activities

1. Determine not-for-profit policies and procedures on fund-raising activities made by decentralized individuals or operating units, through direct solicitation as to:
   - Limits of authority
   - Reporting responsibility
   - Review or control by central fund-raising activity
2. Select a number of such decentralized fund-raising activities for review. Analyze a selected number of such transactions as to compliance with existing not-for-profit policies related to decentralized fund raising.

Note: The purpose of this portion of the review is to learn of the policies and general conditions under which the fund-raising activity operates. The sources of information will usually be the head of the fund-raising activity, other fund-raising staff, and not-for-profit manuals.

Where policies are lacking or indefinite, there may be weakness in control, duplicating fields of responsibility, or other deficiency that will be evidenced in the course of the review. Also evidenced will be variations between policy and actual operations.

Fund-Raising Activity Operations

Fund-Raising Activity Procedures

1. Obtain or prepare a copy of the fund-raising activity operating procedures.
2. Prepare flowcharts of the major fund-raising operations, such as the handling of donor pledges, processing of contributions received, control over open pledges, receipt of contributions and donations (cash, in-kind, and noncash) and donor payment procedures.
3. Review procedures related to fund-raising solicitations:
   - Dollar amounts of contributions and donations solicited
   - Requests for pledges and follow-up
   - Form of contributions pledged and received (cash, in-kind, or noncash)
   - Summarization of solicitation efforts—costs and results

Fund-Raising Activity Forms

Obtain a copy of each form (specialized and individualized) used by the fund-raising activity. These should be studied so that the purpose and usage is thoroughly understood. Areas to be considered include:

   - Contribution pledge form clear and complete, so that the donor understands all terms and conditions
   - Protection of blank contribution receipt forms
   - Routing of copies of fund-raising forms
   - Necessity of each copy of the form
   - Forms designed for efficient and simple completion
   - Use of specialized forms to eliminate repetitive processing such as:
     - Time-phased contributions for repetitive contributions against the same pledge (e.g., $200 per month)
     - Repetitive solicitations from the same donor or organization

Note: It is common to find overelaborate routines relating to the preparation of fund-raising forms, particularly the pledge form. The not-for-profit wants to make it as simple as possible for potential donors—not scary or confusing forms that may change the donor's mind about making a contribution.

Physical Facilities

Prepare a layout flow diagram of the fund-raising activity if appropriate (i.e., if it is a large area, rather than one individual at a desk) showing its layout and general facilities, with particular attention to:

- Work flow efficiencies and inefficiencies
- Arrangements for reception of and interviews with donors
- Office layout for effective/ineffective operations

Collateral Operations

1. Determine and describe all operations performed by the fund-raising activity that are not directly concerned with fund raising. For example, the fund-raising activity may be assigned responsibility for such operations as:
   - Planning the annual meeting
   - Special services for large donors such as making reservations or acquiring special items such as books
   - Sale of materials and equipment
   - Match-making donors and employees

In the review of the collateral operations of the fund-raising activity, the reviewer will have a twofold concern: (1) the effect that the inclusion of these operations under the responsibility of the fund-raising activity will have, as far as internal control is concerned; and (2) the review of the assigned collateral operations.

Because of the many variables, it is not possible to specify any definite program for the review of specific collateral responsibilities of the fund-raising activity. The reviewer must shape his or her study to cover each situation, and it may develop that a supplementary study of a particular function or activity should be made.

Review of Fund-Raising Activity Transactions

Selection of Transactions

Examine files covering all fund-raising activities (e.g., pledges, contributions received, etc.) over a period of XX months. From these files, select, for detailed examination, transactions that include some of each of the following:

- Pledges and contributions made by each fund raiser
- Pledges and/or contributions made by each major donor
- A number of "rush" or "emergency" contributions
- Single contributions divided between several donors
- Contributions that differ from the original pledge—over or under
- Contribution receipts in which dollars, quantities, or specifications are revised from the actual contribution
- Contributions in which a number of payments are made over a period of time

Note: The selection of an adequate sample of donor transactions is of utmost importance. The objective is to set aside for detailed examination a group of contributions that will adequately represent both the "normal" and the "abnormal." There must be enough of the "normal" for the reviewer to verify general policies and procedures and reveal situations that may call for more extensive examination.

Examination of Transactions Selected

The examination of each type of transaction selected should be completed in enough detail, through examination of all supporting records, to enable the reviewer to acquire sufficient knowledge as to how each of the operations, from origination and approval of the contribution to the completion of the contribution, was handled. The reviewer must be constantly concerned with what was done and why; to achieve satisfaction that each contribution was placed and handled in the best interests of the not-for-profit.

It is through this examination that the reviewer may become aware of situations, in the fund-raising activity or in other areas of the not-for-profit, that require further study. The objectives are (1) through verification, to provide the basis for appraisal of current policies and procedures, and (2) to give a basis for constructive recommendation. The following list is intended only as a sample of questions that will occupy the reviewer's attention and may be the subject for further inquiry:

- Where a pledge or contribution was divided among several donors, what was the reason?
- On donor receipts, did some other operating area within the not-for-profit really assume the fund-raising function?
- If contributions are placed for such items as memberships or merchandise, just what is gained by clearing these through fund-raising routines?
- Are there any indications of favoritism to donors?
- Where changes are made from original pledge specifications, are these adequately approved and brought to the attention of those who should be concerned?
- How are allowances and adjustments, such as increases or decreases to a pledge or contribution, handled and approved?
- Does the employee approving a contribution pledge or contribution appear to have adequate information to enable intelligent approval?
- Does it appear that effort is made to make contributing to the not-for-profit by the most economical methods?
- What consideration is given to the tax status of contributions—gifts, noncash items, in-kind, real estate, securities, and so on?
- Are there proper safeguarding procedures for noncash contributions, such as art, negotiable securities, materials, and equipment?
- Can each contribution be traced to the books of record—backward and forward with a clear audit trail?

Records and Reports

The various records that are used in current operations will have been reviewed and appraised in the study of fund-raising procedures. This will include such records as those showing sources of contributions and listings of pledges and contributions received.

Beyond these will be a variety of records and reports that are not required in the normal flow of work but are maintained to provide information considered valuable for administrative response. Examples of this type of record or report are:

- Records of pledges made by each donor
- Records of pledges and contributions placed by each individual, showing number and total value
- Reports of future expected commitments—pledges and contributions
- Reports of fund-raising operations to management
- Reports of contribution trends
- Reports that have been rendered to management covering special contributions, lost contributions, cost savings, or other accomplishments

The examination and appraisal of records and reports has two objectives:

1. First should come verification of the accuracy of the records of statements that are maintained or reported. This should be done on a test basis. For example, if a saving was claimed, there should be a test to be sure that the claimed saving was actually realized.
2. After verification of the general accuracy, the second step is appraisal of the value to the operating area or management member using or receiving the record or report. In this appraisal, the reviewer should ascertain the answers to such questions as:
   - Is each record really used?
   - Does each report serve a useful purpose?
   - Does each report give a complete and accurate picture?
   - Are reports incomplete, so important factors are not brought to management's attention?

The answers to these and other questions that arise will require discussions with those who prepare the records and reports and with those who receive and use them.

OPERATIONAL REVIEW ENGAGEMENT BUDGET

At this point, the operational review team has finalized the initial work program. This was accomplished by identifying the specific work steps and techniques to use for the significant operational areas selected for review. Now the amount of time necessary to complete each work step must be determined to arrive at an overall engagement budget. For those work steps and techniques that have been used in previous operational reviews, there is some experience on which to base budget estimates. For new work steps or techniques, however, best professional judgment will have to be used in arriving at budgeted hours.

Keep in mind that an operational review budget must be flexible and is subject to change. Such flexibility in budgeting is necessary because of the greater possibilities of budget changes. These changes result from activities performed in the field workphase, requiring either additional time for areas warranting more attention or less time for areas found to be less critical than expected.

For instance, additional field work may be needed when the area under review requires more analysis to identify findings and recommendations for operational improvements; or additional significant operational deficiencies may be identified that were not included in the initial work program scope, which require additional budget hours or reallocation of existing budget hours. It can also happen that an area under review may also not yield significant review findings to the extent originally expected. If that happens, the reviewer should stop operational review efforts as soon as this situation is determined and reallocate any hours remaining in the budget for these planned work steps to other work steps.

It is important to understand the significance of the planning phase activities and not to look for budget shortcuts. A well-defined and -performed planning phase not only helps to focus correctly on the right operational activities to review during the field work phase, but it also assists to reduce unnecessary field work steps. Bear in mind that both of these work programs (planning and field work phases) are front-end estimates as to the necessary work steps and budget hours required. These are subject to change, based on actual conditions found as a result of the performance of the work steps themselves. Accordingly, the work program could be changed dramatically upward or downward.

The review team needs to be flexible about shifting work steps, as well as the assigning of review personnel, estimated budget hours, and scheduled start and completion times. This requires the exercise of proper and adequate management control over the operational review engagement, together with sufficient reporting from operational review staff to provide timely identification of any work scope changes. For the greatest effectiveness in conducting and controlling the work program, there must be cohesive team effort between operational review management, staff, and client personnel.

A sample operational review engagement budget for the field work phase is shown in Exhibit 3.1. Note that this budget is prepared prior to the actual work and consists of best estimates, subject to change.

Note that the budget shown earlier in Exhibit 3.1 is for a relatively large review of a large not-for-profit's fund-raising function. It is presented as an example of a work program for the field work phase including the development of findings and the reporting phases. The scope, extent, and number of hours needed to perform a specific operational review in a given situation would, of course, need to be scaled downward or upward as appropriate. The estimated hours shown in the work program budget are intended as representations. They are not meant to imply or relate to actual hours required. Note that the planning phase normally takes an estimated factor of time as compared to the field work phase. A rule of thumb is that the planning phase is approximately one-tenth of the field work phase—in this case, about 60 hours.

Note also that the personnel assigned to the operational review should consist of internal personnel responsible for conducting such reviews, personnel from the user's area, and outside consultants where necessary. As shown in Exhibit 3.1, Edie, Ted, Sue, and Joe are members of the internal review staff; Phil, Meg, Ellen, and Evie are members of the fund-raising activity; and John is an outside consultant. The management of the review is also shared between the review team (e.g., Edie) and the user area (e.g., Phil) to ensure its effectiveness and inclusion with the operating area. In effect, this shared approach to conducting the operational review helps in making the review owned by the operational area with the internal (or outside) review team in the role of helpers or catalysts for change. It then becomes the user's responsibility for change, not the review team's.

**THE OPERATIONAL REVEW BUDGET
IS A HELPFUL SYSTEM**

ASSIGNMENT OF STAFF

Once the work program has been developed and work steps have been identified, the next procedure in the work program phase is to assign appropriate staff personnel to conduct each work step. In other projects, assigning personnel to specific work steps is a fairly simple matter, as there is great interchangeability between staff members in their ability to perform required work steps. In addition, many of the work steps are repetitions of those of similar reviews and even of those of the same project performed in previous years. But not so in an operational review. First, some of the required work steps for a particular operational review may be one-time activities, whereby they are being performed for the first time and may or may not be done again. Second, certain work steps may require specific specialized skills, such as analytical ability, communications skills, knowledge of specific systems and procedures, perceptual ability, organizational and personnel structure skills, and specific technical abilities.

Accordingly, it is extremely important in the performance of an operational review to match the skills and abilities needed to perform effectively a specific work step with staff members' expertise in performing a particular work step.

Theoretically, the closer the match between the skills needed for a particular work step and the skills possessed by the staff member doing the work, the greater the results. In reality, there is not always the luxury of having sufficient staff to assign to optimize such a matching of skills. What normally happens is that an effort is made to optimize such skills matching based on staff personnel available, while dealing with the constraint of having to perform work steps requiring similar skills within the same time frame. The critical task of assigning the right staff members to the right work steps often becomes a case of "making the best of the situation."

THE OPERATIONAL REVIEW IS ONLY AS GOOD
AS THE OPERATIONAL REVIEWERS

OPERATIONAL REVIEW MANAGEMENT

The initial consideration in assigning staff to the operational review is review management. Where possible, it is always best to divide such management responsibilities between the operational review staff and the not-for-profit's operational personnel. The operational review staff manager should be clearly responsible for the technical content and timely completion of the operational review work steps, and the not-for-profit's staff person should be responsible for ensuring the cooperation of departmental management and operational personnel, as well as providing liaison, coordination, and integration between operational personnel and the operational review staff. The specific individuals selected to manage the operational review are extremely critical to its ultimate success. They should be selected most carefully, considering such attributes as:

- Past performance on operational reviews
- Knowledge and experience relative to the area being reviewed
- Ability to effectively manage for results
- Ability to recognize operational deficiencies, identify the causes, and recommend realistic positive improvements
- Communication skills with operational review staff members, client management and operations personnel, and organizational decision makers
- Expertise or understanding in required technical skills such as interviewing, flowcharting, and so on
- Ability to work together with the operational review team and client personnel
- Flexibility as to changes in identified critical areas, work steps, and staff assignments

- Persuasiveness required to convince client management to implement developed recommendations
- Organizational skills to keep the various pieces of the operational review together in a cohesive and understandable framework

The managers assigned to the operational review, usually at least one from the review team and one from operations staff, are then responsible for assigning the staff to work on the operational review. In most instances, the starting point is to determine which review team staff members, client personnel, and outside technical assistance are available for assignment during the time required to conduct the operational review. The process then becomes one of scheduling the best fit between work steps and personnel attributes.

Note that the preparation of the planning phase work program would most likely be done by the operational review managers with additional assistance as requested (e.g., other review team staff, client personnel, outside consultants), while the field work review program would be prepared by all concerned. Many times, the field work program must be submitted to management prior to the start of the operational review. However, in most instances, it will be changed as a result of the planning phase. The preparation and submission of field work review programs prior to the completion of the planning phase is particularly difficult to achieve with any degree of accuracy. It is good practice to request that management wait until completion of the planning phase. This is even more critical for outside consultants, because they may be forced to provide budgets and fees before they are aware of the scope of the work.

Review management would then assign the work steps of the planning phase and field work phase, based on the personnel available. It is good practice to document the operational review team on an organization chart, showing reporting relationships and time availability. To help review managers assign staff to work steps based on time availability, they could use a review program calendar showing the available work days. Once staff assignments are made for the work steps, the planned dates for completion and the staff assigned to each work step are noted on the review budget.

**THE BEST MANAGER IS THE ONE
WHO MAXIMIZES RESULTS**

CONCLUSION

These operational review work steps will be followed up in the next chapter on the field work phase, but for now, remember—not all work steps developed in the work program phase result in the development of significant operational review findings. However, because the reviewer does not know which work steps will provide the most significant findings, all work steps in a work plan must be followed through.

OPERATIONAL REVIEW SITUATION: CLIENT CASE RECORDS DEFICIENCIES

As part of the operational review of The Counseling Agency, the following deficiencies as related to the handling of client case records were disclosed:

1. **Noncompliance—Return Client Case Records to Files.** Counselors are not returning clients' case records to the appropriate folders and files after use, causing other counselors and interested parties to recreate many of the records and spend considerable time searching for file folders that are not in the files. This was found to exist for almost 50 percent of all client folders. This practice was a result of noncompliance with established procedures, whereby client folders were to be checked out and then immediately returned to the files after use.
2. **Improper Updating of Case Records.** Of the 37 counselors in all service areas of the Agency, it was found that 34 were over a month behind on the current posting to client case records. Present Agency policies state that such case records must be updated within the same day as the service provided. The current practice has caused ineffective treatment to many clients as well as the inability to properly process third-party payments for reimbursements. It is estimated that the Agency is behind in such billings by over $400,000. This has resulted in major cash flow problems, the necessity to borrow for operating needs, and the recent downsizing of eight counselors. The Agency is no longer able to provide services in compliance with their major funding sources.

Question and Solutions for Consideration

Document one work step to include in your work program.

1. **Noncompliance—Return Client Case Records to Files**
   a. Analyze sample to determine incidence and amount of noncompliance as to returning client case records to the file. Review procedures in counseling areas to determine where this practice is being performed.
   b. Determine whether the present procedure is effective and whether any changes need to be made to ensure that case folders are in the files or able to be found quickly.

2. Improper Updating of Case Records

    a. Analyze sample number of case records from each of the counseling areas to determine the extent of the practice of improper updating of case records—that is, which areas and which individuals, and to what extent.

    b. Review procedures within the Agency to ascertain whether practices allow for the effective communication of services provided and the billing of third-party payments.

    c. Review the present policy of updating case records within the same day as services by the counselors and ascertain whether the current policy should be changed.

Note: This may be only indicative of the real problem—a tip of an iceberg situation—the amount of case recordings required together with the workloads by counselor and the reasons underlying the situation.

The correction of these deficiencies resulted in an annual net savings of more than $140,000, as well as in identifying a significant problem area in the increasing amount of improperly maintained client case records. The review scope was therefore expanded to determine the causes for the increase in case record deficiencies, and a recommendation was made for major case recording and related quality control systems and procedures changes.

A Museum Operation

Santa Fe Children's Museum

BACKGROUND

The Santa Fe Children's Museum (SFCM) was founded by four local educators who perceived a need for educational opportunities in Santa Fe that would be distinctly different from those provided at home or school. Convinced that experiential learning is a necessary complement to traditional education, the four founders sought to create a dynamic, hands-on, informal learning environment for children. It was incorporated in 1985. For the next three years, museum activity centered around prototype exhibits that were installed in public places such as shopping malls and community centers. In February 1989, SFCM opened its doors to a permanent facility and became the first children's museum in New Mexico.

SFCM primarily serves children ages 2 through 12, their families, and their teachers. More than 65,000 individuals participated in museum activities in the past year, including 6,000 member visits, 10,000 schoolchildren visiting with classes, and 10,000 individuals participating in outreach activities.

SFCM serves all children living in or visiting the Santa Fe area; outreach programs also serve the Albuquerque and northern New Mexico areas. SFCM is a community-based, client-centered organization. Approximately 65 percent of its clients are children, and 35 percent are parents or teachers. SFCM employs six full-time staff and 12 part-time staff as well as 15 teen interns per year and uses over 200 volunteers between the ages of 12 and 85 in its operations.

MISSION AND PHILOSPHY

SFCM's stated mission is "to build upon a child's natural sense of joy and discovery by cultivating habits of inquiry in the arts, sciences, and humanities." SFCM's informal learning environment fosters interactions among children and families and encourages active participation in the learning process through interactive exhibitions and programs.

SFCM believes that children have the right to reach their greatest potential and that children have the capacity to construct their own knowledge in an environment that provides for honest inquiry and real discovery and the human need to socialize. To that end, SFCM has created a place of warmth and color, a learning laboratory whose exhibits and programs are designed to cultivate habits of inquiry that will last a lifetime, invite manipulation, exploration, and experimentation, and present challenges to children and adults alike.

SFCM'S PROGRAMS AND ACCOMPLISHMENTS

Working within their mission, SFCM has become an established and successful children's educational resource within their community. Some of their programs and accomplishments include the following:

- An informal learning environment within their facilities where families can play and learn together and children can take responsibility for their own learning.
- Quality educational exhibits designed to intrigue the mind and elicit questions about learning
- The Education Connection, a field trip program that serves over 10,000 school-children per year
- Art and science education programming that is free with museum admission
- Monthly family performances designed to introduce children to the magic of live theater
- Informal parent education programming with a bilingual child development specialist on site
- Publication of *Voices of Violence/Vision of Peace*, a book documenting Santa Feans' experience with violence, including a section for parents on raising caring children
- Outreach project, Museum on Wheels, located at hospitals in Santa Fe and Albuquerque
- Coordination of community educational events such as workshops with nationally recognized child development experts
- Professional development programs and opportunities for educators
- Teen volunteer and paid teen intern program serving over 100 youth per year, including referrals from Teen Court.
- Outreach programs to expand the number of people served such as free Sundays, free passes, and sponsored low-income family memberships
- Outdoor education classroom including family and social group programs in garden-based biology and environmental awareness
- Summer day camp program for 100 five-, six-, and seven-year-olds at a local elementary school

ATTENDANCE STATISTICS

The following represents a comparison of attendance statistics for the last two years:

	Year 1	Year 2
Onsite attendance	58,000	57,500
Visiting schoolchildren	11,500	8,000

(Decrease attributed to lack of funding for school buses)

	Year 1	Year 2
Museum member visits	7,300	8,500
Arts programming	6,000	7,500
(Increase attributable to program expansion)		
Special Sunday science programs	2,000	2,000
Monthly performance series	1,500	1,500
Preschool prime time	1,000	3,500
(Increase attributable to expanding the program to weekly)		
Babes in the Woods (nature hikes for toddlers and parents)	50	100
Special education programming—teachers and parents	200	2,000
(Increase attributable to "The Hundred Languages of Children" exhibit)		
Birthday parties	1,500	2,040
	(100 parties)	(120 parties)
(Increase attributable to opening of new party room)		
Museum on Wheels	4,500	4,500
Summer day camp	94	114

In general, attendance has stabilized, with member visitation increasing while paid attendance decreased. SFCM continues to seek new ways to increase attendance. The fee for a museum visit is $2 for children and $3 for adults, and children under 12 must be accompanied by an adult. Basic museum membership is $50 per family per year, which entitles members to unlimited visits, free admission to Monthly Performance Series, a monthly calendar, a quarterly newsletter, and a 10 percent discount in the museum store.

SFCM ORGANIZATION

The SFCM organization chart is shown in Exhibit CS2.1. It depicts a full-time staff of four and a part-time staff of 11 as follows:

- Co-directors: three full-time founders/directors fulfilling the role of executive director as well as co-directors of operations/exhibits, administration/education, and programming/special events. This team approach to management models the collaborative decision-making process used throughout SFCM.
- Business manager: full time, with a part-time bookkeeper and an administrative assistant as support personnel.
- Head floor manager and two floor managers: 23 hours part-time, with the assistance of teen and other floor volunteers.
- Store coordinator: 30 hours part-time, with admissions and store volunteers as support.
- Public relations coordinator: 30 hours part-time, responsible for publicity, promotion, newsletter production, and editing of all printed material.
- Volunteer coordinator: 25 hours part-time, responsible for recruiting, training, and scheduling over 100 volunteers and hiring and training teen interns.

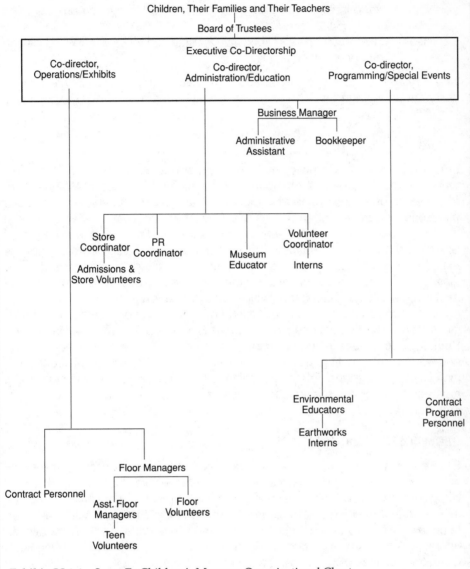

Exhibit CS 2.1   Sante Fe Children's Museum Organizational Chart

- Environmental educators (2): part-time, responsible for science programming within the Earthworks program.
- Museum educator: 30 hours, responsible for staff and volunteer training, liaison to schools, and program scheduling.

SFCM relies on a core of over 200 adult and teen volunteers to help interpret exhibits and to work in the store and at the admissions desk. SFCM experiences very little employee turnover.

BOARD OF TRUSTEES

SFCM is governed by a policy-making board of trustees composed of not less than nine or more than 22 members—presently at 19 members. Members are recruited to bring a balance of professional and community-based affiliations that ensure representation of the widest possible range of needed skills and abilities. Trustees are responsible for the legal and financial commitments of SFCM and the annual evaluation of each co-director. Each board member is expected to act as an advocate on behalf of SFCM, attend monthly board meetings and annual retreats, participate in policy-making decisions, participate in fund-raising events, museum activities, and special projects, visit the museum at least once per month, make an annual donation according to his or her ability, and serve on at least one committee—it is a very active and involved board. Standing committees include executive (also serves as the finance committee), endowment, nominating, speakers' bureau, Friends of the SFCM, education, exhibits, and programs. Ad-hoc committees (which may also include non–board members) are formed to plan special events such as the always successful annual auction.

SFCM FINANCIAL CONDITION

SFCM is in a sound financial position. It has ended each year of its operations with a positive addition to net assets or reserves—never having ended a year with a deficit. SFCM tends to expand its budget based on conservative income estimates and overly realistic expenditure predictions. Staff and public visitation hours are increased only as revenue flows make it possible. As SFCM shows an operating surplus, these funds are included in the budget for the following year. Operating revenue excesses for the past five years are as follows:

Year 1 $20,300
Year 2 $39,900
Year 3 $11,675
Year 4 $11,900
Year 5 $38,457

The SFCM board has ultimate financial control and responsibility for SFCM's fiscal condition. The co-directors and the board's executive committee develop an annual budget. Staff members develop proposed budgets related to their departments with subsequent co-director analysis and approval as to feasibility. To anticipate grant-driven program increases and decreases and possible drops in foundation funding, SFCM uses a three-year budget-planning process.

The co-directors are responsible for monitoring the budget—revenues and expenses—and reporting any budget discrepancies to the board for action. Such discrepancies have been minor in the past. An annual audit is conducted by a local CPA firm. The auditors' Statement of Financial Position and Statement of Activities (with a detail of functional expenses) for the previous year is shown in Exhibit CS2.2.

STRATEGIC LONG-RANGE PLAN

In 1997, the board of trustees, developed a five-year strategic plan based on SFCM's mission together with identified demographic trends in the community. The plan attempts to build on the three interconnecting circles of SFCM operations: the inside environment, the outside environment, and outreach programs.

Inside Environment

Consensus among board, co-directors, staff, and visitors is that the SFCM experience is very successful for children and their families. Based on this, the goal for the inside environment is to deepen the quality of the visitor experience and ensure that SFCM continues to be a setting for all to learn and play together. Objectives established to meet this goal are:

- To intensify training of paid and volunteer floor staff to better interpret the educational content of exhibits
- To provide additional daily programming
- To provide more exhibits to keep the SFCM environment vital and interesting
- To hire a director of operations within the next three years to oversee the upkeep of exhibits and exhibit change-outs (currently a co-director responsibility)
- To hire a director of education (currently a co-director's responsibility) to ensure that the educational integrity of all exhibits and programs remains SFCM's primary focus.
- To continue to offer a low admission ($2 for children, $3 for adults) and free programming, based on the perceived lack of educational enrichment in the schools and a large percentage of low-income residents (along with a high percentage of high-income residents).

Outside Environment

The goal for this area is to become as inviting as the indoor environment, filled with interactive exhibits and spaces for quiet reflection and active engagement. Objectives established to meet this goal are:

- To increase the number of outdoor interactive exhibits
- To develop a water catchment, storage, and reuse system
- To install a collection of human-powered exhibits
- To demonstrate how a community-based organization can solve the problem of land restoration

Assets	Unrestricted	Temporarily Restricted	Permanently Restricted	XXX2 Total	XXX1 Total
Cash and cash equivalents	$ 74,689	$ 67,293	$10,000	$151,982	$124,179
Accounts receivable	1,181	—	—	1,181	2,556
Contributions and private grants receivable	27,531	60,000	10,000	97,531	97,000
Governmental grants receivable	12,979	—	—	12,979	6,826
Inventory	5,886	—	—	5,886	5,825
Investments	31,816	—	167,028	198,844	140,801
Prepaid expenses	877	—	—	877	583
Property and equipment, net of accumulated depreciation	361,011	—	—	361,011	381,431
Total assets	$515,970	$127,293	$187,028	$830,291	$759,201
Liabilities and Net Assets					
Accounts payable	$9,456	—	—	$9,456	$14,650
Accrued expenses	13,494	—	—	13,494	8,673
Accrued leave	8,432	—	—	8,432	4,879
Note payable	5,364	—	—	5,364	—
Capital lease payable	8,423	—	—	8,423	12,228
Total Liabilities	45,169	$0	$0	45,169	40,430
Net assets:					
Unrestricted:					
Undesignated	447,117	—	—	447,117	471,259
Board-designated endowment	23,684	—	—	23,684	—
Temporarily restricted	—	127,293	—	127,293	62,984
Permanently restricted	—	—	187,028	187,028	184,528
Total net assets	470,801	127,293	187,028	785,122	718,771
Total liabilities and net assets	$515,970	$127,293	$187,028	$830,291	$759,201

Exhibit CS 2.2   Santa Fe Children's Museum Statement of Financial Position December 31, XXX2 (with comparative totals for XXX1)

Statement of Activities
for the Year Ended December 31, XXX2
(with comparative totals for XXX1)

	Unrestricted	Temporarily Restricted	Permanently Restricted	XXX2 Total	XXX1 Total
Support and revenue:					
Contributions and private grants	$268,388	$215,664	$2,500	$486,552	$290,573
Governmental grants	128,739	—	—	128,739	143,452
Special events	104,870	—	—	104,870	93,461
Admissions and membership	137,827	—	—	137,827	126,760
Sales, net of $31,498 cost of sales	27,595	—	—	27,595	26,717
Rent	10,555	—	—	10,555	10,978
Investment return	17,421	—	—	17,421	14,315
Other income	1,533	—	—	1,533	3,332
Donated materials and facilities	60,336	—	—	60,336	34,881
Donated services	12,463	—	—	12,463	16,700
Net assets released from restrictions	151,355	(151,355)	—	0	0
Total revenue and other support	921,082	64,309	2,500	987,891	761,169
Expenses:					
Program services	719,368	—	—	719,368	686,886
Supporting services:					
Management and general	159,855	—	—	159,855	190,096
Fundraising	42,317	—	—	42,317	22,908
Total Expenses	921,540	0	0	921,540	899,890
Change in net assets	(458)	64,309	2,500	66,351	(138,721)
Net assets at beginning of year	471,259	62,984	184,528	718,771	857,492
Net assets at end of year	$470,801	$127,293	$187,028	$785,122	$718,771

(Continued)

Exhibit CS 2.2 *(Continued)*

Functional Allocation of Expenses

The costs of providing program services and other activities have been summarized on a functional basis. Accordingly, certain costs have been allocated among the program and supporting services benefited. Following is a matrix of functional expenses:

	Program Services	Management & General	Fund Raising	Total
Salaries and wages	$299,442	$ 98,447	$12,306	$410,195
Payroll taxes	23,954	7,875	985	32,814
Retirement plan	4,167	1,370	171	5,708
Supplies	41,396	6,559	—	47,955
Repairs and maintenance	51,130	3,559	—	54,689
Depreciation	46,452	5,279	1,055	52,786
Contractual services	63,796	—	—	63,796
Rent	20,952	2,381	476	23,809
Utilities	13,182	1,498	299	14,979
Insurance	16,739	4,064	300	21,103
Outreach and volunteers	25,148	—	—	25,148
Printing and postage	17,622	2,053	280	19,955
Advertising and promotion	13,732	—	2,547	16,279
Professional fees	—	11,057	—	11,057
Other	22,944	9,343	16,181	48,468
Donated materials and facilities	53,212	6,020	1,104	60,336
Donated services	5,500	350	6,613	12,463
Total	$719,368	$159,855	$42,317	$921,540

Exhibit CS2.2   *(Continued)*

- To pursue funding for an art barn to serve as a focal point for visitors' interpretations of their outdoor experiences
- To employ a full-time garden manager and two full-time environmental educators

Outreach Programs

The goal in this area isto bring SFCM's philosophy of education to various community sites and to increase organizational partnerships. Objectives established to meet this goal are:

- To continue summer day camp as a model program, share SFCM's approach, and offer training to city and summer school recreation programs
- To increase professional development activities, workshops, and seminars for teachers
- To bring together groups of educators to determine how SFCM can best serve them
- To expand the successful Museum on Wheels outreach program
- To purchase and equip a van to transport museum-quality exhibits and programs to rural areas

SFCM management understands that meeting these long-range goals means strengthening its internal organizational structure. Accordingly, its plan calls for increased board development, aggressive donor solicitation, and high-profile marketing to attract new audiences. A planned 10% annual budget increase will be allocated to staff salaries, exhibits, and increased programming. Emphasis will be on expanding its funding base and relieving co-directors of some nonadministrative duties so they can play a greater role in community organizations.

SUMMARY OF REVIEW

Based on the review of the above materials, it is apparent that SFCM has been extremely successful in their mission. From the vision of the four co-founders, sitting around a kitchen table a short 10 years ago, they have done what many community not-for-profit dreamers have not been able to accomplish—they have made it happen and have been successful at it. Now it appears that SFCM is at a crossroads: It has accomplished what is has set out to do and needs to be maintained and kept fresh and viable while at the same time decisions have to be made as to where SFCM should be going. Should it continue on its path of continual growth and expansion, should it maintain where it is at and work at being the best it can, or should it retrench and decide how much is really manageable? It appears that SFCM has plateaued quite successfully in what its mission is "to build upon a child's natural sense of joy and discovery by cultivating habits of inquiry in the arts, sciences, and humanities." The question now is where to go from here.

OPERATIONAL REVIEW—AREAS TO CONSIDER

SFCM has indeed been successful in working toward its mission. However, there are always ways to be more successful from a standpoint of operating more economically and efficiently in maximizing its effectiveness and the achievement of desired results. Based on the materials presented above, the review team might want to consider the following 10 areas for inclusion in their operational review of SFCM.

1. SFCM appears to have met its initial mission quite successfully. The review team should consider SFCM's present operations as to areas of ineconomies, inefficiencies, and ineffectiveness. There appears to be an internal struggle as to internal operation maintenance and growth.

2. As part of the operational review, the review team should look at what has worked, what has not worked, and what else is needed. Internal operations, as well as what other children's museums (and others) are doing, should be evaluated in an effort to develop best practices in a program of continuous improvements.

3. The co-directors have quite successfully developed SFCM into a children's museum that is enviable by many much larger towns and cities. They have provided excellent guidance and direction in building this not-for-profit into an

entity that more than meets its mission. However, the review team should look at whether they have imparted this same educational and business savvy onto others within the organization so that SFCM can indeed become a learning organization. Are SFCM employees and volunteers in effect constructing their own knowledge in an environment that provides for honest inquiry and real discovery?

4. SFCM has developed many successful programs in its short existence. These need to be reviewed and evaluated as to which course to take for each and whether to develop additional programs. The review team should survey each of these programs to determine its appropriateness at this time as to expansion, retrenchment, deletion, change, as well as the need for additional supportive programming.

5. Attendance at SFCM appears to have plateaued—that is, each attendance element has either leveled off or made minor increases or decreases. The review team should look at the elements of attendance and ask questions such as:

   • On-site attendance: How can this be increased through additional visits by present attendees or by enticing prospective visitors to attend (hopefully on a regular basis)? Keep in mind that most times it is easier and less costly to build such attendance with a present visitor base than continually marketing for additional prospective visitors.

   • Visiting schoolchildren: This is an important segment of SFCM's program because such visits are usually during the school day, which is a usual slow time for SFCM. This is also an area where SFCM can possibly find funding for such purposes or tie into existing funding sources for such field trips.

   • Museum member visits: Although this is a one-time charge per year for unlimited visits for parents and children, such visits should be encouraged for a number of reasons; for example, members often bring others with them (paid admissions as well as future members and attendees), they are a ready audience for additional programs and sales, and they can become SFCM's best source for word-of-mouth marketing and public relations. A well-satisfied customer is your best marketing—and the least expensive. However, the basic fee structure of $50 per family per year may need further analysis.

   • Programming such as arts, science, performances, preschool prime time, and so on. Each of these programs should be reviewed on such bases as participation, satisfaction, strengths and weaknesses, costs versus benefits and revenues (that is, does it more than pay for itself?), use of facilities, and so on. In addition, other possible programs should be investigated for possible implementation.

   • Birthday parties and special events: This appears to be a growth area and should be looked at for further increases.

6. Use of facilities. SFCM has limited inside and outside space. The review team should look at all avenues for maximizing the use of such limited facilities as

to maximizing exhibit space, attendance at all times (what times are minimally used, what times are used but could be used better, and what times the museum is closed during which it could be used productively), and type of user (i.e., children, parents, teachers, community members, etc.). The more people that have knowledge of SFCM, the greater the chance they will speak favorably of it—again very inexpensive marketing.

7. Review and analysis of organization structure from the board of trustees to teen volunteers. Specific areas that might be considered include the following:
   - Role of the board of trustees
   - Role and use of the three co-directors
   - Complement of paid staff such as business manager, floor management, store operations, public relations, museum educator, volunteer coordinator, and environmental educators
   - Effective use of volunteers—adult and teens

8. Management responsibilities between the board of trustees and the three co-directors. It appears that possibly the board is too involved in operations and the co-directors are too involved in setting policy. Typically in a not-for-profit, the board is responsible for establishing guidelines, setting policy, and reviewing and evaluating the results of operations. Not-for-profit management, in this case the three co-directors, are responsible for carrying out the directions of the board on an operational level. Not-for-profit management provides the feedback system for the board to be aware as to what is being accomplished so as to provide effective guidance and direction.

9. The financial condition of SFCM is sound. However, certain areas should be looked at as part of the operational review, such as:
   - Revenues, with an overreliance on grants—government, foundation, and private. In addition, it appears that other sources of revenues such as contributions and admissions have stabilized. Other sources of revenue also need to be considered such as space rentals, store operations, program fees, possible concessions (e.g., food service), fund raisers, and so on.
   - Salary and related expenses, which is by far the largest part of the budget and actual expenditures (over 50 percent). It needs to be determined whether these expenditures are being spent most effectively—that is, is SFCM getting expected results out of each paid position? Are each of these positions needed, and are other positions needed that presently do not exist?
   - Program expenses which should have some correlation to program revenues and results. These programs should be considered for flexible program budgeting and evaluated for financial as well as operational results.
   - Exhibit expense should be looked at also from a profit center standpoint, that is, which exhibits are attracting the attention of visitors and bringing in additional visitors, which exhibits meet the educational mission of SFCM, which exhibits are being somewhat ignored, and so on.

- Outreach expenses again should be viewed from a profit center concept—are they paying their way financially, educationally, marketing, public relations, and so on.
- Other expenses such as promotional, facilities, general administration, and leasehold improvements should be looked at as to whether they are the most economical ways in which to provide such services and expense items.

10. Planning and budgeting systems. SFCM has a documented strategic long-range plan in existence with accompanying action items. Not only should this process be reviewed, but the review team should also determine whether SFCM develops short-term plans that include organizational, departmental, and program goals and objectives as well as detail plans that support departmental and program budgets. These plans and budgets should then be automatically changed based on actual activity levels and effectively evaluated by management and the board.

Based on the analysis of SFCM materials as presented above, the operational review team should consider the following 10 critical areas for inclusion in the operational review:

1. Guidance and direction—that is, board of trustees and co-director responsibilities and processes for developing such direction.
2. Planning and budgeting systems—the development of both long-range and short-term plans (goals, objectives, and detail plans) providing integration of flexible budget procedures based on real activity levels.
3. Revenue enhancement—looking at less dependence on outside grants and increasing other areas of revenues such as contributions, fund raisers, donations, store and concession operations, space rental, memberships and admissions, and so on.
4. Development and increase of endowment funds. The goal for these funds should be a sufficient amount of investment income to guarantee a large part of the operating budget—hopefully 100 percent eventually.
5. Exhibits and programs—development of a system to enable management to determine which of these are being effective and ineffective and whether there are other programs that should be considered.
6. Operating practices—looking at current practices as to whether they are most economical, efficient, and effective from a financial and mission basis. SFCM should be looking to develop a program of best practices in a program of continuous improvements in their development as a learning organization. Best practices can be determined both from internal appraisal as well as benchmarking against similar organizations.
7. Organization and personnel—to determine whether the current organizational structure of a mix of full-time, part-time, and volunteers is accomplished the maximum results.
8. Use of facilities—to maximize revenues generated by the use of facilities considering such aspects as maximizing attendance at present times and events, using the facility at other times for other purposes, space rentals, fee-based programming, use other than children, and so on.

9. Attendance enhancements—looking at present programming and exhibits and uses of inside and outside areas as to maximizing attendance at all times. Also looking at other creative ways to increase attendance such as theme days, bring a friend day, special events, adult activities, snack areas, school programs, and so on.

10. Expenditure review—to determine whether expenses are being used most economically to produce maximum results. Analyzing which expenditures are program related or non-value-added and can be reduced or eliminated and whether there are better ways of providing these services or materials at less or no cost.

CHAPTER FOUR

The Field Work Phase

INTRODUCTION

The operational review work done in the planning phase should produce indications of possible management weaknesses or significant operational areas for improvement in a particular area or activity. However, more information is usually needed to determine that there definitely is a management or operational weakness. The work program, then, is the plan for conducting the operational review work steps in the field work phase. In this phase, additional information is gathered relative to management and operational controls and activities to identify those areas in which to expend time and effort on an in-depth examination. Then the work program steps are performed, and, as a result, areas are identified in which to develop specific findings to present to management.

If the operational review team decides to proceed with an in-depth development of a finding, the information gathered in the field work phase provides a basis from which to proceed. Besides providing an understanding of particular inefficiencies within the organization or department being reviewed, field work also helps the review team to understand the departmental organization and how it functions. Such an understanding is usually necessary in the event that additional information is needed in the development of the finding.

This chapter discusses the field work phase of an operational review. It is in this phase that the work steps are performed, as defined in the work program phase. The operational review team makes a determination, based on the performance and results of these work steps, as to whether those areas of possible weaknesses identified in the planning phase are worth going into in greater detail. If they are, any additional analytical work is done to fully develop the finding for presentation to management. There may also be additional critical areas discovered that require further analytical work. In addition, this chapter reviews some of the procedures and techniques that can be used by the operational review team in the conduct of the field work phase.

FIELD WORK CONSIDERATIONS AND TASKS

Based on the critical areas identified in the planning phase and the work steps designed in the work program phase, the following two items are considered in the field work phase:

1. Whether the reviewee's policies and the related procedures and practices actually followed are in compliance with basic authorities, statutes, legislative intent, grants and contracts, and so on.
2. Whether the system of operating procedures and management controls effectively results in activities being carried out as desired by top management in an efficient and economical manner.

General tasks that would be performed to assist in reaching the correct conclusions include the following:

- Fact-finding or verification—for example, are management procedures being followed?
- Evaluation—for example, analyzing deviations from procedures and determining whether the cause is the policy or procedure itself, or other factors.
- Review of findings—for example, meeting occasionally with the review supervisor and other members of the review team to assist in getting a better understanding of matters requiring interpretation.
- Recommendations as to the areas having sufficient significance to warrant a more detailed examination directed toward the development of an operational review finding.

Operational review recommendations resulting from effective field work are based on the reviewer's determination as to the adequacy and effectiveness of management and operations.

FACTORS IN REACHING CONCLUSIONS

In reaching conclusions in the field work phase, the operational reviewer must consider some specific factors, including:

- Management's use of standards or goals for judging accomplishment, productivity, efficiency, or utilization of goods or services. For example, the reviewer may observe the use of staying within the budget only, as a measure, as opposed to evaluating controllable results such as services provided, effective use of personnel, quality control, and so on.

- Lack of clarity in written instructions, which may result in misunderstandings, inconsistent applications, or unacceptable deviations. An example is the policy of the timely updating and control of client case records that is not being followed.
- Capability of personnel to perform their assignments. For instance, the reviewer may observe individuals who are unable to complete their assignments, such as a backlog of unprocessed service or treatment requests.
- Failure to accept responsibility. For example, there may be persons who do not do what is expected of them in their functional job descriptions, such as preparing periodic reports or providing customer/client services.
- Failure to properly control operations and activities. For example, there may be a work unit in which some individuals are overloaded and others are underloaded.
- Duplication of efforts within departments and across departmental lines. An example might be handling ticket requests by the receptionist, by artistic area personnel, and by box office personnel.
- Improper or wasteful use of financial resources. An example could be the presence of computer processing equipment and procedures, while the same operations are still being performed manually.
- Cumbersome or extravagant organizational patterns, such as an overburdened hierarchy of supervisors and managers or an excessive number of staff personnel.
- Ineffective or wasteful use of employees; for example, the use of administrative assistants or staff personnel to perform functions that could and should be performed by the person to whom they report.
- Work backlogs that are inappropriate to the activity. For instance, the reviewer may find incompletely processed service requests more than 6 months old, owing to an individual's processing the easy requests first.
- Necessity for, and effectiveness of, various operating and service units in relation to the costs of maintaining them. For example, the reviewer may discover a third-party reimbursement unit that was established at the outset of the not-for-profit but is, for the most part, no longer used because such procedures are now totally accomplished by automatic computer data transfer.
- Relevance and validity of criteria used to judge effectiveness in achieving operating results. An example might be an oversupply of exhibit display materials, caused by the inability to plan effectively and to modify that plan based on the reality of the situation.
- Appropriateness of methods used to evaluate effectiveness of achieving results. For example, the reviewer may observe insufficient reporting that does not relate the performance of activities to the achievement of results.

**IN REACHING CONCLUSIONS,
CONCLUDE WHAT IS RIGHT**

SPECIFIC FIELD WORK TECHNIQUES

The reviewer can use various methods to gather the necessary information to identify weaknesses in management and operational systems. The reviewer follows the previously mentioned adage: Whatever works, use it. However, there are certain tools and techniques that are used consistently from one operational review to another.

Many different field work techniques are used in the field work phase, depending on the particular circumstances of the operational review. However, the best tools are common sense and analytical ability. It is not necessary for the reviewer to have mastered all the various technical tools before beginning an operational review. But the reviewer should be able to analyze problems logically, and in many cases this is the only tool needed.

The review team should also be aware of the various management and operational techniques—in both the public and private sectors—that have been used effectively in the past or are currently in vogue, such as the following:

- Total quality management (TQM)
- Participative management
- Benchmarking strategies—internal and external
- Restructuring, reengineering, and reinventing
- Principle-centered leadership
- Learning organizations
- Revision of mental models
- Spirituality in the workplace
- Activity-based costing and management (ABC/ABM)
- Strategic, long-term, short-term, and detail planning
- Flexible (versus static line item) budgeting
- Systems theory
- Complexity theory (complex adaptive systems)

Some of the more common of these field work techniques were mentioned in Chapter 3 relative to developing work program work steps. It is these work steps using these tools and techniques that are carried out in the field work phase. Often, however, further work steps are added in the field work phase. It is to the operational reviewer's advantage to be familiar with as many of these techniques as possible. The more effective the technique and the one using it, the more effective the review results. Moreover, to be able to use a specific technique, the reviewer needs to be familiar with it. These field work techniques and others are documented again in Exhibit 4.1.

One or more of these techniques may be used in each work step assignment. The techniques used will depend on the particular circumstances encountered and the objectives established for each work step. Therefore, there are no hard-and-fast rules as to the work to be done or the techniques to be used in the field work phase. The most effective approach is to individualize the field work steps and related techniques to meet the needs of the particular situation. The operational reviewer's expertise is to know under what circumstances which technique to apply to achieve desired results.

Although there are many tools and techniques that can be used in the field work phase, there are a number that are used consistently. The operational reviewer should be most aware of these techniques, including:

- Analysis of planning and budget systems
- Interviewing
- Internal benchmarking

1. Review of existing documentation, such as policy and procedures manuals
2. Preparation of organization charts and related functional job descriptions
3. Analysis of personnel policies and procedures related to hiring, orientation, training, evaluation, promotion, and firing
4. Analysis of organizational policies, and related systems and procedures; both administrative and operational, particularly planning and budget procedures
5. Interviews with management and operations personnel
6. Flowchart preparation:
   - Systems flowcharts, showing the processes of a functional area, and
   - Layout flow diagrams, showing the physical layout of a work area and its related work flow
7. Ratio, change, and trend analysis
8. Questionnaires, for use by the reviewer or client's personnel
9. Surveys, by phone or in written form, for customers or clients, vendors and so on to respond to
10. Questions within the review work program
11. Review of transactions, in which the different types of normal and abnormal transactions are considered
12. Review of operations, by techniques such as observation, work measurement, time studies, work performance forms or logs, and so on
13. Forms analysis
14. Analysis of results
15. Review and analysis of management information system and related reports
16. Compliance reviews; as to compliance with laws, regulations, grants and contracts, policies, procedures, goals, objectives, and so forth
17. Use of computer processing; using "through the computer" techniques or review and analysis of computer produced information.

Exhibit 4.1 Field Work Phase: Field Work Techniques

- Systems flowcharts
- Layout flow diagrams
- Ratio, change, and trend analysis

THE BEST FIELD WORK TECHNIQUE
IS THE ONE THAT WORKS BEST

ANALYSIS OF PLANNING AND BUDGET SYSTEMS

A good starting point for the operational review team in the planning phase, in order to understand the not-for-profit, why it is in existence, and what it is trying to accomplish (i.e., its goals, objectives, and service results) was to review the not-for-profit's strategic, long-term, and short-term planning methods and related budgeting and control processes. In the field work phase, the review team focuses on the not-for-profit's approach to planning and its integration with the budget system. The not-for-profit's planning and budgeting techniques are a means for the not-for-profit to achieve improved effectiveness. The review team should be aware of the elements of an effective planning and budgeting system as a benchmark to compare with the practices of the not-for-profit under review.

There should be interaction and interdependence of the strategic, long-term, short-term, and detail planning systems with the not-for-profit's budgeting and control systems. The planning process should be an essential first step in the preparation of the not-for-profit's effective budget. By learning and understanding effective planning and budget procedures, the reviewer will be able to more effectively review and analyze such procedures as part of his or her organization-wide, departmental, or specific function operational review.

Although most not-for-profits plan and budget, many consider these processes as separate. In reality, they should be one process. Planning comes first until the organization defines its goals and objectives. Knowing where to allocate its resources based on its plans constitutes the budget process. All not-for-profits plan—some formally, most informally; all not-for-profit's budget—some integrated with their plans, most not integrated with their plans. The advantages of formalizing and throwing open the planning and budgeting process provides an open, integrated, and reasonably structured process that significantly benefits the long-term visibility of the not-for-profit. It is for these benefits that this area is considered a critical function to include in the planning and field work phases of the operational review.

Every organization—whether a manufacturer, Internet business, service provider, or not-for-profit—must plan for its future direction if it desires to achieve its goals and objectives. The organizational plan is an agreed upon course of action to be implemented in the future (short- and long-term) and directed toward moving the not-for-profit closer to its stated goals and objectives. The planning process, if exercised effectively, forces the not-for-profit to:

- Review and analyze past accomplishments and results
- Determine present and future needs
- Recognize strengths and weaknesses

The planning process also enables the organization to:

- Identify future opportunities
- Define constraints or threats that may get in the way
- Establish organizational and departmental goals and objectives
- Develop action plans based on the evaluation of alternatives
- Prioritize the selection of action plans for implementation based on the most effective use of limited resources

The first step in the planning process is to determine why the not-for-profit is in existence. Although many not-for-profit managers would quickly say "To provide our services to as many users as possible," there are many other reasons as well, including:

- To provide the best quality services to our customer or client base
- To provide our services at the least possible cost
- To provide our customers or clients with the best service possible
- To maintain or enhance our favorable position among other similar not-for-profits
- To provide employment or volunteer opportunities within our community
- To achieve personal satisfaction and gratification for members of the board of directors, management, employees, and volunteers
- To create a creative atmosphere in which caring people can grow and develop innovative services and methods for delivery
- To be the service leader in our community

[handwritten margin note: Estab. the why]

The above process of identifying the reason why the not-for-profit is in existence sounds almost too elemental to merit discussion, but it can be one of the most wrenching and difficult processes for a not-for-profit to go through because of the widely diverse mental models and belief systems held by not-for-profit management as to just what this not-for-profit is all about. Each member of the board and management may each have its own reason for being a part of the not-for-profit—to meet each individual's personal needs. Reaching consensus is rarely easy and never quick if it is done correctly. Articulating the not-for-profit's purpose in a paragraph of a very few sentences can be done only with significant intellectual effort—and many, many drafts. The best statements of not-for-profit mission or purpose are like the Gettysburg Address—brief, immediately clear, compelling, and totally unambiguous. This is not easy to accomplish. Such a statement, however, provides clear communication to all of the not-for-profit's stakeholders as to the direction and purpose of the not-for-profit—enabling all concerned to move the not-for-profit in the correct direction.

Once the not-for-profit has identified all of the reasons that it is in existence and has articulated them by means of a mission statement, the next step is to identify related organizational goals—both long- and short-term. These goals are typically formulated by top management (i.e., the board of directors and the executive director), although it is a good practice to obtain feedback from lower-level managers, supervisors, and operating personnel (employees and volunteers) as to the appropriateness, practicality, reasonableness, and attainability of the stated goals. A good rule to keep in mind in the development of an effective organizational plan is that in most not-for-profits it is the employees or volunteers closest to day-to-day operations who usually know the most about present problems and what needs to be done to correct them. Accordingly, the not-for-profit that wishes to be most successful over the long term must have *everyone* (i.e., representatives from all levels) in the not-for-profit involved in the planning process from beginning to end. Many not-for-profits have been unsuccessful in their planning efforts and their ability to survive because of lack of foresight and their inability to use operating level personnel's input creatively.

In addition, operating personnel need to know how to plan properly and operate according to such plans (putting the plans into action) in order to conduct their operations successfully as part of an integrated organizational plan. Operations personnel cannot plan for their own areas effectively unless they understand and agree with the not-for-profit's long- and short-term goals—and have had the opportunity to provide significant input and feedback concerning these plans. It is not sufficient that operations personnel be allowed merely to provide input and feedback; top management must also encourage their input and seriously consider it in the finalization of organizational goals. The development of organizational goals must be internalized as a system of top to bottom agreement for it to be most successful.

Yet the reviewer must understand the principle that members of top management have the ultimate decision-making power and therefore may still decide to do whatever they desire, regardless of operations personnel input. The result of such exclusive top management decision making, however, is organizational goal setting by directive rather than by participation. Because operations staff will see these organizational goals as top management's and not their own, they will not only be less inclined to direct their efforts toward achievement of these goals, but may also tend to sabotage or work openly against the accomplishment of the goals. In an effective planning system, it is extremely important to have everyone in the not-for-profit working toward the same goals. In this manner, management and operations staff are far more likely to make decisions that are consistent with the not-for-profit's overall plans and direction.

Within this framework, how then does a not-for-profit plan effectively for its future? A schematic of the organizational planning process is shown in Exhibit 4.2. Note that in the development of long-range plans, which includes the development of detail plans and related budgets, a top-to-bottom approach is used, whereby top management and operations management and staff interact and communicate, resulting in an agreed upon set of organizational plans (i.e., strategic plans, organizational goals and objectives) and departmental or program (segment) goals, objectives, detail plans, and budgets.

Strategic (Long-Range) Planning

Strategic (long-range) planning usually encompasses a future period of three to five years or more, although the actual period will vary with the specific not-for-profit. Traditionally, the strategic planning process is accomplished by upper management, although other operating employees and volunteers, as well as outside assistance, can be used to enhance the resultant quality of the plan. In such long-range planning, all aspects of the not-for-profit's activities are addressed, including such areas as:

- Not-for-profit expansion or contraction—overall, departments, or programs
- Services to be provided—additions, changes, and eliminations
- Areas in which to provide services—geographic, client base, types of services
- Capital expenditures—facilities, equipment, vehicles, and so on
- Facility requirements—rent, own, renovate, additions, and so on
- Personnel requirements—employees, volunteers, relations, benefits, and so on
- Funding and financing requirements—grants, contracts, contributions, endowments, borrowings, and so on

Strategic planning focuses on the identification and use of strategic thrusts and competencies within the not-for-profit in the development of organizational plans. A basic assumption is that extrapolations made from past data and experience alone are inadequate bases for future planning. As the external and internal environments change, there will be departures from past patterns, requiring strategic adjustments such as new or changed services, additional facilities, new processes, and so on. Strategic planning focuses on the entire environment of the not-for-profit, requiring knowledge of all the factors that have an impact on the not-for-profit. The emphasis is on continued recognition of current operating conditions, but with added ability to anticipate the need for strategic changes.

The development, evaluation, and implementation of strategic planning and related operating strategies is the heart of successful and effective management. Strategic planning is the cornerstone of a management system that assists not-for-profit management to:

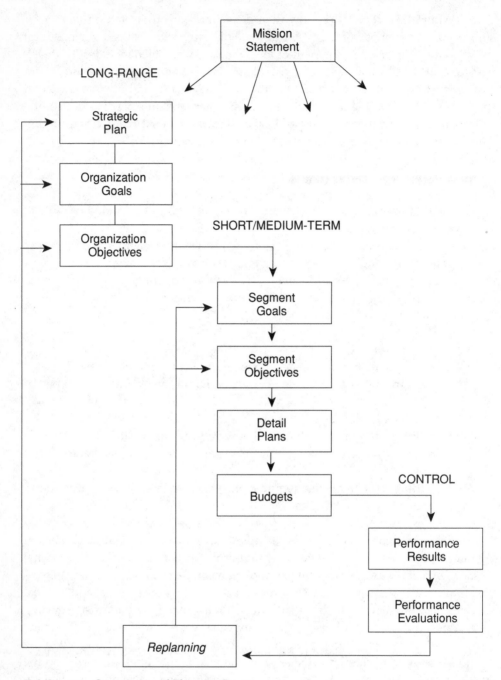

Exhibit 4.2 Organizational Planning Process

- Develop vision for their organizations
- Understand the dynamic and changing environment in which the not-for-profit is managed
- Consider and decide on strategic alternatives that are responsive to the environmental conditions (both internal and external) affecting the not-for-profit
- Adopt strategies that are based on competitive advantages and that will be sustainable

Long-range planning tends to be a complex undertaking because of the many uncertainties of the future. The farther out the planning period from the present, the greater the risk of uncertainty. Because of this uncertainty and because even ordinary conditions change over time, long-range plans must be periodically reviewed and adjusted by appropriate not-for-profit management personnel. In addition, top management must take many other risk factors into consideration in planning for the future, which increases the possibilities of uncertainty, including:

- Economic factors—for example, inflation or deflation, cost of borrowing, public and private funding, level of contributions, and so on
- Client demands—for example, increased or decreased demands for services, addition or contraction of client base, and so on
- Other not-for-profit servicers—for example, level and type of services offered by other not-for-profits in the area, addition and contraction of services, competition for clients from other not-for-profits and outside organizations, and so on
- Political factors—for example, new and changed legislation, increase or decrease in public funding, prevailing attitudes, and so on

The not-for-profit strategic and long-range planners must collect, analyze, and interpret all available information to be used in forecasting the future. Sources of such data include:

- Historical data and reports—changes and trends in dollar and service data
- Revenue trends—grants, contracts, contributions, earned revenues, and so on
- Cost trends—by line item (e.g., personnel, materials, supplies, travel, etc.), by program (e.g., events, displays, services, locations, etc.), by function (e.g., management, artistic, service delivery, nonrelated business, fiscal, personnel, etc.), by grant or contract, and so on
- Financial data—statement of position, statement of operation, analysis of cash flow, and so on
- Service delivery data—increases, decreases, changes, additions, deletions, and so on

The not-for-profit's long-term plan, which is often referred to as its strategic plan, takes into account the following elements:

1. Services to Be Delivered
   The scope of the not-for-profit is defined by the services it offers to its publics, by the population it seeks to serve, by other not-for-profits offering similar services within the same area, and so on.
2. Strategic Thrust
   This area encompasses decisions to be made as to such things as growth or expansion into other areas or the increase of present services, stability of services offered (maintain present position), retrenchment or downsizing the level of services and related activities, and divestiture or curtailing the providing of certain services.
3. Functional Competence
   Looking at the not-for-profit's competence in areas such as services offered, client base (particularly related to other not-for-profits offering similar services), charging or billing or reimbursement for services provided, distribution of services (i.e., central location, various locations, traveling outside of the area), quality and procedures for service delivery, client satisfaction and repeat use, service delivery competence, and quality and reliability.
4. Unique Advantage
   A strategic skill is something that a not-for-profit does exceptionally well, such as client service delivery, operating systems and procedures, quality control, marketing and promotion, fund raising, and client satisfaction, and that has strategic importance to that not-for-profit. A strategic asset is a resource such as name recognition or well-satisfied customer or client base that creates an exceptional advantage over other not-for-profits offering similar services.

   When developing the not-for-profit's strategic plan, not-for-profit management must be fully aware of all of the factors to be considered in the development of their strategic plan. Each factor may result in one or more desirable organizational goals to be integrated into the not-for-profit's strategic plan. These factors include:
   - *Not-for-profit mission.* That is, why the not-for-profit is in existence, which services it will provide, who its customers or clients are, what it desires to provide to each of its customers or clients, its basic operating principles on which it will operate, and so on
   - *Not-for-profit goals and objectives.* The overall results desired to be achieved, directions to be moved toward (increase, decrease, status quo), definitions of desired best practices, critical areas for improvements
   - *Stakeholders' concerns.* Board of directors, contributors, funding sources, management, employees, volunteers, customers or clients, vendors, and so on

- *Environmental issues.* Economy, competing not-for-profits, political concerns, service users, funding availability, legislative conditions, and so on
- *Organizational requirements.* Personnel—employees and volunteers (selecting, hiring, training, downsizing, transferability), facilities (increase, decrease, combine), equipment (service delivery, computer processing, administrative), systems and procedures (service delivery, management, administration)
- *Control and reporting systems.* Identification of key operating indicators (e.g., revenues by source and type, on-time service delivery, service quality, cost considerations), evaluative criteria (e.g., good or poor service and client satisfaction), reporting format (e.g., real-time online, daily summary, weekly recap), follow-up procedures
- *Resource requirements.* Personnel, facilities, equipment, funding, revenues, outside assistance, cash flow requirements

As an output of the strategic planning process, not-for-profit management should develop broad goals for the long-term operations of the not-for-profit, and these goals should be communicated to all lower levels of management and other operations personnel as appropriate. The not-for-profit's long-term goals should address areas such as:

- Desired size and scope of operations
- Customer or client relations
- Personnel, employee, and volunteer relations
- Services to be offered—existing, new, changes, and eliminations
- New services development or enhancements
- Quality control considerations
- Capital investment plans
- Customer or client base—existing, additions, and deletions
- Fund-raising efforts
- Marketing and promotion efforts

By determining such long-term direction, not-for-profit management provides an effective framework within which operations management and staff can then make informed and intelligent decisions relative to developing their own short-term plans and budgets. Keep in mind that strategic planning can be a very complex and time-consuming undertaking for not-for-profit top management. Although operations management and staff may have no direct responsibility for strategic planning decision making, they should be encouraged to provide input and ideas to be considered by not-for-profit management in the strategic planning process.

Top management should also solicit from operating personnel the identification of present problems and causes as well as recommendations to correct the situation, change and trend data, revenue and cost statistics, delivery of service conditions, personnel conditions, and so on. If effective communication systems between top management and the rest of the organization have not been established, the strategic planning process may result in long-term not-for-profit goals that do not fully relate to the not-for-profit's reality. Furthermore, operating personnel may then have to work with goals with which they disagree and believe will not work. In today's competitive not-for-profit world, not-for-profits of all sizes must become more effective planners if they are going to prosper and grow—or even survive.

Short-Term Planning

The strategic plan and long-range goals established by not-for-profit management then have to be translated into more specific segment (departmental, program, function, or project) goals and objectives. The definitions of goals and objectives are shown in Exhibit 4.3. Note that goals are broad directions or targets that the not-for-profit or segment desires to move toward—they may or may not be achievable. Objectives are specific desired results, relating to one or more goals, that can be attained within a given time frame. Normally, short-term goals and objectives are developed for a specific planning cycle (for most not-for-profits, a one year annual cycle) for both the not-for-profit and each operating segment. As top management is responsible for development of the long-term organizational goals, so operating managers and staff are responsible for developing and implementing the short-term goals and objectives within the framework of the overall long-term plans.

GOALS

Statements of broad direction that:

- describe future states or outcomes of the not-for-profit to be attained or retained
- indicate ends toward which the not-for-profit's effort is to be directed

OBJECTIVES

Measurable, desired accomplishments related to one or more goals whose attainment is desired within a specified time frame and can be evaluated under specifiable conditions.

   The characteristics of objectives are:

- *Measurable*—attainment (or lack thereof) can be clearly identified
- *Explicit*—clear indication of who, what, when, how
- *Time Specific*—to be accomplished within a stipulated period of time
- *Realistic*—capable of being attained within the time frame specified and with the expenditure of a reasonable and cost effective amount of effort and resources

---

Exhibit 4.3 Planning Definitions

The following example demonstrates the relationship between long-term goals and short-term goals and objectives.

- *Not-for-profit long-term goal:* To become the leading service provider of substance abuse counseling services within our geographic area
- *Not-for-profit short-term goal:* To increase client contact hours in the providing of substance abuse group counseling services
- *Not-for-profit specific objective:* To increase substance abuse group counseling client contact hours by at least 10 percent over last year

This specific objective can then be translated into specific detail plans and related performance expectations for the substance abuse counseling program. In effect, these short-term objectives and related detail plans become the starting point for the budget process. The beginning budget will then reflect what is necessary (in terms of personnel, materials, facilities, equipment, and other costs) to meet the agreed-upon short-term objectives. When each segment budget is approved by not-for-profit management, it will reflect the authorized level of expenditures needed to fulfill the objectives by following through on agreed-upon detail plans. At this point, each manager, supervisor, staff employee, and/or volunteer has theoretically been delegated the authority to incur the expenditures to make each detail plan workable. Finally, each individual (manager, supervisor, employee, volunteer) can be evaluated based on his or her ability to effectively work his or her plan to achieve the short-term objectives. Exhibit 4.4 depicts these short-term planning steps.

THE PAST IS MY HERITAGE
THE PRESENT IS MY RESPONSIBILITY
THE FUTURE IS MY CHALLENGE

The Budget Process

The budget is a detailed plan depicting the manner in which monetary resources will be acquired and used over a period of time. The budget should be a quantitative manifestation of the next year of the not-for-profit's strategic plan. It is part of the short-term operating plan. Note that budgeting in itself is not planning. The master budget summarizes the not-for-profit's plans (goals and objectives) for the future time period—providing for the allocation of financial resources to agreed upon short-term operating plans. It is a statement of not-for-profit management's expectations and establishes specific targets relative to such things as revenues, fund raising, operating costs, service levels, general and administrative expenditures, and other monetary transactions for the time period covered.

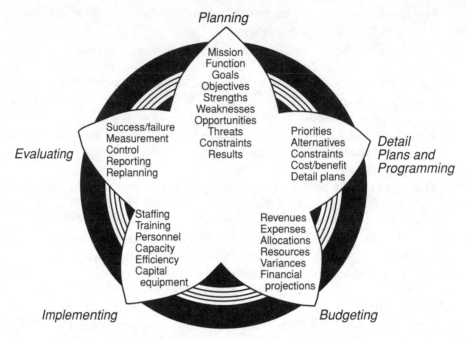

Exhibit 4.4   Short-Term Planning Steps

To be fully effective, the budgeting system must provide not-for-profit management with tools for both planning and control. At the beginning of the budget cycle, the budget is the plan or standard to be met based on the development of organizational short-term goals and objectives and the detail planning steps to achieve these objectives.

During the budget cycle, not-for-profit management uses the budget as a control device to measure results against the planned objectives so that corrective action can be taken to improve continuing performance. At the end of the budget cycle, not-for-profit management uses the final results to measure against the plan to determine if the goals and objectives were met, and, if not, why not. The results of this analysis helps to establish a new and better budget for the next operating cycle. Good planning without proper control produces poor results, and budgeting without proper planning provides no legitimate objectives against which to measure progress.

The chances for success of the not-for-profit's budget program is determined in large part by the method used to develop the budget. Normally, the most successful budget programs are those that allow segment managers and other operations personnel who have the responsibility for related operating costs to prepare their own budgets—based on agreed-upon organizational and segment goals and objectives. This bottom-up budgeting method can be very effective if, as is usually the case, the budget is to be used subsequently to control the segment's operations. If the budget is developed by upper management and enforced entirely by management directive, it will most likely be resented, and will foster animosity toward rather than cooperation with upper management.

When not-for-profit segment managers and their staffs prepare their own budgets, they have more invested in making the results work and feel more supportive toward budget-related goals. Other advantages of such participative budgets include:

- Recognition of staff input at all organizational levels, creating more of a "we're in this together" atmosphere
- Feeling by personnel that their input is valued by top management, and that they can make some of their own decisions
- More accurate and reliable budget figures since those directly involved in the operation are normally able to make better estimates
- A greater likelihood that individuals will work toward the budget objectives if they have been involved in preparing the budget themselves as opposed to dealing with a budget imposed from above
- The creation of a situation in which, if budget is not met, the preparers can blame only themselves, whereas with budgets imposed from above the individuals tend to blame others (e.g., budget was unrealistic, unreasonable, impossible to meet, etc.).

Even these self-imposed or participative budgets will be reviewed and approved by not-for-profit management. If changes are necessary, they can be discussed and acceptable compromises reached. In this type of budget system, all levels of the not-for-profit work together to produce the budget, but since not-for-profit management is typically less familiar with day-to-day operations, they rely on operational management and staff to provide necessary detailed budget data. Not-for-profit management is more aware of the broader organizational goals and objectives and can provide vital input to the budget process to help coordinate the overall requirements of the not-for-profit. The budget process, then, becomes one in which each organizational level cooperates with the others to develop a fully integrated plan of action.

Not-for-profits are more likely to budget on the basis of cash flows (i.e, receipts and expenditures) than private-sector organizations that typically budget based on sales, cost of sales, other expenses, and net profits (or losses). Not-for-profit budgeting is more likely to start with expenditures than with receipts. In fact, many not-for-profits do little, if any, receipt planning and budgeting—they work with expected funding and estimated other revenues as their receipt budget. In effect, the budgeting problem becomes one of determining the amount of revenues necessary to support the level of budgeted expenditures desired or perceived to be needed. This is the reverse of the more typical budgeting situation in which revenues are the principal driving force in the budgeting process, and costs necessary to be incurred as a result of the budget level of revenues are then calculated.

Such an expenditure-driven budgeting process used by most not-for-profits normally lends itself to a *line item* type of budget, with standard line item expenses (e.g., personnel, fringe benefits, materials and supplies, equipment, etc.) for each segment that expects funds. Such line item–type budgets normally require a line-by-line expenditure submission and approval. Due to these line item budget constraints, this type of budgeting system usually prevents individual managers form exercising their discretion in using budgeted funds to achieve stated goals and objectives. Often, managers are not allowed to increase spending on a line item even though they may be able to make corresponding decreases on other line items. This inflexibility can produce actions that may be inconsistent with not-for-profit objectives or even good common sense and business judgment. The inherent problem with line item budgeting is the emphasis on individual expense items and types of costs as opposed to concentration on objective to be accomplished.

Another concern with line item budgeting is its tendency to encourage current budget setting based on prior years' (usually last year or an average of the past few years) budgets or actual expenses for each line item. This type of budgeting methodology is known as incremental budgeting. Using this technique, a not-for-profit segment may be allowed a 5 percent or 10 percent increase (or forced toward a 5 percent or 10 percent decrease) in the budgeted line items. Sometimes, not-for-profit management may grant an overall budget increase and then allow segments to use the total increase for whatever line items they desire. These options do not adequately focus on the achievement of objectives or the differences among line items. Also, this type of budgeting fosters exercise of certain budgeting games such as:

- Creating unnecessary expenditures this year to justify a bigger budget for next year
- Spending up to the budgeted line item's limit, whether the full amount is necessary or not
- End-of-year panic purchases to ensure the expenditure of the full budget allotment so that no money will be taken away from the following year's budget amount
- Use of the budget as a status symbol (the larger the budget, the more powerful the segment)
- Assuming that overall budget approval by not-for-profit management means blanket spending approval for each line item

The line item budgets discussed presume a single level of activity and are thus static in nature. A flexible budget, however, recognizes the probability of a range of activity and is dynamic in nature. The primary use of flexible budgeting is to measure performance accurately by comparing actual costs for a given level of service with budgeted costs for the same activity level. The key to developing the flexible budget is identifying and isolating the variable costs that move proportionately with changes in levels of operating activity from fixed costs that change independently from changes in activity levels.

An example of a static budget and a flexible budget for The Counseling Agency are shown in Exhibits 4.5 and 4.6.

PLANNING AND BUDGETING
ARE THE SIAMESE TWINS OF EFFECTIVENESS

As part of the budget process, not-for-profit management looks at ways to maximize their revenues as well as to minimize their expenditures. While their goal may not be to increase net profits, there is a goal to maximize the not-for-profit's contribution to net assets and reserves (i.e., the difference between revenues and expenditures). A helpful method for ensuring such a maximization of net asset increases is to also consider methods of turning the way things are done in the not-for-profit into cash. Some tips for accomplishing this are shown in Exhibit 4.7.

	Budget	Actual	Better (Worse) Than Budget
Revenues:			
• Units of service	600	540	($1,800)
• Average charge per hour	$ 30	$ 26	(2,160)
Total revenues	$18,000	$14,040	($3,960)
Expenses:			
Personnel	$13,968	$12,440	$1,528
Materials and supplies	767	1,682	(915)
Rent	500	500	—
Utilities	667	783	(116)
Insurance	300	1,460	(1,160)
Transportation	100	180	(80)
Contracted services	50	400	(350)
Other expenses	60	12	48
Total expenses	$16,412	$17,457	(1,045)
Excess of revenues over or (under) expenses	$ 1,588	($ 3,417)	($5,005)

Exhibit 4.5 The Counseling Agency—Example Static Budget

	Original Budget	Adjusted Budget	Actual	Better (Worse) Than Budget
Revenues:				
Units of service	600	540	540	—
Average charge per hour	$ 30	$ 30	$ 26	($2,160)
Total revenues	$18,000	$16,200	$14,040	($2,160)
Expenses:				
Personnel	$13,968	$12,351	$12,440	(89)
Materials and supplies	767	690	1,682	(992)
Rent	500	500	500	—
Utilities	667	600	783	(183)
Insurance	300	243	1,460	(1,217)
Transportation	100	90	180	(90)
Contracted services	50	400	400	—
Other expenses	60	12	12	—
Total expenses	$16,412	$14,886	$17,457	($2,571)
Excess of revenues over or (under) expenses	$ 1,588	$ 1,314	($ 3,417)	($4,731)

Notes To Flexible Budget:

Revenues:

1. Units of service budget adjusted to 540 hours of units of service, which is the activity level on which to base the remainder of the flexible budget.
2. Average charge per hour stays at $30 per hour as long as this stays the expected charge per hour.

Expenses:

1. Personnel budget adjusted for position not filled. The amount of this difference is adjusted from the budget and is no longer available.
2. Materials and supplies budget is adjusted to expected costs based on the new level of activity—that is, 540 hours rather than 600.
3. Utilities also adjusted to expected costs based on new level of activity.
4. Insurance costs are adjusted to expected costs based on activity level. The actual cost may also be adjusted on a periodic basis rather than as cash is disbursed. That is, one twelfth of 1,460 (assuming level pro ration) or $122 per month
5. Transportation costs are also adjusted to the new activity level.
6. Contracted services are adjusted based on present needs. It costs the agency $400 to provide the services that the person who was not replaced would have provided. The reviewer should analyze this practice as to a best practice and whether it could be used elsewhere to make operations more economical, efficient, and effective.
7. Other expenses are also adjusted to expectations under the present circumstances.

Exhibit 4.6   The Counseling Agency—Flexible Budget

1. Become a consultant to other not-for-profits.
2. Subcontract to other not-for-profits—do something for others.
3. Sell excess supplies and materials.
4. Develop an educational presentation that others might purchase.
5. Share your network or mailing list—for a price.
6. Rent time and space—for example, your conference room or client counseling areas
7. Perform a service such as a seminar or workshop.
8. Sell off your excess inventory.
9. Run workshops or training programs.
10. Use your space as a showroom for other not-for-profits.
11. Cost share equipment—computer systems, power tools.
12. Produce a series of similar work—books, posters.
13. Barter for materials and services.
14. Acquire in-kind and donated services.
15. Bulk purchasing of materials and use of sharing arrangements.
16. Look for professional discounts.
17. Piggyback your trips.

Exhibit 4.7   Turning Your Not-for-Profit Operations into Cash

INTERVIEWING

As previously mentioned, interviews in the planning phase are generally limited to management, along with some interviewing of operations personnel. In the field work phase, however, interviews are not limited to management, but primarily include those individuals—employees and volunteers—who actually do the work so as to determine what is going on and why. Exhibit 4.8 provides some notes relative to the operational review interview.

The purpose of the operational review interview is to correlate practice and theory, to gather facts, opinions, and ideas, and to establish a positive image of the reviewers in the minds of the not-for-profit's personnel. To conduct a successful interview, there must be adequate preparation. The reviewer should learn as much as possible about the operation through such sources as policies and procedures manuals, organization charts and functional job descriptions, internal and external reports, prior review reports and working papers, technical journals, and so on. It is the review team's responsibility to do their homework prior to the interview and not spend time asking questions to which they already know the answers.

I. *Importance of the operational review interview*
   A. Correlates practice and theory
   B. Gathers facts, opinions, and ideas
   C. Establishes the reviewer's image in the mind of the client

II. *Preparing for the Interview*
   A. Learn something about the organization through:
      1. Policies and procedures
      2. Operating manuals
      3. Organization charts and functional job descriptions
      4. Legislation: laws, charters, grants, contracts, and ordinances
      5. Reports: internal and external
      6. Prior review reports
      7. Working papers
      8. Technical journals
   B. Prepare an interview agenda.
      1. Write out basic questions
      2. Review and rephrase questions
      3. Organize and consolidate questions
   C. How and what the reviewer asks depends on whom he or she is talking to.
      1. Decision management: Aim at gathering information about policy and objectives
         a. Do:
            • Ask about policy.
            • Ask about goals and objectives.
            • Encourage free exchange of ideas.
            • Sell yourself and the review team.
            • Concentrate on the "big picture."
         b. Don't:
            • Use technical terminology.
            • Get involved in great detail.
            • Inject yourself in the middle of a story; let the interviewee talk.
            • Interrupt.
            • Criticize the operation.
      2. Operating management: Including department managers, supervisors, and the like. Some of the areas to be covered with this group are work flow, present problems, relationship to other departments, and future improvements.
         a. Do:
            • Evaluate work flow.
            • Document functions of departmental personnel.
            • Sell yourself.
            • Anticipate reluctance.
            • Plan ahead and be prepared to discuss operations.
            • Observe operations while you talk.
         b. Don't:
            • Use technical terminology.
            • Inject your ideas in the middle of a story; rather, direct the conversation.

Exhibit 4.8   Operational Review Interview Notes

> • Be reluctant to stimulate the interviewee to action.
> • Ignore the day-to-day problems.
> • Gloss over interdepartmental relationships.
> 3. Operating personnel: These include people responsible for a specific job.
>   a. Do:
>   • Have a list of questions.
>   • Know the general work flow.
>   • Be friendly and complimentary.
>   • Sell yourself.
>   • Concentrate on the areas of responsibility of the interviewee.
>   b. Don't:
>   • Use technical terminology.
>   • Use words that can allow the interviewee to draw the wrong inference.
>   • Criticize the operations or personnel.
>   • Try to overpower the interviewee.
>   • Allow the interview to deteriorate into a complaint session.
> D. Remember, never go into the interview cold and unprepared; do your homework before the interview.
>
> III. **Scheduling the Interview**
>   A. Make advance arrangements.
>   1. Time and place; interviewee's work area most desirable.
>   2. Probable duration of meeting; limit to an hour or less.
>   B. Arrange favorable hours and days.
>   1. Avoid hours immediately before or after lunch.
>   2. Avoid late Friday afternoon, day before or after a holiday or vacation.
>   3. If possible, try for early morning, shortly after workday begins, or mid-afternoon.
>   C. Share the agenda and request materials.
>   1. Indicate generally the subject of the meeting.
>   2. Request materials: sample forms, statements, etc.
>   D. Keep interview generally one-on-one, with no supervisors or supervisees present.
>
> IV. **Opening the Interview**
>   A. Be punctual; it helps your image.
>   B. Put the person at ease, but control the amount of small talk.
>   C. State clearly the purpose of the interview.
>   D. Assure the interviewee you will protect his or her anonymity.
>
> V. **Conducting the Interview**
>   A. Be open, objective, and reasonable.
>   B. Convey to the other person that the review is a matter of joint concern.
>   C. Use your agenda to direct the interview and prevent undue subject wandering.
>
> *(Continued)*

Exhibit 4.8 *(Continued)*

VI. *Questioning the Interviewee*
  A. Ask questions that require more than yes or no answers.
  B. Seek the other person's analysis of causes and effects; statements of things that are of concern to the interviewee.
  C. Do not ask loaded questions:
      1. Those that indicate you have already assumed an answer.
      2. Those that indicate what you would like to hear.

VII. *Note Taking*
  Never record complete minutes.
      1. Adversely affects other person.
      2. Not conducive to good listening; hence, you may not be able to separate material from immaterial items.

VIII. *Effective Listening*
  A. Ask the person to repeat or restate if you do not understand.
  B. Ask for concrete examples if language is general or vague.
  C. Summarize or rephrase in order to encourage elaboration.
  D. Ask the interviewee what he or she would do to correct or improve conditions.
  E. Allow periods of silence in which to think.
  F. Don't:
      • Debate or waste time in disagreeing over any point, no matter how important.
      • Be sarcastic.
      • Jump to conclusions.
      • Contradict a person in front of others.
      • Quote other people you have interviewed; the interviewee will not trust you to keep his or her responses confidential.

IX. *Closing the Interview*
  A. Stick to the time schedule even if you have not finished your agenda; simply arrange for another meeting.
  B. If the other person wishes to extend the interview, then do so; but let this be his or her option, not yours.
  C. Before leaving, summarize the major facts obtained in the interview.
  D. Thank the interviewee for his or her time.
  E. Leave the door open for further questions or information.

X. *Recording the Interview*
  A. Review, organize, and record your notes as soon as possible after the interview; at least on the same day.
  B. Write out enough, so that conclusions are reasonably self-explanatory.
  C. Send a copy of your notes to the interviewee for his or her review and agreement, where appropriate.

Exhibit 4.8   *(Continued)*

Interview Agenda and Whom to Interview

As part of the reviewer's interview preparation, an interview agenda is prepared; which includes the major areas to be covered and the basic questions to be answered. The agenda is used as the reviewer's guideline, not to share the details with the interviewee, but only the general areas to be covered. However, the reviewer should be prepared to deviate from the agenda as required by answers obtained in the actual interview. The questions to be asked depend on who is being interviewed. For example, if the interviewee is decision management, the reviewer would gather information relative to policies and objectives. If operating management, including department managers, supervisors, and the like, are being interviewed, the reviewer might cover such things as work flow, interdepartmental relationships, present problems, and future improvements. If operating personnel, the people responsible for a specific job, are being interviewed, the reviewer might ask about the specific work flow and related systems and procedures.

The interview agenda is used by the reviewer as a guideline to ensure that each agenda item is adequately covered in the interview. If the reviewer needs to deviate from the agenda into unforeseen but more important areas as a result of the interviewees responses, the reviewer makes sure his or her agenda items are covered in this or a subsequent interview.

Scheduling the Interview

Another significant issue is the proper scheduling of the interview. It is the reviewer's responsibility to make advance arrangements as to the time and place, at the convenience of the interviewee. It is usually best to meet at the interviewee's work area so that the person being interviewed is most at ease and the reviewer can observe ongoing operations during the interview.

There should be agreement on the length of time the interview will take—a good rule is to limit the interview to an hour or less. In scheduling the interview, the reviewer should arrange for the most favorable hours and days. If possible, the interview should be conducted in the early morning, shortly after the beginning of the workday; or in the midafternoon, sometime between an hour after lunch and an hour before quitting. Try to avoid those times immediately before or after lunch, first thing Monday morning, late Friday afternoon, and the day before or after a holiday or vacation.

Setting Up the Interview

When setting up the interview, the reviewer should indicate what the general agenda is to be, but should not share the actual agenda with the interviewee. If the reviewer would like the interviewee to provide specific materials either before or at the time of the interview, the reviewer asks for them at this time so that the interviewee has sufficient time to make them available—either prior to or at the time of the interview. The reviewer should not wait until the time of the interview to request such materials. It should also be made clear to the interviewee that the interview should include just that individual and the reviewer. This ensures confidentiality and helps the interviewee to feel free to speak, which might not happen in the presence of supervisors or supervisees. This also ensures getting more honest and correct information from both parties. It is also a good idea not to bring anyone else along because this only increases anxiety. A one-to-one interview can thus be more productive than an attempt to save time by talking to more than one person at a time.

Starting the Interview

It is the reviewer's responsibility to be punctual and to arrive at the interview site a little before the scheduled start time. While it might be inconsiderate of the interviewee to arrive late or to keep the reviewer waiting, remember that it is the reviewer's goal to get information from the other person during his or her work time, and therefore, sometimes the reviewer will be inconvenienced. In addition, being on time helps to enhance the reviewer's professional image and create a favorable impression. From the outset, the interviewee should be put at ease. An effective icebreaker or small talk can be helpful, but the reviewer should control the amount of time used for this purpose. An effective transition can be used to state clearly the purpose and general agenda of the interview. The reviewer should assure the interviewee that his or her anonymity will be protected and confidentiality respected.

When conducting the interview, the reviewer should be open, objective, and reasonable. The interviewee should be assured that the operational review is a matter of joint concern and that the reviewer's role is to help him or her to improve operations and make the job easier. The basic agenda is used to direct the interview, prevent unnecessary wandering, and ensure that all agenda items are covered. Note that the interviewee should not have a copy of the actual agenda. This keeps the reviewer from being constricted by a written agenda if he or she wants to pursue more significant areas of concern that may arise.

Questioning Procedures

When asking questions, it is a good idea for the reviewer to stay away from "yes or no" questions, as they limit the amount of information to be obtained. Rather, the reviewer should ask questions that require the interviewee to analyze causes and effects, state matters of concern, and give opinions. The reviewer should never ask "loaded" questions, those indicating that an answer is already assumed, or those indicating what the reviewer would like to hear (e.g., "Your systems are really lousy, aren't they?").

Note Taking

While conducting the interview, the reviewer should not take full notes or minutes as the interviewee is talking. Such note taking may adversely affect the other person, and no one wants to look at the top of another person's head. Moreover, such minute taking is not conducive to good listening; it can cause the reviewer to be unable to separate material items from those having little impact. A good practice is to take abbreviated notes to trigger subsequent recall, including the recording of facts, source references, rough diagrams, quick flowcharts, key words, and so on.

Effective Listening

Since the purpose of the reviewer is to gather information and learn more, it is important for him or her to be an effective listener and to make sure to get accurate facts and statements. People learn by listening, not by talking. A good technique to increase the effectiveness of listening skills is to ask the interviewee to repeat or restate items that are not completely understood. However, this technique should not be overused, because it may turn off the interviewee. Nor should the reviewer ask the interviewee to repeat something that can be found out easily elsewhere. Another good listening technique is to ask for concrete examples if the person's language is too general or vague. However, the reviewer must be sure these are not areas that should have been known before the interview. Other techniques that can be used include summarizing or rephrasing what the interviewee has stated in order to encourage elaboration, or asking how the interviewee would correct or improve conditions.

During the interview, it is good practice to allow periods of silence in which to think. It is not the reviewer's responsibility to fill in the silent awkward periods. Often, the interviewee needs these silent periods to gather thoughts. It is also important not to antagonize the interviewee by debating a point, making sarcastic comments, jumping to conclusions, or contradicting him or her—particularly in front of others. Moreover, the reviewer should never quote from past interviews with others, as this might get the other persons in trouble, while the present interviewee will not trust the interviewer to keep his or her responses confidential.

Closing the Interview

When closing the interview, the reviewer must make sure to stay within the one-hour time agreement, even if the interview agenda is not finished. In this case, another interview can be arranged. However, if the interview can be completed in a short time—say within 10 minutes—and if the other person wishes to extend the interview, the reviewer can do so, but allowing the decision to continue to be the interviewee's.

At the close of the interview, the reviewer summarizes the major areas covered and the facts obtained to assure their completeness and accuracy. Then the reviewer sincerely thanks the interviewee for his or her time, and asks cordially whether the person may be contacted again should there be additional questions or further information needed.

Note Recording

After the interview, the reviewer should review, organize, and record the notes taken as soon as possible, at least on the same day. This helps to ensure the accuracy of interview records. In recording interview notes, the reviewer must be sure to write out sufficient details so that conclusions are reasonably self-explanatory. A good practice, where appropriate, is to send a copy of the interview notes to the interviewee for review and agreement. This ensures accuracy and completeness while the interview is still fresh in his or her mind and provides more accurate data on which to base conclusions.

Sample Interview

A sample transcription of an interview between an operational reviewer and a department manager is shown in Figure 4.9. To reinforce the materials covered on effective interviewing techniques, review and analyze the interview presentation and document any good or bad points identified. When a point is identified, try to think of how it affects the interview and later relations with the interviewee and the department. Some comments are provided at the end of the interview.

EFFECTIVE INTERVIEWING
IS MORE LISTENING
THAN TELLING

INTERNAL BENCHMARKING

Not-for-profits have been in existence for many years—some successful and long-lasting, others short-lived. Through the years, there has been no clear-cut criteria or formula for success. Many not-for-profits have been successful through such intangible attributes as dumb luck, falling into a niche service area, being the first, client acceptance, and so on. Other not-for-profits using the best available operating acumen and methods have failed miserably. Identifying, implementing, and maintaining the secrets of success is an elusive target. Banking

1. **Reviewer** (walks right into Department Manager's Office unannounced):
    Hi, we're doing an operational review of your area, so I thought you might answer some questions about the case record system.
2. **Department Manager** (looks up and looks at watch):
    What! You caught me by surprise. I have a meeting shortly, but I'll see what I can do for you.
3. **Reviewer** (sits down next to Department Manager and picks up pencil from desk):
    Can you tell me the status of the SRS program?
4. **Department Manager:**
    Huh!
5. **Reviewer** (louder):
    SRS program—Standard Reporting System
6. **Department Manager:**
    Oh. We haven't used that in months.
7. **Reviewer:**
    I know. Can you describe the program?
8. **Department Manager** (obviously disturbed):
    I told you, it's not currently being used.
9. **Reviewer:**
    Could you just describe it?
10. **Department Manager** (more annoyed):
    Okay. The purpose was to record client case data so that the information was recorded in all necessary places at the same time. We dropped it because we couldn't establish an effective reporting system between areas where we could tell . . . (cut short)
11. **Reviewer:**
    Uh huh. So, you have to correct your recording system for SRS to work. What type of client case records do you keep?
12. **Department Manager:**
    We use an on-line computerized record.
13. **Reviewer:**
    I see. It's my experience that whatever records you use, it's almost impossible to effectively record client case data on a current basis. In fact, most case record operations are extremely sloppy. I suppose I'll see for myself how good yours are.
14. **Department Manager** (shocked—sits back in chair):
    Uh huh.
15. **Reviewer:**
    What vehicles do you have in your client transport fleet?
16. **Department Manager** (looks confused and disturbed):
    Four passenger vans, two station wagons, and four passenger cars.
17. **Reviewer** (writes down answer and asks manager to repeat):
    Run that by me again.
18. **Department Manager** (in a very annoyed tone):
    Four passenger vans, two station wagons, and four passenger cars.
19. **Reviewer:**
    Is that all?
20. **Department Manager** (extremely annoyed):
    Yeah, that's all!!!
21. **Reviewer:**
    Who schedules the pick ups?
22. **Department Manager:**
    The counseling shift supervisor schedules pickups and returns and dispatches drivers.
23. **Reviewer:**
    Is the schedule formally written?

(Continued)

Exhibit 4.9   Sample Interview

24. **Department Manager:**
No, its not formal! Its just a day-to-day–type thing.
25. **Reviewer:**
Do you have any transport records and time spent on them?
26. **Department Manager** (really disturbed):
No!
27. **Reviewer:**
Have you ever calculated the cost to make a pickup and return?
28. **Department Manager:**
No!
29. **Reviewer:**
That's funny, Tony Maroney, the counseling unit's administrative assistant told me that they keep detailed records and costs of all client pickup and returns. He thinks we could save a bundle of money if we got out of the pickup business.
30. **Department Manager:**
(quite disturbed—turns away)
You don't say.
31. **Reviewer:**
Where do you get your authority over treatment plans?
32. **Department Manager:**
(picks up large loose-leaf binder)
Look, it's right here in the *Agency Policies and Procedures Manual.*
(flips through the book).
Here are the sections.
33. **Reviewer:**
That's okay. I'll read my copy when I get back to the office.
Do you have an organization chart I can have?
34. **Department Manager:**
Sure, just a minute. I'll call my assistant. (Calls out)
Al, get me a copy of our organization chart.
35. **Al** (enters room):
I have a chart you can have, but it's about three years old.
36. **Reviewer:**
You don't have a current organization chart? How can you run your department without one?
37. **Department Manager** (upset and embarrassed; pauses and stutters):
We'll, uh, I'll get you a copy when we update it (nods to Al, who leaves).
38. **Reviewer** (starts to gather up his papers—puts the Department Manager's pencil in his bag):
Uh, I've written down the forms I'd like to have copies of (hands piece of handwritten paper to Department Manager).
39. **Department Manager** (looks over paper):
Uh huh, Client Application, Log of Counseling Assignments, Treatment Order, Client Addition Record, Client Status Report, Completed Treatment Form, After Care and Follow-Up Documents.
Look, I can't get them for you now (looks at watch). I'm already 20 minutes late for my meeting. I'll have to send them to you.
40. **Reviewer:**
Okay. I didn't think it was that much trouble (grabs paper back and copies down forms on pad).
41. **Department Manager** (gets up to leave):
If you have any more questions, contact my secretary (leaves the office with the reviewer still sitting there).

Exhibit 4.9   *(Continued)*

SAMPLE INTERVIEW COMMENTS

OVERALL WEAK POINT

The interview was not planned; it skips from one area to another without any logical sequence. The question of authority over client case records is asked at the end of the interview instead of at the beginning, which would be the most logical place.

1. No appointment was made. The reviewer called on the department manager without making an appointment, establishing a time limit, or reviewing the general agenda. This is a result of lack of proper planning. If the department manager was contacted in advance and given the general agenda or areas to be covered, he or she could have been prepared for the interview. In addition, the department manager might have been able to raise some points the reviewer may not have thought about.

2. The department manager mentions having a meeting shortly but will see what he or she can do. However, the reviewer not only fails to respond to this issue, but offers no apology for just stopping by unannounced, producing an immediate negative image of the reviewer and the review team.

3–6. The reviewer jumps right into the interview with no preliminary ice breaking; again putting the department manager ill at ease. In addition, the reviewer starts out with the SRS program—obviously a sore point in the department. This creates a good possibility of putting the department manager immediately on the defensive.

7. The reviewer's question "Can you describe the program?" is the type of open-ended question to be asked in an operational review interview. However, there is the point of whether this might not be a too detailed question for a department manager and whether the reviewer could have acquired such detailed information prior to the interview.

8–10. The department manager, although obviously disturbed, starts to respond to the question quite adequately, providing good information. However, the reviewer cuts the department manager short and jumps immediately to a conclusion. Had the reviewer allowed the department manager to continue, instead of being presumptuous and dismissing his or her opinions, the reviewer might have gained some valuable information and recommendations.

11. The reviewer, after cutting the department manager short, jumps right into another area (client case records) without properly concluding the discussion on the SRS Program or introducing the new discussion area.

12–13. After the department manager responds that the department uses an online computerized record, the reviewer interjects his or her own poor opinion of any and all case record operations—again putting the department manager on the defensive. As the interview is unfolding, the department manager will probably hold back and not provide as much complete information as possible.

14. The department manager, although shocked, allows the interview to continue.

(Continued)

Exhibit 4.9   *(Continued)*

15–18. The reviewer does not properly close the discussion on client case records, but instead jumps right into the transport fleet. The reviewer writes down what the department manager says about the transport fleet and then asks him or her to repeat. This can be annoying and distracting, especially to a department manager. Such detailed information should be obtained from someone other than the department manager, and prior to the interview.

19–20. The reviewer asks the department manager "Is that all?". This again implies displeasure and the point that there should be more. The department manager is justifiably "extremely annoyed."

21–22. The question "Who schedules the pickups and returns?" is again detail data that should have been known prior to the interview. This type of question only puts the person on the spot, implying, "You should know the answer, or how can you be running the department?"

23–28. These questions tend to be of the yes or no type, allowing the department manager to offer no additional information, opinion, or analysis. In addition, the staccato-style questioning suggests a scene in which a bright light might be shone on the department manager as the interrogation gets heavier.

29–30. The question "Have you ever calculated the cost to make a pickup and return?" is a set-up, and the department manager provides the expected "no" answer. The reviewer, however, rather than pick up on the thread of the discussion and ask for an analysis or opinion of why not, disputes the department manager's information by bringing another employee's (Tony Maroney) input into the discussion. This is not only a breach of confidentiality of the other employee, but it also undermines the confidence of the department manager being interviewed. For, if the reviewer is that quick to bring someone else's opinion into the discussion, he or she will do the same with the present discussion. In most instances, the other person will be either a supervisor (as in this case) or a supervisee; such a situation creates possible trouble and conflict. This practice also destroys the interviewee's trust in the reviewer and inhibits the openness of the interview.

31–32. The reviewer asks "Where do you get your authority over case records?" This question should have been asked at the beginning of the interview. In addition, it points to the reviewer's having done insufficient advance preparation. When the department manager offers to show the policies and procedures manual, the reviewer says, "That's okay, I'll read my copy when I get back to the office." This not only discounts the department manager's offer, but also reemphasizes the lack of preparation.

33–37. The reviewer asks for an organization chart, which should have been requested at the time the interview was scheduled or obtained from other sources prior to the interview. What results here is the necessity to engage someone else in the interview (Al, the assistant), ultimately resulting in the reviewer's criticizing the department manager in front of the supervisee. This causes the department manager to become upset and embarrassed, certainly not conducive to a good working relationship, which is necessary for the rest of the operational review.

Exhibit 4.9 *(Continued)*

38.	The reviewer begins to end the interview by gathering up papers and walks off with the department manager's pencil—rude on both counts. The reviewer then requests certain forms via a handwritten piece of paper. Note that any forms or documents needed should be requested at the time the interview is scheduled. This allows the department manager to have them ready so as to explain their use at the interview. The reviewer should know what to request by proper planning and research in preparation for the interview. Should other items come up in the interview, of which the reviewer was not aware, these could be legitimately asked for. The department manager needs to read the handwritten note to make certain of the request and responds that he or she will have to send such copies to the reviewer, which is quite doubtful based on the content of the interview thus far.
39.	The department manager also says "I'm already 20 minutes late for my meeting." Remember, the department manager had originally stated that he or she had a meeting to go to shortly. However, the reviewer has shown no regard for the department manager's needs during the entire interview.
40.	The reviewer's response, "Okay. I didn't think it was that much trouble," is probably the last straw. Not only has this final comment sent the department manager out the door, but the reviewer has also not left the door open for the future.
41.	The department manager's closing, "If you have any more questions, contact my secretary," while cordial under the circumstances, is more likely a brush-off; and the chance of the department manager's cooperating with the reviewer in the future is remote.

Exhibit 4.9 *(Continued)*

on what has worked in the past and your own intuition are ineffective substitutes for objective internal appraisal and external comparison and analysis—what we call benchmarking. Benchmarking is becoming the tool of choice for gathering data related to programs of continuous improvement and to gain competitive advantage.

Benchmarking, like the process of operational review, can be defined as a process for analyzing internal operations and activities to identify areas for positive improvement in a program of continuous improvement. The process begins with an analysis of existing operations and activities, identifies areas for positive improvement, and then establishes a performance standard on which the activity can be measured. The goal is to improve each identified activity so that it can be the best possible and stay that way. The best practice is not always measured in terms of least costs, but may be more what stakeholders value and expected levels of performance (i.e., effectiveness).

Benchmarking processes are directed toward the continuous pursuit of positive improvements, excellence in all activities, and the effective use of best practices. The focal point in achieving these goals is the customer or client—both

internal and external—who establishes performance expectations and is the ultimate judge of resultant quality. A not-for-profit customer or client is defined as
anyone who has a stake or interest in the ongoing operations of the not-for-
profit—anyone who is affected by not-for-profit results (type, quality, and timeliness). Stakeholders include all those who are dependent on the survival of the
not-for-profit, such as:

- Management (board of directors, operations): external/internal
- Funding sources: external (public and private)
- Employees/volunteers/subcontractors: internal/external
- Customers/clients/end users: external
- Suppliers/vendors: external

Benchmarking results provide the not-for-profit—management, funding
sources, and employees—with data necessary for effective resource allocation
and the strategic focus for the organization. The benchmarking process provides
for those objective measures to determine the success of the company's internal
goals, objectives, and detail plans as well as external and competitive performance measures. Benchmarking the company's performance against stakeholder
expectations enables the not-for-profit to pursue its program of continuous improvement and the road to excellence. Effective benchmarking encompasses both
internal and external needs. Some examples of internal and external benchmarks
for a not-for-profit include:

- Increased revenues: in total, by funding source, and by service
- Increased reserves or net assets
- Total services delivered: in total, by type, by period, by event
- Services delivered compared to cost of services
- Cash flow changes
- Survival and growth
- Internal excellence (positive changes)
- Competitive excellence (compared to similar not-for-profits): quality,
  timeliness, cost, responsiveness)
- Supplier excellence: preferred vendors
- Employer excellence: employee participation, empowerment, and so on

While not-for-profit management may be most concerned with short-term
benchmarking criteria, such as funding and service delivery increases, other
stakeholders may be more concerned with longer-term criteria such as real service and operational growth, customer and client satisfaction, and ongoing positive cash flow. There needs to be a meaningful balance between such
short-term and long-term goals of divergent stakeholders for the benchmarking
process to be most successful. Some benchmarks for not-for-profit organizational growth include:

- Cost reductions: short-term gain for long-term pain
- Price of services increases: may create more external competition
- Revenue volume increases: present and potential customers and clients
- New service expansion: present and additional services
- New distribution channels: other locations, Internet, collaborations
- Service delivery increases in existing service areas
- Close a losing operation/location: decrease or lack of funding, lessened demand for services offered
- Merge or collaborate with another not-for-profit
- New service development
- Efficiency and productivity improvements: achieve more with less
- Non–value-added activities eliminated

Internal benchmarking analyzes existing practices within various operating areas of the not-for-profit—to identify activities and drivers and best performance. Drivers are the causes of work or triggers (e.g., a client service request) that set in motion a series of activities. Internal benchmarking focuses on looking at the not-for-profit's operations before looking externally. Significant positive improvements can be made as the reviewer question such things as:

- Is that activity needed?
- Why do we do that?
- Is that position/material really needed?
- Can the activity be done better in another manner?
- Is that step necessary? Does it provide added value?

Internal benchmarking is the technique used in the field work phase of the operational review because it provides the framework to compare internal practices within the not-for-profit as well as to external best practice benchmark data.

**INTERNAL BENCHMARKING
IS THE FIRST STEP
TO INTERNAL APPRAISAL**

EXTERNAL BENCHMARKING

External benchmarking is used to compare the not-for-profit's operations to other not-for-profits, particularly in developing operational review recommendations, and includes the following types of benchmarking:

- *Competitive benchmarking:* Looks to the outside to identify how other simi-lar not-for-profits are performing. Competitive benchmarking identifies the strengths and weaknesses of competing not-for-profits and is helpful in determining its own successful competitive strategy. It can also help to prioritize specific areas for improvement such as customer or client ser-vice, operating efficiencies, cost data, performance results and so on.
- *Industry benchmarking:* Extending beyond the typical one-to-one compari-son of competitive benchmarking, industry benchmarking attempts to identify trends, innovations, and new ideas across the service fields of the not-for-profit. Such identification can help to establish better performance criteria, but may not lead to competitive breakthroughs. Remember that other not-for-profitss may be going through the same benchmarking process as you.
- *Best-in-class benchmarking:* Looks across multiple types of not-for-profits to identify new, innovative practices, regardless of their source. This search for best practices should be the ultimate goal of the benchmarking process. It supports continuous improvement, increased performance lev-els, and movement toward best practices and identifies opportunities for positive improvements. The review may even consider best-in-class prac-tices from the private sector where appropriate.

**EXTERNAL BENCHMARKING
IS THE SEARCH FOR BEST PRACTICES
WHEREVER THEY CAN BE FOUND**

PERFORMING AN INTERNAL BENCHMARKING STUDY

In performing an internal benchmarking study as part of an operational review, there area number of bases on which to compare to present practices, such as:

- Comparisons between individuals performing similar functions within the same work unit
- Comparative analysis between different work units within the not-for-profit that perform similar functions
- Comparisons to overall not-for-profit (i.e., industry) standards
- Comparisons to published benchmark standards
- Comparisons to tests of reasonableness

In analyzing present conditions, the reviewer must be aware of what condi-tions are expected to meet not-for-profit organizational goals and objectives. In determining the proper benchmark for comparison to a specific activity, the reviewer could review such areas as relevant legislation and laws, existing grants and contracts, policy statements, systems and procedures, internal and external regulations, responsibility and authority relationships, standards, schedules, plans and budgets, principles of good management and administration, and so on. In determining the correct benchmark for a specific function, the reviewer should answer the following questions for the activity:

- What should it be?
- What do you measure against?
- What is the standard procedure or practice?
- Is it a formal procedure or an informal practice?

This results in comparing what is to what should be—the benchmark.

In evaluating operating practices, the reviewer should be aware that procedures are formal methods of doing things, usually documented in writing, and prescribed by management. Practices are the actual way that work activities are performed and are rarely documented in written form.

Some examples of internal benchmarks that can be used for such comparison purposes include the following:

Internal to the Organization

- Organizational policy statements
- Legislation, laws, and regulations
- Grant and contractual arrangements
- Funding arrangements
- Organizational and departmental plans: goals and objectives
- Budgets, schedules, and detail plans

Developed by the Internal Benchmarking Team

- Internal performance statistics: by individual or work unit
- Performance of similar organizations
- Not-for-profit industry or functionally related statistics
- Past and present performance
- Engineered standards
- Special analysis or studies
- Review team's judgment
- Sound business practices
- Good common business sense

Comparing individuals performing similar functions (i.e., production workers, engineers, salespeople, accounting personnel, etc.) is not an exact science, because each individual's function is not exactly the same. However, the reviewer can identify better practices as to how to use one's expertise and ways of doing the job with others. However, such automatic transference of how one performs an activity to another is usually not that easily accomplished. Some areas for the review team to consider in making not-for-profit employees and volunteers more effective include:

- Making employees entrepreneurs (i.e., in business for themselves), responsible for their own level of accomplishment and related compensation.
- Fostering cooperation (and eliminating competition) among employees as it is now to all of their benefits to increase productivity and resultant services at the least cost.
- Creating an atmosphere of self-disciplined behavior characterized by individual responsibility, working together, and self-learning.
- Elimination of too many so-called management and supervisory personnel with the use of coaches and facilitators (in less numbers than managers and supervisors) to create a program of continuous improvement and productivity rather than stagnation and unnecessary costs.

**COMPARING INDIVIDUALS
IS NOT AN AUTOMATIC TRANSFER**

In many cases, internal benchmarks may not be available and must be developed. In the absence of existing internal standards or benchmarking criteria with which to evaluate performance, three alternative approaches are available to the reviewer:

1. Comparative analysis
2. The use of borrowed statistics
3. The test of reasonableness

Comparative Analysis

Comparative analysis is the technique that can be used, where specific internal standards do not exist for comparison, to compare the reviewed activities to similar situations within the not-for-profit. This analysis can be accomplished in two ways:

1. Current performance can be compared to past performance.
2. Performance can be compared with that of another similar work unit within the not-for-profit.

Comparing current to past periods has the advantage of possibly disclosing trends in performance. For example, if the cost per client contact rises from year to year, one may question whether (1) prices have risen, (2) inefficiencies in service delivery procedures have increased, (3) clients are being given increased service, or (4) a better quality of service is being delivered. The situation can then be analyzed further to determine exactly why the cost per client contact has increased.

In this example, the criteria by which actual performance is evaluated is not a predetermined plan or a formal set of performance standards; but simply that which was done in prior years. Using such comparisons does not provide sufficient data to tell whether the rise in cost per client contact is good or bad, or whether costs are too high. This method does, however, identify the causes so that not-for-profit management can judge performance as it occurred. Although trends are possible to note and examine by this method, meaningful comparisons of alternative methods or procedures cannot usually be accomplished.

The comparison of two different but similar work units normally provides the opportunity to evaluate different approaches to operations management. By determining the results of different operational approaches, the reviewer can make some helpful recommendations for improving efficiency and effectiveness. There are, however, some disadvantages in comparing two separate but similar work units. The major disadvantage is the failure to recognize factors which justify differences between the two units. For example, it is difficult to compare service delivery locations, as no two facilities may have exactly the same type of service delivery systems, hire the same type of employees, use the same type of equipment, or have the same type of clients and other essentials. Each service delivery location would, however, have many of the same types of problems regardless of their differences. The similarity of problems can enable the reviewer to analyze how each location's management group handles these common problems. The reviewer can then analyze such alternatives for improving the efficiency and effectiveness of operations and resultant recommendations can reflect the review team's judgment based on the results produced by each alternative.

Use of Borrowed Statistics

Many not-for-profit groups and organizations throughout the country, such as health providers, hospitals, colleges and universities, arts organizations, museums, and so on, provide uniform and comparable industry and benchmark standards for evaluating performance. In addition, many professional associations and journals publish benchmarking results and standards on an ongoing or periodic basis. These borrowed standards can then be used to compare performance of not-for-profits in similar endeavors. Although such comparisons would make performance evaluation quicker and easier, there are some disadvantages to this procedure as well.

One disadvantage is that national, state, or local averages and broad-based statistics rarely relate to specific situations. Thus, while such statistics provide some indications of the organization's performance, they cannot be used for precise measurement or evaluation. Another disadvantage is that very few national averages or uniform statistics actually exist. In those cases in which such statistics do exist, such as by standard service code, hospitals, health service industries, schools, libraries, and so on, they either relate to only a small portion of the areas subject to review or internal benchmarking, or they are limited to very restricted areas and are of minimal use.

Test of Reasonableness

When there are no internal standards, and comparisons with other not-for-profits are impossible, or borrowed benchmarks are unavailable, the reviewer can still test organizational performance on a benchmark based on the test of reasonableness. Through experience, members of the review team may have become familiar with how things are done economically, efficiently, and effectively in other not-for-profits. The review team should then be able to relate these experiences to the current functions included in the present operational review.

Accordingly, the operational review team can often spot operational irregularities and weaknesses that might escape the notice of others without such a background. In an operational review, perceptions of a situation are based on the eyes of the beholder—in this case, the cumulative experience of the review team. In addition, there exist what may be termed *general standards of society* that apply to good management in any field, public or private. For example, reviewers can often spot work being done in a loose, unsatisfactory, and inefficient manner, even without specific standards or benchmarks. Many times, this work has been considered acceptable—"that's the way we've always done it."

Obsolete records, excessive materials, personnel who are continually absent from work, abuse in the use of resources such as automobiles and expense accounts, or negligence in processing documents or handling cash funds are all examples of items that can be evaluated through the test of reasonableness. The test of reasonableness is also an appropriate tool to quickly review operating areas not subjected to detailed analysis. Even where the operational review team has analyzed in detail, the individual reviewer should still examine their conclusions for reasonableness. This ensures that the team has not become so engrossed in statistics that they have overlooked important items or placed too much weight on minor ones. The test of reasonableness can also be viewed as application of good common sense or prudent business practice to the situation. Some indicators of internal benchmarking deficiencies are shown in Figure 4.10.

1. **Management and Organization**
   - Poor planning and decision making
   - Too broad a span of control
   - Badly designed systems and procedures
   - Excessive crisis management
   - Poor channels of communication
   - Inadequate delegation of authority
   - Excessive organizational changes

2. **Personnel Relations**
   - Inadequate hiring, orientation, training, evaluation, and promotion procedures
   - Lack of clearly communicated job expectations
   - Idle, excessive, or not enough personnel
   - Poor employee morale
   - Excessive overtime and/or absenteeism
   - Unclear responsibility/authority relationships

3. **Service Delivery Operations**
   - Poor service delivery methods
   - Inefficient facility layout
   - Excessive poor quality services resulting in redo, poor satisfaction, and so on
   - Idle service delivery personnel
   - Insufficient or excessive equipment
   - Excessive service delivery costs
   - Lack of effective service delivery scheduling procedures
   - Poor housekeeping
   - Excessive, slow-moving, or underdemand for services

4. **Purchasing**
   - Not achieving best prices, timeliness, and quality
   - Favoritism to certain vendors
   - Lack of effective competitive bidding procedures
   - Not using most effective systems such as blanket purchase orders, traveling requisitions, telephone ordering, and so on.
   - Excessive emergency purchases
   - Lack of a value analysis program
   - Purchasing unnecessarily expensive items
   - Excessive returns to vendors

5. **Financial Indicators**
   - Poor revenue to cost ratios
   - Poor return on revenues: services delivered per revenue dollar
   - Unfavorable cost ratios
   - Unfavorable or unexplained cost/budget variances

6. **Complaints**
   - Customers or clients: poor service creating dissatisfaction
   - Employees: grievances, gripes or exit interview comments
   - Vendors: poor quality or untimely deliveries
   - Service delivery: schedules not met, material not available, untimely delivery, poor quality, and so on.

Exhibit 4.10   Indicators of Internal Benchmarking Deficiencies

> **COMPARATIVE ANALYSIS**
> **IS NOT THE SAME AS COMPARING**

SYSTEMS FLOWCHART

Another technique that is widely used in the field work phase is systems flow-charting. The purpose of systems flowcharting is to document general and specific procedures to help the reviewer understand operations and activities. Flowcharts show the work that is actually being performed, who is doing it, how it is done, and how much is done. Flowcharting provides far more satisfactory results than reviewing operating manuals and documentation, because the reviewer gains a better and more accurate understanding of operating activities. In addition, the process of flowcharting, which requires obtaining and documenting an understanding of operating systems, helps stimulate the reviewer's interest, enthusiasm and imagination, resulting in a more realistic identification of weaknesses.

The systems flowchart is a graphic representation of the sequence of operations in a process. It is especially useful in showing where documents, equipment, reference materials, files, and new paperwork are introduced into the process. It documents what work is performed and how.

The systems flowchart provides information relative to (1) how operations are actually carried out, (2) the necessity or usefulness of the work steps included in processing transactions, and (3) the effectiveness of the process and controls provided in the process.

The systems flowchart also helps the reviewer to identify the system's inefficiencies, such as the following:

- Unnecessary handling
- Inefficient routing
- Unused information on documents or records
- Inadequate planning or delegation
- Inadequate instruction
- Insufficient or excessive equipment
- Poor use of computer processing facilities
- Poorly planned reports
- Inadequate or improper scheduling

A systems flowchart that could be prepared during the field work phase for a not-for-profit's purchasing–receiving–accounts payable–disbursement system is shown in Exhibit 4.11. This is a systems flowchart for a fairly sizable not-for-profit and it shows worksteps and volumes that would not be present at a much

Procedure	Personnel	Purchasing	Receiving	Accounts Payable
1. The originating dept. initiates a purchase by preparing a requisition. The requisition is approved by the dept. head who also specifies the account coding. The requisitions are not prenumbered.	Department Head			
2. Upon receipt of requisition, a prenumbered purchase order (approximately 30,000 per year) is prepared in accordance with the NPO's purchasing manual.	Purchasing Clerk #1			
3. Recheck entries on PO and verify math calculations. The prices are compared to current price lists maintained by purchasing.	Purchasing Clerk #2			
4. Review and approve PO. If new vendor or item is involved, determine that competitive prices are obtained by comparison to industry price lists. POs not approved are returned to originating dept. for correction or clarification.	V.P. Purchasing			
5. Distribute copies of PO and requisition as follows: PO 1. Vendor 2. Originating Dept. 3. File (numeric) 4. File (vendor) 5. Receiving 6. Accounts Payable Dept. Req. Receiving copy #5 includes quantities and prices.	Purchasing Check Clerk #1			
6. Account for numerical sequence and file	Secretary to the V.P. of Purchasing			

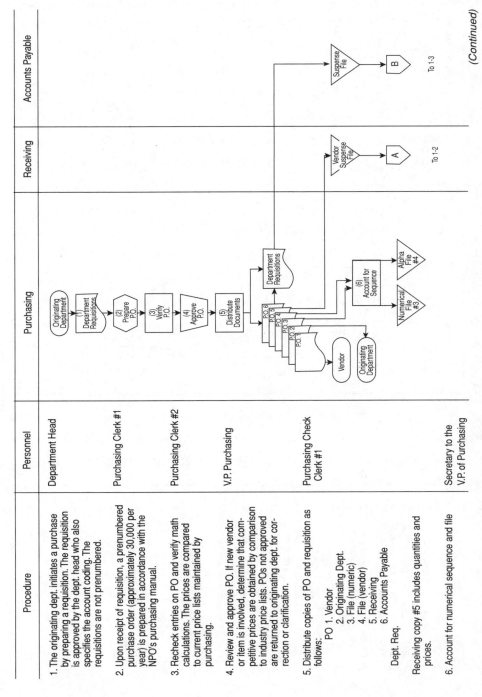

Flowchart labels — Purchasing column: Originating Department; Department Requisitions; (2) Prepare P.O.; (3) Verify P.O.; (4) Approve P.O.; (5) Distribute Documents; Department Requisitions; P.O. 6, P.O. 5, P.O. 4, P.O. 3, P.O. 2, P.O. 1; Vendor; Originating Department; (6) Account for Sequence; Alpha File #4; Numerical File #3.

Receiving column: Vendor Suspense File; A; To 1-2.

Accounts Payable column: Suspense File; B; To 1-3.

(Continued)

Exhibit 4.11 Systems Flow Chart: Purchasing–Receiving–Payables–Disbursement System

193

Purchasing–Receiving–Payables–Disbursements System

Procedure	Personnel	Receiving	Accounts Payable
7. When goods are received, count and check for damaged items. (See separate narrative write-up.) Prepare, sign, and date three part prenumbered receiving report. Attach to bill of lading and PO 5.	Receiving Clerk #1		
8. Review and compare receiving report, bill of lading, and PO 5 for completeness and any discrepancies. Distribute as follows: 　　P.O. 5. Accounts Payable 　　B of L 　　R.R. 1. File 　　　　2. Accounts Payable 　　　　3. Head of receiving dept. Note: the two receiving clerks may rotate steps 7 & 8 as both are involved.	Receiving Clerk #2		
9. Check numberical sequence of receiving report. Prepare daily listing of receiving reports and forward to accounts payable.	Head of Receiving dept.		
10. Route Receiving Documents to Accounts Payable 　• R.R. 1 　• R.R. 2 　• B of L 　• P.O. 5 　• Purchase Requisition 　• P.O. 6	Accounts Payable Clerk #1		

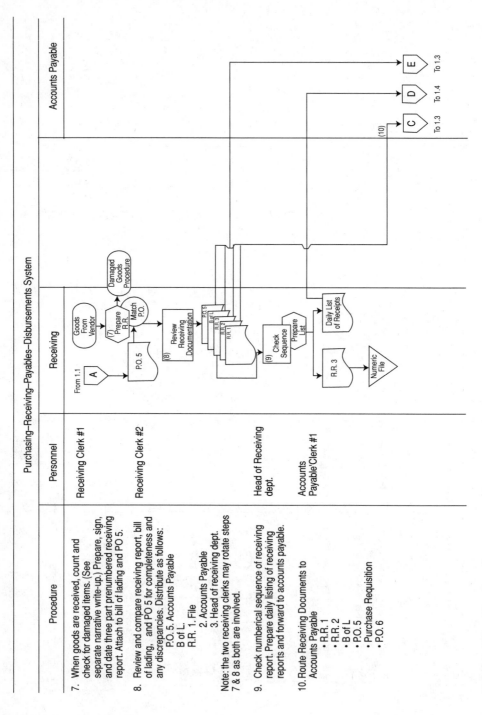

Exhibit 4.11 *(Continued)*

194

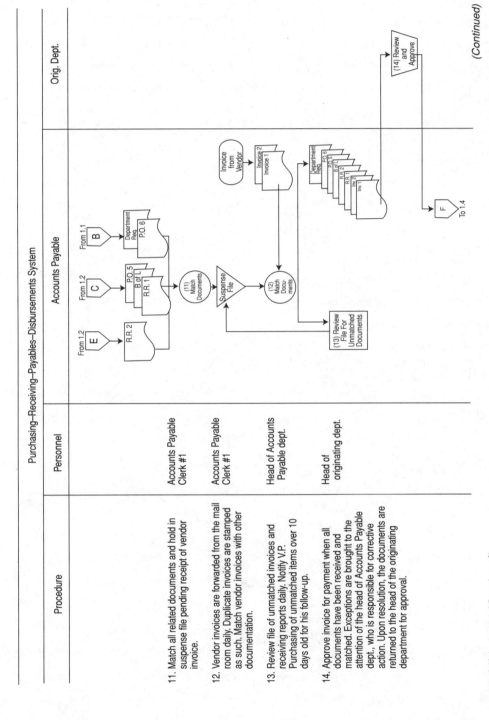

Purchasing–Receiving–Payables–Disbursements System

Procedure	Personnel	Accounts Payable	Orig. Dept.

11. Match all related documents and hold in suspense file pending receipt of vendor invoice.

Accounts Payable Clerk #1

12. Vendor invoices are forwarded from the mail room daily. Duplicate invoices are stamped as such. Match vendor invoices with other documentation.

Accounts Payable Clerk #1

13. Review file of unmatched invoices and receiving reports daily. Notify V.P. Purchasing of unmatched items over 10 days old for his follow-up.

Head of Accounts Payable dept.

14. Approve invoice for payment when all documents have been received and matched. Exceptions are brought to the attention of the head of Accounts Payable dept., who is responsible for corrective action. Upon resolution, the documents are returned to the head of the originating department for approval.

Head of originating dept.

Exhibit 4.11 (Continued)

(Continued)

Purchasing–Receiving–Payables–Disbursements System

Procedure	Personnel	Accounts Payable	Cash Disbursements

Procedure

15. Match Invoice and supporting documentation to related entry on daily listing of goods received and indicate that items have been matched by initialing the list. Check all documentation, verify math computations, agree quantities, check for proper discount, verify account distribution, check for approval, and indicate work by initials. At end of month, prepare accrual on the basis of open items on daily receipts list.

16. Prepare prenumbered voucher (approximately 35,000 per year). Includes all information necessary for posting to accounting records and preparation of check by E.D.P. Accumulate net amount of vouchers on adding machine tape as a control total for each day's transactions. A supply of prenumbered checks is given to computer operator.

Personnel

Accounts Payable Clerk #2

Cash Disbursement Clerk #2

Accounts Payable

From 1.2 — D

From 1.3 — F

(15) Match to List of Receipts

Verify Calculations, Coding, Etc.

Daily List Dept of Receipts.

E.O.M

Prepare Accounts Payable Accrual

Chron. File

Dept. Req.
PO 6
B 4
R.R. 2
INV 2
INV 1

Cash Disbursements

Locked File of Blank Checks

(16) Prepare Vouchers

Voucher Blank Checks

Control Total

G — To 1.6
H — To 1.6
I — To 1.5
J — To 1.5

Exhibit 4.11 *(Continued)*

196

Procedure	Personnel	EDP
EDP documentation consists of the source programs, operator instructions, and record layouts.		
17. The vouchers are entered via data terminal in EDP. An interactive edit routine is performed as data is entered.	Data Terminal Operator	
18. Computer operator processes data file through an edit program. The edit program checks that all numeric fields are numeric and checks for missing voucher numbers. The conversion process is verified by the use of record counts. Any vouchers which are detected as errors are returned to cash disbursements clerk #1. The voucher is corrected within two days and sent back to EDP for reprocessing.	Computer Operator (all operators are capable of running this series of programs)	
19. The daily transaction data file is used to prepare the checks and the check register. In addition, a month-to-date transaction file of checks issued is maintained to accumulate and prepare the monthly posting to the general ledger by account. The daily transaction data file and the month-to-date file are maintained for one week. The final MTD file is kept for 13 months.	Computer Operator	
20. End of the month procedure: The end of month file is processed to prepare a summary of the checks issued which serves as the source document to post the journal entry in the general ledger.	Computer Operator	

EDP flowchart labels:

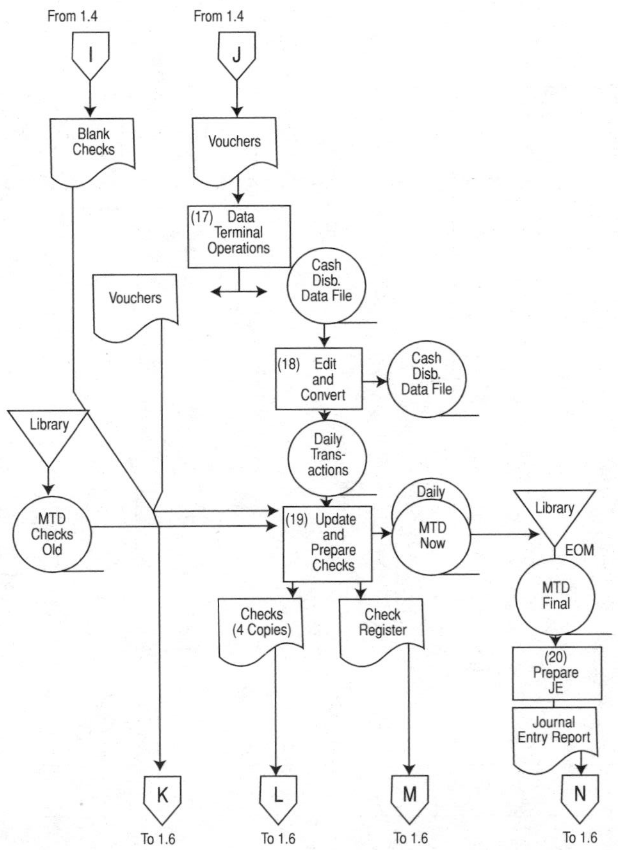

From 1.4 — J — Vouchers — (17) Data Terminal Operations — Cash Disb. Data File — (18) Edit and Convert — Cash Disb. Data File — Daily Transactions — Daily — MTD Now — (19) Update and Prepare Checks — Library — EOM — MTD Final — (20) Prepare JE — Journal Entry Report — N — To 1.6

From 1.4 — I — Blank Checks — Vouchers — Library — MTD Checks Old

Check Register — M — To 1.6

Checks (4 Copies) — L — To 1.6

K — To 1.6

Exhibit 4.11 (Continued)

(Continued)

197

Purchasing–Receiving–Payables–Disbursements System

Procedure	Personnel	Accounts Payable	Mail Room

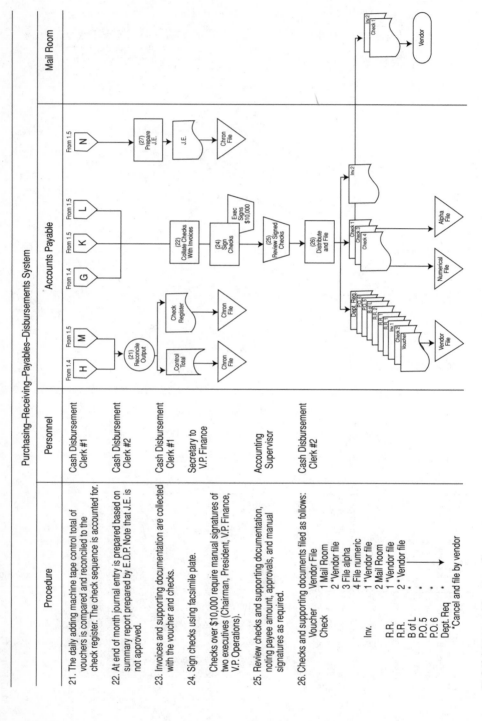

Procedure

21. The daily adding machine tape control total of vouchers is compared and reconciled to the check register. The check sequence is accounted for.

22. At end of month journal entry is prepared based on summary report prepared by E.D.P. Note that J.E. is not approved.

23. Invoices and supporting documentation are collected with the voucher and checks.

24. Sign checks using facsimile plate.

25. Checks over $10,000 require manual signatures of two executives (Chairman, President, V.P. Finance, V.P. Operations).

26. Review checks and supporting documentation, noting payee amount, approvals, and manual signatures as required.

26. Checks and supporting documents filed as follows:

Voucher	Vendor File
Check	1 Mail Room
	2 *Vendor file
	3 File alpha
	4 File numeric
Inv.	1 *Vendor file
	2 Mail Room
R.R.	1 *Vendor file
R.R.	2 *Vendor file
B of L	*
P.O. 5	*
P.O. 6	*
Dept. Req	*

*Cancel and file by vendor

Personnel

Cash Disbursement Clerk #1
Cash Disbursement Clerk #2
Cash Disbursement Clerk #1
Secretary to V.P. Finance
Accounting Supervisor
Cash Disbursement Clerk #2

Exhibit 4.11 *(Continued)*

smaller not-for-profit. The intent of the flowchart and its related analysis is to depict the process and value of flowcharting and related analysis.

The detailed operating procedures demonstrated in the systems flowchart example do not represent recommended procedures but, rather, procedures that a reviewer might uncover in an operational review. Consequently, the reviewer's focus should not be on these detailed procedures, but on how the flowchart is structured, to identify strengths and weaknesses in the operations. The reviewer should question each step in the process as to the following:

- Necessity—can the step be eliminated? Can the entire process be eliminated?
- Is the step a value-added or non–value-added process?
- Economy—is the step being performed in the most economical manner?
- Efficiency—is the method of performing the step the most efficient?
- Effectiveness—does the step provide for desired results? Are the desired results necessary?

The systems flowchart is also the starting point for documenting systems and processes as part of an internal and external benchmarking study to identify inefficient processes, leading toward recommended best practices in a program of continuous improvement. In addition, as process steps are identified, they can begin to be assigned costs as part of an overall activity-based costing or management system by service, customer or client, and function. Such costs enable the reviewer to quantify the costs of inefficiencies in the development of a review finding and recommendation.

The systems flowchart shown in Exhibit 4.11 depicts a suggested format for such a presentation that classifies procedures by departments or work units and relates their flow across these lines. Although it is important that the reviewer know how to prepare such flowcharts, it is equally important that the reviewer know how to analyze them. To make the flowchart complete, the reviewer might want to add the names and titles of personnel involved in each work step, related work volumes (transactions processed and backlog sitting at their work stations), and support it with copies of all source documents (blank and filled in) and reports mentioned.

As each numbered item on the flowchart is analyzed, the review team should document their comments as to operational deficiencies which could be corrected immediately or proposed for future correction (e.g., development of computerized procedures), areas of criticalness as to the development of a review finding, areas for further review at this time, and areas for review in the future. An analysis of Exhibit 4.11 showing suggested responses is shown in Exhibit 4.12.

LAYOUT FLOW DIAGRAM

A layout flow diagram is a schematic diagram of the existing or proposed physical arrangement of a work area to which has been added the flow lines of the

> **IT IS NOT AN EXERCISE IN**
> **DRAWING PRETTY SYSTEMS FLOWCHARTS**
> **BUT IN ANALYZING THEM FOR IMPROVEMENTS**

principal work performed there. This type of diagram is used to document the existing layout and paths of movement of people, paperwork, or materials. The layout flow diagram also enables the reviewer to disclose certain inefficiencies in the system, such as:

- Unnecessary functions or work steps
- Unnecessary handling or inefficient routing of certain documents
- Inadequate planning or delegation of work
- Inadequate instruction to employees
- Insufficient or excessive office equipment and computers
- Poor use of computer processing capabilities
- Bad work scheduling
- Inefficient work area layout
- Unnecessary personnel
- Excessive or inadequate facilities and work space

In addition, the layout flow diagram also enables the reviewer to identify certain potential personnel roadblocks to economical, efficient, and effective operations. Among these are:

- *Isolates* —individuals or work units that appear to be unconnected to the rest of the work area
- *Controllers* — individuals whose major function appears to be controlling or overseeing the work of others without any appreciable value added
- *Dispatchers* — individuals or work units whose main purpose is to receive work from one work unit or individual and pass it to another work unit or individual without appreciably adding to the work.
- *Hierarchical pyramids*—in which there is a reporting relationship either upward or downward, and in which the individuals appear to be mainly reviewing and/or redoing the work that was passed to them prior to passing it further up or down the pyramid.

Most organizational pyramids are constructed so that each higher level can police and control the lower level, while often providing no other benefits than to ensure that the lower levels do their work. If these hierarchical levels can be elim-

1.a. Procedure and control question as to whether the department heads should be doing the account coding (is this the best use of time?). Normal procedure calls for the requisitioner and/or an account coding clerk to provide such coding. This may also be a tip of the iceberg situation suggesting a larger problem—an organizational pattern of management performing clerical tasks.

  b. Purchase requisitions are not prenumbered. Numerical control over purchase requisitions ensures that all purchases are processed by the Purchasing Department and no requisitions are processed more than once. Normally, such control is exercised by the requisitioning department and, accordingly, must be performed uniformly throughout the organization.

2. Approximately 30,000 purchase orders are prepared annually by one purchasing clerk. This appears to be a large number for one person to handle. The reviewer would want to analyze the procedures for preparing purchase orders to clarify this situation.

3.a. Another purchasing clerk rechecks entries on the purchase order and verifies math calculations. The preparation of purchase orders (particularly for 30,000 per year) is usually done on a computerized basis with today's technology. If so, this step could be eliminated. This may also suggest a larger problem (another tip of the iceberg situation), in which computer equipment and resources are available, but not properly utilized.

  b. The prices are compared with current price lists maintained by the Purchasing Department. The operational reviewer should note this as an area for further analysis to determine accuracy and up-to-dateness of the price list.

4.a. The vice president of purchasing reviews and approves all purchase orders, which again is not the best use of management time.

  b. If a new vendor or item is involved, the vice president determines that competitive prices are obtained by comparison with industry price lists. This is another area for further analysis.

  c. Purchase orders not approved are returned to the originating department for correction or clarification. The operational reviewer should determine what reasons constitute disapproval.

    There is also no mention of whether a check is made against the approved plan/budget prior to the preparation of the purchase order. Other than this, there would not appear to be any other reason to return purchases to the issuing department, particularly after the purchase order is prepared.

5. Distribute copies of purchase order and requisition.

  a. The purchase requisition should be returned to the issuer as proof of processing (or some other method of notification), and not to accounts payable.

  b. The originating department needs to receive notification of its open purchases, but not necessarily a copy of the purchase order. With a computerized system this could take the form of a data file or open purchase listing. These data are then used to control the processing of open purchase requisitions and subsequent open purchase orders.

  c. Two copies of the purchase order (one maintained in numeric sequence and one in alphabetic sequence) are kept in the Purchasing Department. Again, with a computer system, only one copy (filed numerically) is needed, as the computer system can enable the user to go from numeric to alphabetic and back.

  d. The receiving department normally receives a copy of the purchase order as its authorization to receive the goods. However, it has no reason to have prices on its copy. Quantities usually are on the receiving copy, so that the receivers know

(Continued)

Exhibit 4.12   Analysis of Systems Flowcharts: Suggested Responses

what is authorized for receipt and proper control is maintained over partial receipts. Another method is not to provide quantities, thereby forcing receivers to count everything. However, this method does not provide an open item quantity with which to reconcile to the actual receipt. The operational reviewer should determine which method works best in a specific situation.

6. The secretary to the vice president of purchasing accounts for numerical sequence of the purchase orders and files both the numerical and alphabetical copies. The computer system should maintain strict numerical sequence and eliminate the sorting and filing of alphabetical copies. In addition, at the present time this does not appear to be a function that needs to be done by the secretary to the vice president of purchasing.

7.a. Damaged items procedure. This is an area for additional analysis to determine whether proper control and handling is exercised for damaged items upon receipt.

   b. Prepare a three-part receiving report. Good business practice is never to re-record information that already exists in the system. In this instance, receiving data are already shown on the purchase order copy. Therefore, this document should be used as the receiving report without any unnecessary re-recording. At all times, the open purchases awaiting receipt should equal the open purchases maintained in the Purchasing Department.

   For partial receipts (where the full quantity of an item or all the items on the PO are not received at the same time), a copy is made of the purchase order to be used as the receiving copy, the partial shipment data is noted on the original copy of the receiving PO, and the original PO is refiled as a purchase awaiting receipt for the remaining open items.

8. Review and compare the receiving report and the PO copy. With the use of the PO itself, there is of course no need to compare with receiving reports.

9. Check numerical sequence of receiving reports and prepare daily listing of receiving reports by the head of the Receiving Department. This step would also be eliminated by the use of PO receiving copies, greatly reducing the amount of paper within the system.

10. Route receiving documents to accounts payable. The accounts payable department winds up with a considerable amount of paperwork to wade through and match-up in order to process a purchase for payment. The reviewer should consider how many of these payments really need to be routed through the purchasing, receiving, and accounts payable systems—where a more efficient system would be much less costly and more effective. Can the not-for-profit greatly reduce or even eliminate these functions?

11. Match all related documents and hold them in a suspense file pending receipt of vendor invoice. This step is necessary; but notice the number of documents already accumulated in the process.

12. Vendor invoices are forwarded from the mail room. The reviewer may want to review mailroom procedures to determine whether this is the most efficient manner of receiving and processing vendor invoices. An effective alternative might be to receive vendor invoices directly by the Accounts Payable Department or via a lockbox system.

13. Review unmatched invoices and receiving reports. Analyze the current situation and determine whether unmatched items are proper. Note that unmatched invoices more than 10 days old may indicate the nonreceipt of receiving reports from the receiving department (inefficiency in the receiving department); and unmatched receiving reports may indicate the nonreceipt of vendor invoices from the mail room

Exhibit 4.12 *(Continued)*

(inefficiency in the mail room). In addition, this is not a function that the head of accounts payable, nor the vice president of purchasing, needs to be involved with.

14.a. Approve invoice for payment. This is a necessary step; however, note the number of documents which need to be reviewed and filed.

   b. Exceptions brought to the attention of the head of accounts payable for corrective action. Analyze what types of exceptions are being experienced and how they are being corrected.

   c. Upon resolution, the documents are returned to the head of the originating department for approval. This step is unnecessary, and the documents should not leave the accounts payable department.

15.a. Matching invoice and support documentation and verifying math, discount, account distribution, etc. This procedure should be tested on a sample basis to determine the accuracy of such operations.

   Consider reduction and elimination of these procedures by changes in receiving procedures and computerization.

   b. End of month accrual based on open items on daily receipts list. Computer system should provide this automatically.

16.a. Prepare prenumbered voucher (approximately 35,000 annually). As the purpose of the voucher is to provide the necessary data in an orderly manner for subsequent data entry, alternative procedures might be considered for this purpose, such as circling the original document, recording data onto a rubber stamp impression directly on the document, etc.

   b. Data entry control procedures should be reviewed to ensure that the present process of controlling by the total net amount of the vouchers is the most efficient and best.

   Reference to EDP (computer systems) documentation:

   This is the first indication in the system that data processing procedures are in existence. The operational reviewer should determine the extent of computer processing used, the overall capability of present computer resources, the effectiveness of use, and the efficient use for present systems concerns. In this situation, the operational reviewer might recommend the increased use of computer procedures for the present system under review to provide for the economies, efficiencies, and effectiveness previously discussed.

   In the development of his or her recommendations for the increased use of computer procedures, the operational reviewer should consider the providing of a computer systems design for the implementation of recommended computer procedures. The systems design document should include items such as input formats, offline and online controls, data record layouts, processing procedures, information and report layouts, and so on.

   In regard to the present procedures being reviewed on the systems flowchart, the operational reviewer should:

17. Review data terminal operations to determine that proper computer controls exist to ensure that only authorized transactions are processed and no others, that error identification and correction procedures are adequate, and that edit routines contain all necessary checks and validations.

18.a. Review edit routines embedded in the computer edit program to ensure that all edit checking is proper and that there are not other edits that should be included in the program.

   The edit program should also be tested (possibly "through the computer") to determine that it is working as documented.

(Continued)

Exhibit 4.12   *(Continued)*

    b. Review all internal processing controls, such as the use of record counts in the conversion process, to ensure that no data records are lost, added, or suppressed during processing.

    c. Review error detection and correction procedures to ensure that all error conditions are properly identified, controlled, and resubmitted back into computer processing correctly. This is an extremely critical area, as it is subject to abuse and laxity if not properly controlled.

19. The present systems flow within computer processing should be reviewed as to efficiency and the production of necessary operating and management information. The various data files used in computer processing and their physical and processing controls and purposes should also be reviewed.

      As part of this review, computer processing procedures relative to system run-to-run controls should be determined as to their operating properly. In addition, offline control total procedures should be reviewed to ensure that the computer system is being properly controlled by the users.

20. The end-of-month procedure consists of computer processing preparing a monthly check summary listing. This listing then serves as the source document for reinputting the same data for computer posting to the general ledger. This is an indication of the improper use of computers; as the principle to be applied is to use the same data sources for all integrated purposes. In this case, computer processing should automatically post to the general ledger without such re-inputting.

21. Off-line daily control procedures to reconcile the results of computer processing should be reviewed to determine that controls over the results of computer processing are adequate.

22. An end-of-month journal entry is prepared, based on the summary report prepared by computer processing. This processing should be done automatically by the computer system with integrated processing procedures.

23. Invoices and supporting documentation are collected with the voucher and checks. This is another point at which the reviewer should look at the accumulation of documents and determine what can be eliminated.

24.a. Sign checks, using a facsimile plate. The controls and safeguards for the use of this plate should be reviewed.

      In addition, review the check signing procedure and determine whether the secretary to vice president of finance needs to be involved.

    b. Checks for more than $10,000 require manual signatures of two executives. Determine whether this is a proper limit and whether procedure is working.

25. Review of checks and supporting documents by accounting supervisor. Determine whether this step is necessary and, if so, whether the accounting supervisor needs to be involved.

26. Checks and supporting documents filed. As can be seen, the present systems and procedures have created an enormous amount of paperwork necessary for the purchasing, receiving, payables, and vendor payment functions. Each document that can be eliminated results in the reduction of forms cost, preparation costs, handling time, filing time, and file costs. In looking at the documents to be disposed of, the following could be considered for elimination:

- Voucher
- Check copies
- Receiving report
- Department requisition

Exhibit 4.12 *(Continued)*

inated, it can greatly reduce the cost of operations without sacrificing results; in fact, results are often increased. What is really needed is to motivate each worker's self-disciplined work behavior—in effect, to make the worker responsible for results.

An example of a layout flow diagram is shown in Exhibit 4.13. Note that the solid lines between numbered blocks represent direct reporting relationships and

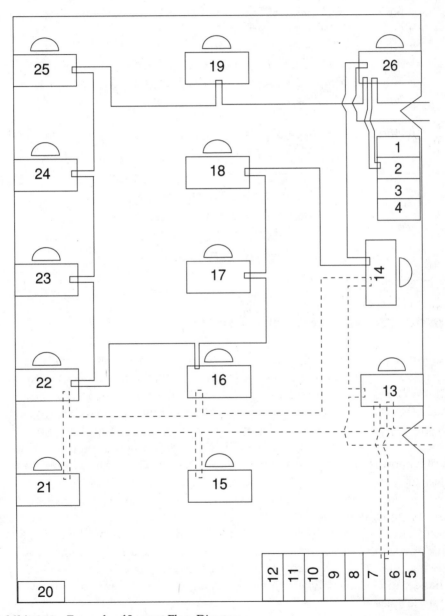

Exhibit 4.13 Example of Layout Flow Diagram

the dotted lines represent indirect relationships. The numbers on the layout flow diagram correspond to the following:

- Numbers 1 through 4: Client intake unit
- Numbers 5 through 12: Consulting counselors and therapists
- Number 13: Counseling coordinator
- Number 14: Counseling director
- Number 15: Case record reviewer
- Numbers 16 through18: Treatment plan and aftercare unit
- Number 19: Director of services
- Number 20: Consulting psychiatrist
- Number 21: Third-party reimbursement reviewer
- Numbers 22 through 25: Third-party billing unit
- Number 26: Admissions director

Inefficiencies or potential personnel roadblocks are shown in Exhibit 4.14.

**LAYOUT FLOW DIAGRAMS
ARE NOT AS MUCH CONCERNED
WITH THE LAYOUT
AS WITH INEFFICIENCIES**

RATIO, CHANGE, AND TREND ANALYSIS

Ratio, change, and trend analysis is another technique used in the field work phase to strengthen and supplement other operational review tools and procedures. Using this technique, the reviewer critically examines, interprets, and explains relationships between sets of operating and financial data at a given point in time by comparing them over a number of periods. Ratios have no intrinsic significance; they are primarily useful in highlighting significant changes and relationships. They do not, in and of themselves, form a basis for reaching informed decisions.

Ratio, change, and trend analysis may be used for a variety of purposes. For example, grantors and contributors may be interested in financial strength and the ability of the not-for-profit to stay in business, creditors in solvency, management in performance and deviation from what was planned or considered normal. Within the scope of the operational review, the reviewer uses ratio, change, and trend analysis to identify managerial and operational problems and trouble areas.

The identification and analysis of a problem situation is the initial step in

Note: The following responses correspond to the numbers shown on the layout flowchart for each person/job function.

1–4. These employees in the client intake unit are all performing the same function, with number 2 the titular "supervisor" or head worker. This function should be reviewed as to efficiency. In addition, reporting relationships should be analyzed, including their reporting to number 26 the admissions director, who acts as a controller.

5–12. These consulting counselors and therapists are performing an offline or staff function in an "isolate" capacity to the remainder of the work group. Their only reporting, which is indirect (as shown by the dotted lines), appears to be with number 13, the counseling coordinator, who appears to be performing the role of "dispatcher."

13. The counseling coordinator is performing the role of dispatcher on an indirect basis. He or she is interfacing in this capacity with number 5 through 12 (consulting counselors), number 14 (counseling director), and number 21 (third-party reimbursement reviewer). The detailed tasks of this function should be looked at as far as necessity.

14. The counseling director is performing the role of "controller." He or she is controlling materials from number 22 (third-party billing unit) and number 16 (treatment plan and aftercare unit) on an indirect basis, and from number 26 (admissions director) and number 18 (treatment plan and aftercare unit) on a direct basis, and is then routing to number 13 (counseling coordinator) on an indirect basis. The operational reviewer should determine whether there is any value-added effort being made or whether this is strictly controlling.

15. The case record reviewer appears to be an "isolate" with only an indirect interest in materials coming from the outside and from number 13 (counseling coordinator), and then routing them on to number 21 (third-party reimbursement reviewer).

16–18. The treatment plan and aftercare unit is in an inverse pyramid with materials coming from number 14 (counseling director) and then distributed downward from number 18 to number 16. The function being performed should be reviewed as to necessity of all three employees. Number 16 at the bottom of the pyramid relates to number 22 (third-party billing unit) on a direct basis, and to number 22 and number 14 on an indirect basis.

19. The director of services is performing the role of "controller" between number 26 (admissions director) and number 25 (third-party billing unit—supervisor?). This is a typical role for a manager over two supervisors. That is, there is a review of one area's output prior to routing it to another area. This is often an expensive and unnecessary function.

20. The consulting psychiatrist is an absolute "isolate," bearing no direct or indirect relation to anyone else in the work area. This could be a staff resource person who is sometimes necessary and sometimes just a nice luxury.

21. The third-party reimbursement reviewer is an "isolate" with only indirect relation to number 22 (third-party billing unit) and number 15 (case record rviewer). Ask, again, is this a necessary function?

(Continued)

Exhibit 4.14 Analysis of the Layout Flow Diagram: Suggested Responses

22–25.	The third-party billing unit is another inverse pyramid similar to number 16 through number 18. Work is routed by number 19 (director of services) to number 25 (third-party billing unit supervisor?), who then appears to distribute the work downward through number 24, number 23, and number 22. Number 22 relates directly to number 16 (treatment plan and aftercare unit)—the reviewer should find out what is happening here—and indirectly with number 21 (third-party reimbursement reviewer).
26.	The admissions director performs the role of "controller," receiving work from number 2 in the client intake unit and from the outside and routing it back to the group of employees number 1 through number 4 and, when satisfactory, routing the work to either number 14 (counseling director) or number 19 (director of services).

Exhibit 4.14   *(Continued)*

developing an effective solution. Ratio, change, and trend analysis helps the reviewer to detect problem areas for further analysis. The reviewer should consider for ratio, change, or trend analysis those areas in which most significant change has occurred and those of greatest vulnerability. In applying these techniques, the goal is to determine and measure changes and interrelationships in data, and then to examine critically and evaluate the changes revealed and their significance.

In using ratio, change, and trend analysis, the reviewer considers each situation individually and develops the ratios to use accordingly. There are two prime sources of reference to be used in applying this technique:

1. Comparison with historical internal data and budget data
2. Comparison with external data, such as industry statistics, functional standards, and work performance standards

In using internal data, it is important to make sure that such data are accurate and collected and reported properly. It must also be determined that such data are recorded on a consistent basis from period to period. When using budget data, the reviewer must determine that budgets are constructed in relationship to not-for-profit organizational and departmental plans and that actual data are not just compared with budgets, but that actual and budget numbers are what they should be from the standpoint of economy, efficiency, and effectiveness.

For external data to be used effectively, they should be objective and independent, derived from similar and comparable operations, and, if current, reflect experience during a comparable period with similar common economic factors and conditions. Note that in using such external data there are no two not-for-profits that are exactly the same, even within the same company structure. Accordingly, the reviewer uses external comparisons as a yardstick or indicator, not as a finite measure. These results can indicate possible trouble spots and further field work to be performed.

Incidentally, ratios are but one tool available to the reviewer to determine changes. Others that can be used are indexes, percentages, relationships, variable budgets, correlation analysis, and so on. These tools are often used in conjunction with one another.

The development of ratio, change, and trend analysis as related to a review finding is not an end in itself. Such analysis must be evaluated, integrated, and interpreted as one factor in the development of an operational review finding. Typically, more analysis and field work are required to develop the full dimensions of the finding. The results of ratio, change, and trend analysis provides a measure of significance.

Exhibit 4.15. shows a situation related to a small not-for-profit hospital where the use of ratio, change, and trend analysis was found to be helpful in the measurement of changes and their significance.

**RATIO, CHANGE, AND TREND ANALYSIS
CHANGES THE FUTURE, NOT THE PAST**

OTHER TECHNIQUES

There are many other tools and techniques that the operational reviewer can use in the field work phase, depending on the situation and the objective of the work step—too many to cover in this book. However, two significant techniques of which the reviewer should be aware are tests of transactions and reviewing performance versus plans.

Tests of Transactions

The operational reviewer, in testing transactions, examines the procedures actually applied to specific transactions or items, from beginning to end. The transactions selected for review should represent the operations involved. The character or type of transactions selected is more important than the number of transactions selected. Operational review tests of transactions should be limited in the number of transactions used, but must be representative of actual transactions processed.

In addition to the information provided in flowcharting, the test of transactions provides the reviewer with information relative to the results of transactions in terms of management's objectives, specific requirements, and

During the course of an operational review of a small not-for-profit hospital, the review team realized that the hospital would have to change numerous operating procedures to survive in a changing market for health care services.Part of the review is to identify critical areas in need of positive improvements. As part of the review of the hospital's operating statistics and budget figures, the following was developed:

	Year 1	Year 2	Year 3
Census (in beds)	1,350	1,210	1,060
Maintenance costs (in dollars)	185,000	203,000	285,000
Salaries (in dollars)	31,141,000	42,312,360	54,749,100
Number of positions	2,980	3,018	3,045

Questions for the review team:

1. How would you use these operating statistics to determine the trends at the hospital?
2. Based on these initial indicators, what areas would you suggest for hospital management to consider as critical areas in the operational review?

Suggested Responses:

1. **Use of statistics**
   A. Relationship of maintenance costs to beds:

   $$\frac{\$185,000}{1,350} = \$137/bed \qquad \frac{\$203,000}{1,210} = \$168/bed \qquad \frac{\$285,000}{1,060} = \$269/bed$$

   B. Relationship of salaries to number of positions:

   $$\frac{\$31,141,000}{2,980} = \$10,450 \qquad \frac{\$42,312,360}{3.018} = \$14,020 \qquad \frac{\$54,749,100}{3,045} = \$17,980$$

   C. Relationship of number of positions to number of beds:

   $$\frac{2,980}{1,350} = 2.2 \text{ positions/bed} \qquad \frac{3,018}{1,210} = 2.5 \text{ positions/bed} \qquad \frac{3,045}{1,060} = 2.9 \text{ positions/bed}$$

The analysis of these statistics indicates the following:

1. What is the cause for the rise in the cost per bed for maintenance?
2. Why are the number of beds decreasing and maintenance costs increasing over the three year period?
3. What is the cause in the rise of average salary per position?
4. Why are the number of positions increasing while the number of beds are decreasing?
5. What operational changes are happening in the hospital industry and in particular this hospital? Relate these changes to the statistics above.

Exhibit 4.15   Ratio, Change, and Trend Analysis: A Small Hospital Situation

2. **Suggested Critical Areas**
   a. **Types Of Services Analysis**
      - Inpatient
      - Outpatient
      - Laboratory
   b. **Admissions Analysis**
      - Treatment analysis
      - Demographics
      - Timing (e.g., holidays, weekends and so on)
   c. **Staff Analysis**
      - Types of personnel
      - Turnover statistics
      - Changes in positions
   d. **Usage Analysis**
      - Beds/treatment
      - Inpatient versus outpatient
      - Services used
   e. **Occupancy Analysis**
      - Trends: ups and downs
      - Departmental
      - Length of stays
   f. **Facility Analysis**
      - Use of services
      - Traffic patterns
      - Referrals out
   g. **Market Analysis**
      - Types of patients
      - Demographics
      - Physician statistics
   h. **Payment Analysis**
      - Third party insurer status
      - HMO payments
      - Self payment
      - Private insurers
      - Medical assistance

Exhibit 4.15   *(Continued)*

commonsense practices. The operational review work program given in Chapter 3, Exhibit 3.1, shows a selection of transactions and examination of transactions selected as sample work program steps.

Performance versus Plans

A review of performance versus plans allows the reviewer to examine existing plans that relate to the area being reviewed and the methods operations follows, to compare actual performance with the plans. This technique can provide direct insight into the ability of management to effective plan for the not-for-profit, as well as the relative strength and effectiveness of management control. This is a good technique to use in most operational reviews, to help analyze management controls over operations—primarily to help ascertain how management personnel themselves determine whether plans, policies, and procedures are being followed, and whether they are effective and efficient.

In many not-for-profits that come under operational review, there exist no effective planning procedures whatsoever. These organizations are typified by "seat of the pants" and crisis-type management, which attempts to operate without adequate short-term detail plans and, in many instances, without a budget. Those organizations that are found to have budgets often use the budget as a constraining and punitive tool, rather than as part of a helpful system. In these instances, this practice not only constitutes a review finding, but also makes it incumbent on the reviewer to help management develop an effective planning and budgeting system. This is often one of the first steps of the operational review, as the definition of planning goals and objectives is necessary to effectively evaluate the results of operations.

OPERATIONAL REVIEW SITUATION: CASE MANAGEMENT PROCEDURES

During the planning phase of the operational review, the reviewer observed that the case management area of The Counseling Agency appeared to be grossly overstaffed. Accordingly, the review team wanted to perform operational review procedures during the field work phase and included such techniques in their work program. Although the Case Management Manager agreed that there might be a little overstaffing, she pointed out that a recent agency report showed their case management expense per client case processed was no higher than that of other similar not-for-profits, including those operating in lower-cost areas.

Question and Solutions for Consideration

What work steps would you perform in the field work phase to substantiate your preliminary finding of overstaffing in the case management area?

Some of the work steps that could be performed include:

1. Expanded review of case management costs including payroll, materials and supplies, consultants, and so on, to verify total case management costs being reported, and to make sure all costs are being included (for example, the case management manager's being charged to the executive payroll)
2. Interviews with each of the case management employees to determine exactly what tasks they perform and to what extent

3. Layout flow diagram of the case management operations area and major operations to determine smoothness of operational flow
4. System flowcharts for each case management operating procedure to determine whether procedures could be simplified, steps eliminated, and duties realigned
5. System flowcharts and layout flow diagrams of proposed systems for increased efficiency with reduced staff

Note: As a result of these review work steps being performed, it was determined that case management costs were understated by $84,000 and that in actuality overall costs were more than similar not-for-profits. Be aware that such comparisons are to be used only as yardsticks and do not actually measure the economy, efficiency, and effectiveness of the entity.

The performance of these work steps provided the following results:

- Case management processing simplified
- Manual procedures eliminated that were the same as computerized
- Number of reports eliminated in which information was duplicated
- Personnel duties realigned, resulting in increased efficiency
- Overall staff to be reduced by six positions

Note: The reviewers do not identify specific personnel to be dismissed, but only document job positions or functions which can be eliminated. It is management's responsibility to decide what to do at that point (e.g., reassign personnel, change responsibilities, and dismiss employees). The dismissal of good employees is to be discouraged.

The total net annual savings resulting from these operational review findings and conclusions amounted to more than $250,000.

A Performing Arts Organization

Santa Fe Chamber Music Festival

BACKGROUND

The Santa Fe Chamber Music Festival (SFCMF) was founded in 1972. During its first performance season in 1973, 14 artists performed six Sunday concerts in Santa Fe and toured to several New Mexico and Arizona locations. Pablo Casals was SFCMF's honorary president that first season. In addition, SFCMF began a 20-year series of Georgia O'Keefe posters and program covers.

The inclusion of guest composers has been an integral part of SFCMF since 1976, and since 1980 SFCMF has commisioned 28 new works, contributing significantly to twentieth century chamber music repertoire. The *Music of the Americas* program was begun in 1988 to explore the musical diversity of the Western Hemisphere. After a five year survey of the music of Bolivia, Puerto Rico, Argentina, Brazil, Peru, and Mexico, the program evolved into an annual jazz and world music series.

SFCMF ensembles have toured regionally since 1973 and nationally since 1980. The 2000 national tour included performances in California, Oregon, and Texas. Regionally, SFCMF tours annually to various New Mexico communities, which as a rule, have little or no live music to offer their residents. Regional tours offer a concert and youth concert at each location. In May 2000, the SFCMF ensemble visited the New Mexico communities of Mountainair, Socorro, Las Cruces, Silver City, and Corrales.

SFCMF performances are regularly broadcast on national radio networks, with radio series ranging from 13-week hour-long broadcasts to segments on National Public Radio's (NPR's) *Performance Today.* SFCMF also has four recordings on compact disc of repertoire from the 1995, 1996, 1997, and 1998 summer seasons.

SFCMF maintains a strong tradition of community service, affirming the belief that music is an international language that can be understood by all people and a heritage that belongs to everyone. Education and outreach programs offered at no charge to the community include "Music in Our Schools," an education series for grades K–6 in the Santa Fe public schools; youth and family concerts; open rehearsals; concert previews; and artist/composer seminars. A typical season for SFCMF consists of one weekend in the spring, a one-week national tour, and a six-week season in Santa Fe (every night except Tuesday). SFCMF offers various subscription and ticket plans for the Santa Fe series with concerts held in the 450-seat St. Francis Auditorium. In addition, SFCMF provides year-around educational programming through its Institute and maintains a year-round gift shop.

MISSION AND PHILOSOPHY

SFCMF's mission statement is as follows:

> To promote the enjoyment and understanding of chamber music through live performances by artists of the highest quality for audiences of all ages in the unique cultural environment of Santa Fe.

In addition to presenting its series of public and touring concerts, SFCMF established the SFCMF Institute in 1998 to elevate its education and outreach activities and strengthen connections between SFCMF and its public and communities.

Specific goals of the Institute include expanding the accessibility of chamber music to the community at large, promoting access to specific, targeted, underserved segments of the community, encouraging long-term and frequent concert attendance by adults and young people, and creating new opportunities for emerging instrumental artists. The SFCMF Institute consists of five component programs: the distinguished young artists program, "Music In Our Schools", youth concerts, festival touring, and adult education.

ORGANIZATION

SFCMF is a not-for-profit incorporated in 1972 under Section 501(c)(3) of the Internal Revenue Code, organized and operating exclusively for charitable and educational purposes including the promotion of chamber music and related arts. During the last year(fiscal year ended 10-31-99), SFCMF produced 34 performances during its summer festival and three performances during its spring weekend mini-festival.

In 1991, the Santa Fe Chamber Music Festival Endowment Foundation was incorporated as a 501(c)(3) not-for-profit operating under the control or supervision of SFCMF for the purpose of securing funds and property by contribution or otherwise in order to establish an endowment fund, the principal and income of which shall be used solely and exclusively for the benefit and support of SFCMF.

SFCMF and the Foundation are codependent entities—that is SFCMF is dependent on income from the endowment of the Foundation and the Foundation exists to support SFCMF. The Foundation will annually distribute between 3 percent and 5 percent of the net assets of the Foundation—$100,000 in the previous year.

SFCMF ORGANIZATION STRUCTURE

SFCMF's organization chart is shown in Exhibit CS3.1. Note that this same chart was used for analysis purposes in Exhibit 2.9 in Chapter 2.

The organization chart shows a large board of directors of 38 members, with an additional advisory council of 22 members, an executive committee of 14

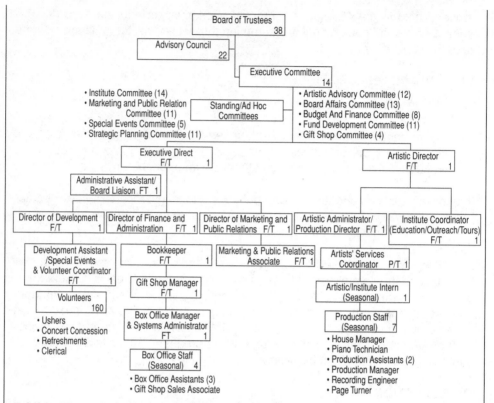

Exhibit CS3.1   Santa Fe Chamber Music Festival Organizational Chart

members and various ad hoc committees. This represents an enormous commitment by board members.

Reporting to the board are an executive director and an artistic director, who are jointly responsible for carrying out the directions of the board and ongoing operations. In addition, there are 26 employees reporting to these two directors as follows:

Reporting to the executive director are:

- Administrative Assistant /Board Liason
- Director of development
  - Development assistant/special events and volunteer coordinator
    - Volunteers (approximately 160 ushers, concert concession staff, refreshments personnel, and clerical)
- Director of Finance and Administration
  - Bookkeeper
    - Gift shop manager (with volunteer sales staff)
    - Box office manager and systems administrator
    - Box office staff (seasonal) (three box office assistants and gift shop sales associate).

- Director of marketing and public relations
  - Marketing and public relations associate

Reporting to the artistic director are:

- Institute coordinator (education/outreach/tours)
- Artistic administrator/production director
  - Artists' services coordinator
    - Artistic/institute intern (seasonal)
    - Production staff (seasonal) (house manager, piano technician, two production assistants, production manager, recording engineer, page turner)

During the performance season, SFCMF uses approximately 160 volunteers in the roles of ushers, concessionaires, refreshment sales personnel, and clerical functions. In addition, seasonal personnel are hired to perform the duties of box office staff, gift shop sales, and various production staff.

AREAS OF UNIQUENESS

SFCMF recognizes that there are many performing arts organizations in the Santa Fe area and nationally that compete for the attention and funding of the classical music public. In recognition of this, SFCMF management is continually searching for areas where they can be unique and achieve competitive advantage over these other arts organizations. Some of the areas that SFCMF management believes that they are unique include:

- Board of trustees—committed, supportive, and generous (each member commits to a $2,500 contribution—either pay it or bring in a like-amount donation)
- Endowment foundation—now at 2.7 million with a goal to reach 5 million with a present contribution of $100,000 annually to SFCMF.
- Cash reserve—a temporarily restricted net asset of $150,000 in the SFCMF cash reserve account.
- Balanced budget—SFCMF annually operates within its budget and typically provides an addition to net assets for the year.
- Volunteer base—SFCMF uses over 160 volunteers during its season and throughout the year with many of these volunteers returning from previous years.
- Gift shop—operating on a year-round basis at a small profit but providing positive marketing and public relations for SFCMF.
- Regional and national outreach—providing excellent publicity for SFCMF as well as bringing potential patrons and attendees to the SFCMF fold.
- Annual talent search—brings nationally known talent as well as emerging talent to the SFCMF summer festival and other programs.
- Ongoing fairly static revenue stream—made up of approximately 38 percent earned income (e.g., ticket sales from an average of 78 perent of available seats sold, gift shop and concessions, advertising, touring fees, interest income, and in-kind contributions) and 62 percent contributions (e.g., grants, contributions, special events, and endowment transfer).

SFCMF FINANCIAL CONDITIONS

SFCMF's financial statements for its last fiscal year ended October 31 are shown in Exhibits CS3.2 (combined statement of financial position—SFCMF and foundation) and CS3.3 (combined statement of activities—SFCMF and foundation). As can be seen from a quick review of these statements, SFCMF is in very sound financial position with an increase of over $500,000 in assets from the previous year (a total of $3,167,098), an increase of a like amount in net assets (a total of $2,973,142), and increases in net assets for the year in all of their funds.

The board of trustees in July, 1995 embarked on a financial and organizational stabilization plan to establish an equilibrium and integrity to the SFCMF's financial and administrative operations commensurate with its artistic quality and reputation. In the past, SFCMF resorted to emergency measures to meet its operational expenses (and losses) and annual budgeting failed to appropriately confront the realities facing not-for-profits in times of dwindling resources but ever increasing expenses. SFCMF desired to stop the invasion of endowment funds as a viable solution to a budget process that is rooted in unrealistic expectations. The plan was conceived in the following three parts:

1. The elimination of old debt and guarantee of necessary financial resources to complete each festival and fiscal year
2. An in-depth programmatic, administrative, and operational analysis of the Festival, with the intent to "right size" the organization and present an overall program that is budgeted on achievable, realistic sources of income—both earned and contributed—and appropriately sized administrative and operational base.
3. Significant progress over a five-year period (through 2001) toward long-term stability through the establishment of a $250,000 cash reserve and an increase in the endowment fund to a minimum of $5,000,000.

SFCMF SELF-ANALYSIS

In 1999, the members of each standing committee were asked to respond to the following questions relative to the nature of SFCMF's business and various internal and external processes and functions. The questions and consensus responses are summarized below:

1. What business(es) are we in?
   Entertainment, education, audience and donor development, special events, retail and wholesale merchandise sales
2. What are our products?
   Concerts, educational materials/services, music-related merchandise
3. Who are the customers for each of our products (current and potential)?
   Concert-goers, Santa Fe residents, tourists, schools/children, funders, advertisers, shoppers.
4. What are the major activities that make up our operating costs?
   Concerts, recordings, educational programs and community outreach, merchandising
5. What are the major components of our cost structure?

Combined Statement of Financial Position
October 31, 1999 and 1998

Assets	Festival	Foundation	Elimina-tions	1999 Total	1998 Total
Cash and cash equivalents	$ 79,079	$ 4,154	$ —	$ 83,233	$ 203,775
Investments	—	2,549,809	—	2,549,809	2,006,364
Interest receivable				—	9,402
Accounts receivable	21,900			21,900	7,448
Grants receivable	111,500			111,500	16,250
Contributions receivable	85,114	134,165		219,279	230,997
Due from the Festival		20,065	(20,065)	—	—
Inventory	106,814			106,814	92,540
Prepaid expenses and deposits	15,398			15,398	4,768
Equipment, net of accumulated depreciation for 1999 of $182,275 and for 1998 $174,789	59,165			59,165	34,548
Total assets	$478,970	$2,708,193	$(20,065)	$3,167,098	$2,606,092

Liabilities and Net Assets					
Liabilities					
Accrued expenses	$ 47,861	$	$	$ 47,861	$ 47,628
Accounts payable	126,773			126,773	29,388
Due to the endowment	20,065		(20,065)	—	—
Deferred revenue	19,322	—		19,322	42,059
Total liabilities	214,021	—	(20,065)	193,956	119,075
Net assets:					
Unrestricted	114,949			114,949	103,188
Temporarily restricted	150,000	1,905,663		2,055,663	1,581,299
Permanently restricted	—	802,530		802,530	802,530
Total net assets	264,949	2,708,193		2,973,142	2,487,017
Total liabilities and net assets	$478,970	$2,708,193	$(20,065)	$3,167,098	$2,606,092

Exhibit CS3.2   Santa Fe Chamber Music Festival, Ltd. and Santa Fe Chamber Music Festival Endowment Foundation

Combined Statement of Activities
Year Ended October 31, 1999 and 1998

	Festival			Foundation				Combined Tools	
	Un-restricted	Temporarily Restricted	Total	Un-restricted	Temporarily Restricted	Perma-nently Restricted	Total	1999	1998
REVENUES									
Ticket sales	$ 416,517	$	$416,517	$	$	$	—	$ 416,517	$ 390,203
Gift shop, concessions, and poster sales	69,110		69,110					48,989	48,989
Advertising	42,732		42,732					42,732	33,060
Contributions, grants, and special events	902,643	74,500	977,143		212,392		212,392	1,189,535	1,160,373
Contributions from the endowment	100,000		100,000					100,000	65,000
Touring fees	25,500		25,500					25,500	31,090
Dividend income		—			119,748		119,748	119,748	26,210
Interest income	4,656		4,656		3,935		3,935	8,591	50,776
Gain (Loss) on sales of asssets	—		—		(469)		(469)	(469)	1,508
Miscellaneous	356		356					356	534
Unrealized gain on investments					170,846		170,846	170,846	36,975
In-kind contributions	78,752		78,752					78,752	68,516
Total revenues	1,640,266	74,500	1,714,766		506,452		506,452	2,221,218	1,913,234
Release of temporarily restricted net assets				106,588	(106,588)				
Total support and revenues	1,640,266	74,500	1,714,766	106,588	399,864	$	506,452	2,221,218	1,913,234

EXPENSES

Administrative	383,507	6,588	390,095					344,208
Artistic and production	568,191	—	568,191					528,502
Box office	45,617	—	45,617					
Development	198,124	—	198,124					164,124
Institute (education and outreach)	164,603	—	164,603					80,872
Marketing, public relations, publications	190,575	—	190,575					244,267
Gift shop, concessions, and posters	67,903	—	67,903					27,391
Interest	—	—	—					281
Bad debt expense	2,500	—	2,500					51,631
Contributions to the festival		100,000	100,000					65,000
Depreciation	7,485	—	7,485					11,949
Total Expenses	1,628,505	106,588	1,735,093					1,518,225
Change in net assets	11,761	74,500	86,261	399,864		399,864	486,125	395,009
Net assets at beginning of year	103,188	75,500	178,688	1,505,799	802,530	2,308,329	2,487,017	2,092,008
Net assets at end of year	$ 114,949	$150,000	$ 264,949	$1,905,663	$802,530	$2,708,193	$2,973,142	$2,487,017

Exhibit CS3.2 (*Continued*)

Artistic, the Institute, marketing/public relations, box office, gift shop, concessions, fund development, special events, general administration (e.g., salaries and benefits, office rental, postage, telephone, etc.).

6. What are the principal sources of our revenue?

   Ticket sales, contributions/grants, touring fees, special events, advertising sales, in-kind contributions, merchandise sales, endowment, planned giving.

7. Who are the major competitors for each of our sources of revenue?

   Other Santa Fe performing arts organizations, all other Santa Fe not-for-profits, other not-for-profit gift shops, retail stores, other popular tourist destinations, other music festivals, other programs and magazines (e.g., advertising), organizations in cities where Santa Fe second homers have principal residences

8. Who are our peers (i.e., other summer festivals that present chamber music)?

   Taos School of Music and Chamber Music Festival, Chamber Music Albuquerque/June Music Festival, Music from Angel Fire, La Jolla Summerfest, Aspen Music Festival, Bravo! Colorado (Vail) Music Festival, Tanglewood (Massachusetts), Chamber Music Northwest (Portland, Oregon), Spoleto Festival USA (South Carolina), Round Top Music Festival (Texas), Seattle Chamber Music Festival, Grand Teton Music Festival (Wyoming).

9. What are our competencies?

   Artistic and administrative quality, strong education and community outreach programs, active board participation, strong committee structure, competent proactive financial management, ability to attract financial support, contributions to chamber music repertoire through commissioning program

10. What are the six factors that are most important to our success?

    Maintain (and improve) artistic quality and attract top artists, performance values, committed trustees and volunteers, competent administration and financial stability, stable economy and tourism, a growing audience.

11. How do we measure success?

    Critical reviews/positive audience reaction, participation of top talent, ticket sales/expanding audience, quality of board, fund-raising success, end each fiscal year with operating budget surplus

12. What are major opportunities for improvement?

    Enhanced national presence, expand audience, enhanced local presence and increased integration into the community, more collaboration with other Santa Fe organizations, more education/community outreach activities, more touring/residences, increased endowment, more business and foundation support, attract youth and diversity to board of trustees, cyber innovations, more support staff

13. What will be the status of the Santa Fe Chamber Music Festival in three years if we are successful during this time period?

    Heightened local and national reputation, diversity in all areas, solid organizational and financial base, endowment of $5 million, cash reserve of $250,000, Festival is core element in cultural awareness of (young) people, concerts/events that are more consistently sold out.

SFCMF STRETEGIC PLAN

SFCMF, in August 1999, issued its Strategic Plan 2002, which was the culmination of many hours and efforts by the board and staff in developing a strategic plan for the next three years. The plan encompassed all major operational areas of SFCMF showing objectives and action items (ongoing and by annual period). These objectives by operational area are summarized below:

1. *Administration*
   - To promote accountability and fiscal responsibility in a supportive operating environment, in which issues are openly communicated and effectively addressed.
   - To establish more accurate information systems for SFCMF operations
2. *Artistic*
   - To present programs of intrinsic value by talented musicians who enthusiastically perform the core chamber music classical repertoire, neglected works of quality and new music, together with other musical genres—such as world music, popular songs, and jazz—that have interested and influenced classical composers and musicians.
3. *Board affairs*
   - To continue to develop SFCMF's board of trustees.
   - To provide the support and information needed to carry out the board's responsibilities and activities knowledgeably and professionally.
   - To develop and refine policies of the board and the executive committee to facilitate SFCMF's operational effectiveness.
4. *Box office*
   - To establish policies and procedures for ticket sales that promote and maximize staff facility and customer satisfaction
5. *Endowment foundation*
   - To adhere to the purposes for which the foundation was established
6. *Endowment fund campaign*
   - To establish SFCMF's endowment at $5 million by October 31, 2002
7. *Fund development*
   - To maintain and develop a strong and diverse mix of sources of income from individual contributions, corporate contributions, foundation grants, government grants, special events, and planned giving
8. *The Institute*. The Institute will encompass all SFCMF educational and outreach activities, and will be integrated fully with all artistic programming. Through the Institute, SFCMF is:
   - To develop and provide quality music education and outreach programs that communicate the intrinsic value of music and create new concert audiences
   - To provide educators with workshops on integrating music education into their overall program
   - To provide children of every age with ongoing live musical experiences that will instill in them a genuine appreciation and understanding of music
   - To foster national and international young musicians beginning their professional careers, as well as talented, young musicians from New Mexico

- To offer high-quality chamber music performances and education programs to New Mexico communities
9. *The Internet*
   - To utilize latest internet technology to maximize opportunities in areas of ticket sales, fund raising, public relations, and mailing list maintenance
10. *Marketing and public relations*
    - To increase earned income and heighten SFCMF's public visibility and stature
11. *Merchandising*
    - To increase earned income and heighten visibility of SFCMF through sale of SFCMF logo merchandise and other music related items
12. *Special Events*
    - To consider all special events as integral to broadening of constituencies and heightening of local and national image of SFCMF
13. *Volunteers*
    - To make maximum utilization of volunteers for artistic, gift shop, concert concessions, and administrative assistance.
    - To regularly recognize and demonstrate value of and appreciation for volunteers.

SUMMARY OF REVIEW

SFCMF, for a performing arts organization in today's climate of eroding support, is in an enviable position. Revenues from all sources continually exceed expenditures on a fiscal year basis providing for a positive contribution to net assets each year. In addition, SFCMF is well on its way to achieve its two major financial goals directed toward being operationally independent—that is, an endowment fund of $5 million dollars and cash reserves of $250,000. Operationally, SFCMF appears to have a committed board of trustees as well as management competency in both administrative as well as artistic areas. SFCMF has developed well-thought-out strategic plans for the next three years in all areas of operations. They have defined the direction they would like to go toward, now they need to define the manner in which they will move toward that direction. In other words, they are in the right vehicle pointed in the right direction, but will they be able to drive the vehicle correctly to arrive at the right destination. This is where the economy, efficiency, and effectiveness of internal operations comes in. That is what an operational review is all about.

OPERATIONAL REVIEW—AREAS TO CONSIDER

Based on the case materials presented, the review team might want to consider the following areas for inclusion in their operational review of SFCMF. Keep in mind that although SFCMF appears to be a successful performing arts organization, they can be even more successful, do better by doing the right thing at the right time, and maximize results at less cost, with greater efficiencies.

1. What business is SFCMF in?
   While functionally SFCMF is primarily a performance arts organization, it is also in the following businesses:
   - Education
   - Outreach
   - Fund raising
   - Endowment fund management and investment
   - Merchandising
   - Volunteer training and use
   - Board of trustee management
   - Retailing—gift shop operations
   - Special event planning and implementation

   The review team needs to look at each of these businesses (and others) as to the best practice approach for each. At present, each of these businesses are directed within the same SFCMF management and operations model.

2. Organization concerns
   Although the present organization structure appears to be effective in moving SFCMF in the right direction, the review team should analyze the present organization as to how it could become more effective and efficient—and as a result more economical. It is possible that in certain areas it is overstaffed, in other areas understaffed, in other areas overly dependent on volunteers, in other areas improperly organized, and so on. Some specific areas of organization that the review should consider include:
   - Board of trustees—while they appear to be helpful in guiding SFCMF, the review team should look at the following areas for review:
     - Size of the board, both in number of board members and committees—is this setup effective or merely getting in the way of operations?
     - Roles and functions—helpful in providing overall direction and setting policies or too involved in overseeing and managing operations.
     - Purpose of the board and how it can be used effectively—that is, is it mainly a fund-raising board and an adjunct to operational activities or other things?
   - Executive and artistic directors—top management considerations such as:
     - How effectively these two individuals work together
     - Roles and expectations of each position
     - Authority and responsibilities—autonomous to achieve desired results
   - Director's level positions—development, finance and administration, marketing and public relations, artistic administrator/production director, institute director—to be questioned as to:
     - Functions, purpose, and expected results of each one
     - Is each position necessary?
     - Are other positions at this level more necessary?
     - Can these functions be performed with increased results in some other manner?
   - Other full-time positions to be analyzed as to:
     - Are these the right ones as to full time?
     - Does each function need to be performed by a full-time employee?

- Can these functions be accomplished more effectively in some other manner?
- Is each of these positions necessary?
  - Seasonal staff and volunteers:
    - Efficiency of present procedures
    - Too little or too many
    - Orientation, training, and supervision concerns

3. Uniqueness of SFCMF

    Building on SFCMF's stated areas of uniqueness, how else can SFCMF exploit its uniqueness to maintain and increase their competitive advantage? How can SFCMF use its present areas of uniqueness more effectively and what other areas can be developed?

4. Planning and budget systems

    SFCMF's strategic plan was reviewed in these materials. Although it appears to be well thought out and inclusive, it may be only a starting point. While some semblance of action items are documented as part of the plan, the review needs to cover the entire planning and budget system to determine if other desired aspects of such systems are present, such as:

    - Overall statements of organizational direction, coordinated with SFCMF's mission statement and philosophy, by the board and the executive and artistic directors together with statements of basic business principles and philosophies that can be agreed upon by all organizational levels. It is important that such overall organizational agreement be achieved before moving any further—that is, that everyone in the organization is singing from the same song book.
    - Organizational goals and objectives as stated by top management. While some of these can be extrapolated from the strategic plan, it is not always clear what is a goal, an objective, or an action item, and what is organizational, departmental, or program.
    - Departmental and program goals and objectives—that is, what direction each department or program is moving relative to organizational goals and objectives and what are their short-term specific results.
    - Detail plans—that is, how is each objective planned to be achieved as to resources needed, activities to be done and when, and results expected.
    - Budgets constructed related to agreed upon objectives and detail plans. The budget should really be an allocation of scarce resources to such detail plans on some form of prioritization basis.

5. Budget procedures

    The budget process at SFCMF appears to be a typical not-for-profit line item budget process. The budget process should be reviewed to determine if other budgeting concepts could increase its effectiveness, such as:

    - Program budgeting that coordinates program activities and costs to desired plans and results forcing program management to continually replan and rebudget.
    - Flexible budgeting concepts, whereby the original budget is automatically adjusted based on changes in activity levels—upward or downward.

- Profit center concepts in which specific operational areas (e.g., gift shop, concessions) are established both from a revenue as well as an expenditure standpoint. The entity is then held accountable for making its profit plan work.
- Cost center concepts for so-called overhead or non–value-added functions such as accounting and finance, computer processing, box office operations, and so on. The expectation for these areas is to eliminate all unnecessary activities, produce desired operational results at the least cost, and perform their activities most efficiently.

6. Management control and reporting

SFCMF top management needs to review and analyze operations as to the effective achievement of desired results. The review team needs to review present management control and reporting procedures to ensure that top management is receiving sufficient information to make effective evaluations and appraisals. As SFCMF encompasses many different types of operations and activities within its overall structure, such a management and control system should encompass the following features:

- Identification and reporting of key operating indicators—that is, repeat and nonrepeat contributors and subscribers, attendance comparisons, merchandise sale comparisons, achievement of specific results, and so on
- Simplification of reporting in all areas, so that results reported are easily understood
- Exception reporting that highlights over and under conditions for management's attention so that effective corrective action can be taken. Remember the goal is not to fix the blame, but to fix the cause
- Program reporting showing performance data relative to both financial and operational considerations
- Integration of financial and operational information—how well the area did with its allocation of resources (that is its flexible budget) in relationship to producing desired results

7. SFCMF financial condition

SFCMF is in sound financial condition and moving effectively toward its goal of a $5 million endowment fund and a $250,000 cash reserve. However, there are some specific areas that should be reviewed and analyzed as part of the operational review.

- Revenues—made up of 38 percent earned income and 62 percent contributions. Is that a proper mix or can it be improved in both areas? Are there other effective sources of revenues that can be considered?
- Expenditures—although overall within budget limitations, can they be eliminated or reduced? Areas to look at include:
  - Salary and related expenses—by far the largest area of expenditures. Are these expenses being spent most effectively and is SFCMF achieving maximum expected results out of each paid position?
  - Program expenses which should have some correlation to program revenues and results. Such programs should be considered for flexible program budgeting and evaluated for financial as well as operational results.

- Education and outreach expenses—are they being used effectively, particularly where there is no direct relationship to an outside funding source?
- Overhead, support, and non–value-added–type expenditures under a cost center type concept. Are the functions and activities necessary, can they be reduced or eliminated, and are there more effective and less costly ways to provide such services?

CHAPTER 5

Development of Review Findings

INTRODUCTION

The operational review team, considering the critical areas identified in the field work phase for further analysis, begins to develop its significant findings. During the course of the operational review, the review team may have identified certain findings that required no additional analysis. In those instances, the review team would have prepared their findings and presented them directly to management. It is not good practice to hold such findings for the final report. As findings are identified and/or developed, they should be reported to management, so that if management agrees, remedial action can be taken as soon as possible.

Every operational review finding, whether requiring additional analysis or not, has certain common structural characteristics—just as every building, no matter how different from other buildings, has a roof, walls, floor, and so on—which can be regarded as building blocks. The operational reviewer must use these basic building blocks to construct a complete finding, one that gives the reader all the information needed to understand the finding and the reason for the recommendations.

This chapter discusses the development of effective and convincing operational review findings. Using the work steps performed in the field work phase, the operational review team identifies those findings it believes to be most significant. For these findings, the operational review team develops the necessary elements to convince management that a deficiency exists and that there is need to take corrective action. These findings are not intended to be critical, but to help management improve its operations. Establishing a constructive atmosphere helps to ally management with the review team and to ensure greater receptiveness of such findings. Moreover, if operations people are part of the review team, the findings will be more binding.

The most important single element of the operational review is the development of specific findings—this is the heart of the operational review. Furthermore, the acceptance and implementation of these findings by management is the

 placed.

229

yardstick for operational review success. A good rule of thumb is that if the review team can persuade management to accept at least 50 percent of its findings
and recommendations, then the team has been successful. Developing review
findings involves (1) data collection, to get as much pertinent, significant information about each finding as is realistic; and (2) evaluation of the finding; in
terms of cause, effect, and possible courses of corrective action.

In developing such specific review findings and conclusions, the reviewer
must do the necessary amount of analytical work, along with accumulating all
appropriate evidential supporting data.

THE OPERATIONAL REVIEW FINDING
IS THE HEART OF THE OPERATIONAL REVIEW

ATTRIBUTES OF A REVIEW FINDING

To develop a specific operational review finding, the reviewer should be aware
of, and use effectively, the following attributes or building blocks:

- Statement of condition
- Criteria
- Cause
- Effect
- Recommendations

These attributes are summarized in Exhibit 5.1.

Statement of Condition

All operational reviews involve initial fact finding in the field work phase. When
fact finding is used to determine the statement of condition, the reviewer examines and verifies as much of the operations and related data as necessary to establish clearly all pertinent facts. The work steps performed are those that best fit the
situation. In an operational review, this fact-finding process is really the
"what–when–where–how" step. The statement of condition provides a reference
point to the finding as it relates to established criteria.

One difficulty in performing operational reviews is that the condition disclosed by the detailed work in the field work phase often does not turn out to be
quite the same as initially indicated in the planning phase. Thus, developing the
finding sometimes turns out to be an evolutionary process in actual practice,

1. *Statement of Condition*
   What was found?
   What was observed?
   What is defective, deficient, or in error?
   Is the condition isolated or widespread?
   This is the what–when–where–how step.
2. *Criteria*
   What should it be?
   What is it measured against?
   What is the standard procedure or practice?
   Is it a formal procedure or an informal practice?
   This is the comparing what is with what should be step.
3. *Cause*
   Why did it happen?
   What is the underlying cause of the deficiency?
   Why have operations become inefficient or uneconomical?
   This is the identification of the cause and not the symptom step.
4. *Effect*
   So what?
   What is the effect of the finding?
   What is the end result of the condition?
   This is the present or potential impact on the operations step.
5 *Recommendations*
   What could be recommended to correct the condition?
   What recommendations are practical and reasonable for acceptance?
   Who should implement the recommendation?
   Is the recommendation based on a logical connection to the present condition, crite-
     ria, and causes?
   This is the what needs to be done to correct the situation step.

Exhibit 5.1   Operational Review Finding Attributes

which requires the work program to be evolutionary as well. It is in the field work phase that these changes take place, causing the work program to be revised as facts are discovered.

The reviewer should be able to reach agreement with appropriate not-for-profit management on the correctness of the facts; even though there may be disagreement on the reasons, significance, and need for corrective action. The reviewer's failure or inability to agree on the facts with not-for-profit management does not, however, stop the review team from reporting a finding if team members are reasonably certain that the information developed is correct. Bear in mind that although it may be reported to top management, the operational review finding is really intended for operations management.

Note, too, that the condition (or the problem or the finding itself) is always in the singular. However, the related criteria, causes, effects, and recommendations may be multiple in nature. Although there is no absolute order, the attributes of an operational review finding are normally presented in this order: condition, criteria, cause, effect, and recommendation. The reviewer may decide to present review findings in a different order, but always starting with condition and ending with recommendation.

Criteria

In analyzing present conditions, the reviewer must be aware of what conditions are expected to meet organizational goals and objectives. In determining the proper criteria for a specific condition, the reviewer looks at such areas as relevant legislation and laws, existing grants and contracts, policy statements, systems and procedures, internal and external regulations, responsibility and authority relationships, standards, schedules, plans and budgets, principles of good management and administration, and so on. In evaluating procedures and practices, the reviewer should be aware that procedures are formal methods of doing things. Such procedures are documented, usually in writing, and prescribed by management. Practices are the actual ways in which work activities are performed and are rarely documented in written form.

Essentially, in developing the finding criteria, the reviewer compares what is with what should be. The review team has taken the first step toward developing a review finding when it has identified a difference between what actually exists and what should be or what the reviewers think is correct or proper.

Examples of criteria that can be used for such comparison purposes include:

- Written requirements, such as laws, regulations, grants, contracts, instructions, policies and procedures manuals, directives, and so forth
- Stated goals and objectives of the organization and/or department or work unit
- Verbal instructions
- Independent opinion of experts

Some other measures or standards that are used to compare an operational condition with what it should be are shown in Exhibit 5.2.

Alternative Criteria

In many cases, criteria may not be available and must be developed. This is one of the operational reviewer's challenges. In the absence of standards or other effective criteria with which to evaluate performance, three alternative approaches are available to the operational reviewer.

INTERNAL TO THE ORGANIZATION

- Organizational policy statements
- Legislation, laws, and regulations
- Contractual arrangements
- Grant conditions
- Funding arrangements
- Organizational and departmental plans: goals and objectives
- Budgets, schedules, and detail plans

DEVELOPED BY THE OPERATIONAL REVIEWER

- Performance of similar individuals or functions (internal benchmarking)
- Performance of similar organizations (competitive benchmarking)
- Industry or functionally related statistics (industry benchmarking)
- Performance of functions outside the company (best-in-class benchmarking)
- Past and present performance of the organization
- Engineered standards
- Special analysis or studies
- Reviewer's judgment
- Sound business practices
- Good common business sense

EXAMPLE

Objective: To provide meaningful, accurate, and timely operating information

Criteria:

1. Information provided is relevant to not-for-profit management's needs—top management, operations management, and staff.
2. Information supplied is accurate and reflects the period and activities being reported.
3. Information is received in sufficient time after the reporting period to be useful for its intended purpose. Can the information be supplied on a real-time basis?
4. Information is easily understood—not too much detail, not insufficient detail, but just right for decision making and action.

Exhibit 5.2   Operational Review Criteria Standards

1. Comparative analysis
2. The use of borrowed standards
3. The test of reasonableness

Comparative Analysis

Comparative analysis is the technique that can be used, where there are no specific standards for comparison, to compare the reviewed circumstances to similar situations. This analysis can be accomplished in three ways:

1. Current performance can be compared between individuals within the same function or similar functions within the not-for-profit (internal benchmarking).
2. Current performance can be compared with past performance (historical comparison).
3. Performance can be compared with that of a similar not-for-profit (competitive benchmarking).

Comparing current performance between individuals within the same function can provide a yardstick as to what the performance standard can be. However, the reviewer must be careful that he or she does not adapt an unrealistic standard for the others working within the same function. In addition, for others to come up to this standard, they may be inadequately trained, inappropriate for the job, need coaching assistance, and so forth. It may be equally important to determine the cause for the disparity in individual performance and what corrective action may be necessary.

Comparing similar functions (e.g., various service delivery units within the not-for-profit at different locations) within the not-for-profit, using internal benchmarking techniques, again may provide an internal criteria to use. The reviewer must be careful, however, not to use a standard that is merely the best of inefficient practices. In the development of a program for continuous improvement directed toward implementing best-in-class practices, the reviewer should also look at the comparison of these functions with other not-for-profits (competitive and best-in-class benchmarking).

The comparison of two or more different but similar organizations normally provides the opportunity for the reviewer to evaluate different approaches to operations management. By determining the results of different operational approaches, the reviewer can make some helpful recommendations for improving efficiency and effectiveness. Such comparison can be made separately as part of the operational review or as part of a formal external benchmarking study (competitive or best-in-class) connected to the operational review.

There are, however, some disadvantages in comparing two separate but similar organizations. The major disadvantage is the reviewer's possible failure to recognize factors that justify differences between the two organizations. For example, it is difficult to compare two not-for-profit health care providers, because no two not-for-profit health care providers have exactly the same type of service delivery systems, hire the same type of employees, use the same type of equipment, or have the same proximity to support services and other essentials. Most not-for-profit health care providers would, however, have many of the same types of problems, regardless of their differences. The similarity of problems can enable the operational reviewer to analyze how each management group handles them. The reviewer can then analyze alternatives for improving the efficiency and effectiveness of operations, and the resultant recommendations can reflect his or her judgment, based on the results produced by each alternative.

The Borrowed Standard

Many not-for-profit groups and associations throughout the country, such as hospitals, colleges and universities, museums, libraries, and so on, provide uniform and comparable standards for evaluating performance. These borrowed standards can then be used to compare performance of not-for-profits in similar endeavors. Although such comparisons may make performance evaluation quicker and easier for the operational reviewer, there are some disadvantages to this procedure as well.

One disadvantage is that national averages and broad-based statistics hardly ever relate to specific situations. Thus, while such standards and statistics provide some indications of the not-for-profit's performance, they cannot be used for precise measurement or evaluation. Another disadvantage is that very few national averages or uniform statistics actually exist. In those cases in which such standards and statistics do exist, such as by standard industry code, for hospitals, colleges, specific services, schools, libraries, and so forth, they either relate to only a small portion of the areas subject to operational review, or are limited to very restricted areas and are of minimal use to the reviewer.

The Test of Reasonableness

When there are no internal standards, and comparisons with other not-for-profits are not practical or borrowed statistics are unavailable, the reviewer can still test organizational performance on the basis of reasonableness. Through experience, reviewers have become familiar with how things are done economically, efficiently, and effectively in other organizations (and other locations within their own not-for-profit, e.g., the counseling function at various locations). The reviewers should be able to relate these experiences to the current operations under review.

Accordingly, the reviewer can often spot operational irregularities and weaknesses that might escape the notice of others without such a background. In operational reviews, perceptions of a situation are in the eyes of the beholder—in this case, the cumulative experience of the individual operational reviewer. In addition, there exist what may be termed *general standards of society* that apply to good management in any field, public or private. For example, the reviewer can often spot work being done in a loose, unsatisfactory, and inefficient manner, even in the absence of specific standards. Often, this work has been considered acceptable—"That's the way we've always done it."

Unacceptable service delivery with poor client acceptance, excessive materials and supplies, personnel who are continually absent from work, abuse of resources such as automobiles and expense accounts, and negligence in processing documents or handling cash funds—all are examples of items that can be evaluated through the test of reasonableness.

The reviewer can also use the test of reasonableness as an appropriate tool to quickly review operating areas not subjected to detailed analysis. Even where the review team has analyzed in detail, the reviewers should still examine their conclusions for reasonableness. This ensures that the reviewers have not become so engrossed in statistics that they have overlooked important items or put too much weight on minor ones. The test of reasonableness can also be viewed as the operational reviewer's application of good common sense or prudent business practice to the situation.

Cause

The operational review finding is not complete until the reviewer has fully identified the reason or cause for the deviation from the criteria. To analyze the cause, the operational reviewer must answer the following questions:

- Why did it happen?
- What are the reasons for the operational deficiency?

The most important factor of an operational review finding is the underlying cause of the deficiency. This cause is the reason that operations have become inefficient or uneconomical. The reviewer's responsibility is to report what must be done to correct the situation and prevent recurrence of the adverse effect.

Developing the underlying cause of a review finding requires a good amount of judgment on the reviewer's part. If the reviewer analyzes the cause of a problem too deeply, the conclusion may be impractical. Moreover, the reviewer must make sure to identify the cause, not the symptom.

Review tests and procedures should normally be sufficient to show whether the condition is isolated or widespread. This determination is necessary to reach a proper conclusion about the significance of the deficiency and propose adequate recommendations for corrective action if the condition is widespread and/or likely to recur.

The reviewer must be careful in identifying a specific cause, as it often appears to be specific individuals who are the cause. Normally, the reviewer's responsibility is to identify the underlying reasons for resultant deviations from expected criteria, not specific individuals. The review team is wise to avoid identifying specific individuals as the cause of a problem. The real cause could be such things as improper orientation or training, unclear instructions and expectations, poor hiring practices, ineffective supervision and management, or inappropriate systems and procedures. Remember, the operational reviewer is to help achieve positive improvements in the operation, and finger pointing at employees may jeopardize the review team's ongoing credibility.

Some possible types of causes are shown in Exhibit 5.3.

- Ineffective or lack of adequate planning systems and procedures
- Confusing, ineffective, or faulty organizational structure
- Superfluous or unwieldy organizational hierarchy
- Lack of effective delegation of authority, commensurate with related responsibilities
- Inability or unwillingness to change, as exemplified by resistant attitudes: "We've always done it that way"; "It's standard practice."
- Lack of effective or sufficient management or supervision
- Inadequate, misleading, or obsolete policies, procedures, standards, and so on
- Lack of effective personnel procedures relative to hiring, orientation, training, evaluation, promotion, and firing
- Ineffective use of computer processing
- Inadequate management and/or operational reporting systems
- Lack of effective communication
- Personal inadequacies such as negligence, carelessness, unfamiliarity with expected requirements, failure to use good sense or judgment, dishonesty, lack of effort or interest, and so on
- Inadequate resources, including people, equipment, materials and supplies, and facilities
- Ineffective operating systems and procedures
- Deviation from expected standards or criteria
- Lack of knowledge that a problem or condition exists

Exhibit 5.3   Operational Review Finding Causes

Effect

One of the primary goals of the operational review is to persuade not-for-profit top management and operations management and staff to take positive action to correct the findings of operational deficiencies the review team has identified. To help management determine just how seriously the condition affects its operations, the reviewer should quantify the effect to the extent possible. As discussed earlier, economy, efficiency, and effectiveness are good measures of effect. They can usually be stated in quantitative terms such as dollars, time, production, number of items or transactions, and so on. Sometimes, when past effects cannot be fully determined, the reviewer may want to present future effects. In determining an operational review effect, the reviewer should answer the following questions:

- So what?
- What is the effect of your finding?

Effect represents the end result of the condition, actual and/or potential. Effect should convince management that either its policies are working out well and its goals are being achieved, or its goals are not being achieved and therefore something needs to be done.

The operational reviewer should, whenever possible, quantify the financial effects or loss. Such determinations demonstrate to not-for-profit management the need for corrective action, as well as help to convince management in the operational review finding report. Such quantification may consist of:

- Actual or estimated monetary losses or potential cost savings
- Uneconomical or inefficient use of resources
- Actual or estimated loss of potential revenues
- Not achieving as effective operating results as possible
- Job expectations not being met as well as they could be
- Information system not useful or meaningful, resulting in poor decision making
- Decrease in employee morale and organizational atmosphere

A list of possible indicators for quantifying effect is shown in Exhibit 5.4.

Recommendations

The successful completion of the operational review finding is the development of recommendations as to the action that should be taken to correct the present undesirable condition. The recommendations should logically follow an explanation of why the present condition exists, the underlying causes, and what should be done to prevent its recurrence. The reviewers' recommendations should be practical and reasonable, so that not-for-profit management will easily see the merits of adopting them.

In developing recommendations, the reviewer should answer these questions:

- What could be recommended to correct the situation?
- Is this recommendation based on a logical connection to the present condition, criteria, and causes?
- Is the recommendation practical and reasonable for implementation?

In many cases, a workable recommendation seems to suggest itself, but at other times the reviewer may need some ingenuity to come up with a recommendation that is sensible and has a reasonable chance of being adopted. Operational review recommendations should be as specific and helpful as possible, not simply that operations need to be improved, controls need to be strengthened, or planning systems need to be implemented. Review team members should do their best to make certain that their recommendations are practical and acceptable to those responsible for taking action. Each recommendation should be directed to a specific management member, so that it is clear who should take the necessary action to implement the recommendation. In addition, the reviewer

1. *Management and organization*
   - Poor planning and decision making
   - Too broad a span of control and/or poor channels of communication
   - Badly designed systems and procedures
   - Excessive crisis management
   - Excessive organizational changes and/or inadequate delegation of authority
2. *Personnel relations*
   - Inadequate hiring, orientation, training, evaluation, and promotion procedures
   - Lack of clearly communicated job expectations
   - Idle, excessive, or not enough personnel
   - Poor employee morale
   - Excessive overtime and/or absenteeism
   - Unclear responsibility/authority relationships
3. *Service delivery operations*
   - Poor service delivery methods re: excessive redo, client dissatisfaction, loss of clients, decrease in return visits, and so on
   - Inefficient layout and/or poor housekeeping
   - Idle equipment and/or operations personnel
   - Insufficient or excessive equipment
   - Excessive service delivery operating costs
   - Lack of effective service delivery scheduling procedures
4. *Purchasing*
   - Not achieving best prices, timeliness, and quality
   - Favoritism to certain vendors
   - Lack of effective competitive bidding procedures
   - Not using most effective systems such as blanket purchase orders, traveling requisitions, electronic and telephone ordering, and so on
   - Excessive emergency purchases
   - Purchase of unnecessary expensive items
   - Unmet delivery schedules
   - Excessive returns to vendors
5. *Financial indicators*
   - Poor increase in reserves or net assets results
   - Poor service delivery to cost ratios
   - Unfavorable cost ratios to results achieved
   - Unfavorable or unexpected cost/budget variances
6. *Complaints*
   - Customers: bad or poor service
   - Employees: grievances, gripes, or exit interview comments
   - Vendors: poor quality or untimely deliveries
   - Service delivery: schedules not met, material not available, not done on time, quality poor, and so on

Exhibit 5.4   Possible Indicators for Quantifying Effect

should always weigh the cost of carrying out a recommendation against its expected benefits.

Good, workable recommendations are a result of the collective review team's experience. The more alternative systems and procedures team members are aware of, the better the chance to arrive at the optimum recommendation. In developing recommendations, the review team should consider all sources; review team members, outside consultants, departmental personnel, other employees, other review staff, other organizations, professional associations, results of internal and external benchmarking studies, and so on.

Often, the best recommendations come from operating personnel, who need only the reviewer's channel of communication to be heard by decision-making management. In these instances, the reviewers must make sure that such operating personnel are given credit for identifying and/or developing the recommendation. The more involved operation personnel are in developing recommendations, the more committed they will be to make them work most effectively. The reviewer's goal is to identify the systems and procedures for recommendation that will optimize savings, be least costly and most efficient to use, and achieve maximum results, regardless of where they come from.

To reinforce the process of identifying and developing good recommendations, the operational review situation presented in Exhibit 5.5 may help to sharpen the reviewer's skills in this area.

**EACH OPERATIONAL REVIEW FINDING
ATTRIBUTE IS IMPORTANT—
NO ONE IS MORE IMPORTANT
THAN ANOTHER**

REVIEW FINDINGS DEVELOPMENT

The operational review team is responsible for the effective development of the review findings. As an aid in developing adequate and complete review findings, reviewers can use a checklist such as the following:

Are any of the finding attributes—statement of condition, criteria, cause, effect, recommendation—missing? Why? What can or should we do about it? Is it a presentation defect or a symptom of an incomplete review?

Are attributes mixed up with one another in a way that impedes clarity? Are facts distinguishable from opinions?

Is the *condition statement* valid? Have we indicated that it is a fact or that it was told to us?

The review team performing an operational review at The Counseling Agency found that the agency had numerous grants and contracts to provide counseling services to rural residents where other such services were not available. Many of these residents were considered low income under federal guidelines and the agency provided such services at no cost to the client under the conditions of their grants. However, many other noneligible residents were also provided counseling services. As many of these residents had neither credit cards nor checking accounts, the agency agreed to bill them for their service at a later date.

As part of the review team's analysis of such client accounts receivable and collection functions, the review team found that the agency's policy for sending out delinquent payment notices was as follows:

- First notice: 10 days after payment due date (30 days after providing of service)
- Second notice: 10 days after the first notice
- Third through eighth notices: every 5 business days
- After 60 days: to agency management for further action

It was also found that the agency continued to provide such counseling services to these clients regardless of the extent of their delinquency in paying. The counselors stated that these clients needed these services as much as low-income clients and should not be penalized for being above low-income guidelines. They were there anyway and they did not see where it cost the agency anything. The counselors refused to be part of such bill collecting.

The review team analyzed such procedures for the current fiscal year and found the following:

- 22% of these clients paid their bills at the time of counseling service delivery
- 18% of these clients paid a partial amount at the time of service with the remainder at the time of the next service
- 12% of these clients paid their bills eventually (an average of 68 days)
- 48% of these clients never paid their bills

The operational review recommendations were as follows:

1. Eliminate the accounts receivable and collection functions by allowing the counseling function to collect payments at the time of service. This would cover over 22% of this client base.
2. For those who could not pay at the time of service, the counseling function would be responsible for collecting at the time of the next visit. This covered an additional 18% of this client base.
3. Once the client paid their outstanding bill, additional services would be provided—an additional 12% of the client base.
4. If the client still could not pay, additional services could only be provided with management approval under special circumstances.
5. Other clients who did not pay within 60 days would be refused further services until such payment was made.
6. Such collection procedures were to become a part of the counseling functions case recordkeeping function. Service and payment records became part of the counseling supervisory procedures.

The net cost savings of these recommendations were estimated at $87,000 per year.

Exhibit 5.5 Developing Recommendations: Accounts Receivable and Collections

Are the *criteria* unclear or unconvincing? Are they weak or unsound from a professional standpoint? Do they contain subjective bias?

Have we explained the *cause*? Have we given the real cause, or is it a symptom? Is the information on the cause incomplete? Superficial? Does it get to the heart of the matter?

Has *effect* been understated? Exaggerated? Quantified when possible?

Is the *recommendation* unnecessarily vague? Too rigid? Does it take care of the past but not the future? Is it punitive rather than constructive? Is it out of harmony with cause?

APPROACH TO DEVELOPING REVIEW FINDINGS

There are, of course, many different and varied not-for-profit operational review situations. Thus, there is no one approach to use consistently to perform the operational review and develop findings. However, the following steps can be considered as a basic approach:

1. Review and analyze operating policies, systems, procedures, and the practices actually being followed to determine whether they will produce the desired results if performed correctly and adequately. If they will not, the operational reviewer can proceed directly to quantifying the effect and determining the cause.
2. Accumulate valid evidence on the operational area under review and its corresponding transactions. This is done by gathering available documentation such as written correspondence, contracts, authorized forms; through interviews with management and operations personnel; and systems analysis such as via systems flowcharts, layout flow diagrams, work observations, and so on.
3. Compare actual transactions with systems and procedures to determine whether procedures are being followed correctly and desired results achieved. If so, the reviewer stops here and ceases spending any more time in reviewing this area. If procedures are not being followed and results are not being achieved, then the reviewer continues with the development of the finding and identification of the attributes.
4. Quantify the effect in terms of dollars lost, or ineffectiveness resulting from the failure to achieve desired results. If the effect is insignificant, the reviewer curtails spending more time in finding development. Nevertheless, the reviewer may decide to report the area to management and may spend some additional time to develop reporting details.
5. If desired results are not being achieved, determine the cause, together with appropriate and sufficient evidence. Note that it is possible that the

policy or procedure is faulty and the practice correct, in which case it may be that the policy or procedure should be changed.

6. Develop recommendations on improving the situation for economy, efficiency, and effectiveness. If the cost of the proposed recommendations exceeds the projected dollar savings, the reviewer may conclude that the recommendation is not warranted. This situation is not usually the case. Operational review recommendations are not always considered solely on an economical basis. They may also provide for increased operational effectiveness, improved decision making, increased organizational efficiency, higher personnel morale, and so on.

Having completed the steps in this approach, the operational reviewer is then ready to present the finding to management, using the finding attributes.

DEVELOPMENT OF REVIEW FINDING: EXAMPLE—EMPLOYEE-LEASED AUTOMOBILES

The Counseling Agency provides substance abuse, individual and group therapy, suicide prevention, and other counseling services to clients in many remote locations within their service area. The agency's policy is to lease automobiles for those counselors who spend sufficient time on the road where the cost of the lease is less than mileage reimbursement and vice versa. As part of the operational review of The Counseling Agency, procedures were reviewed for administering automobile leasing arrangements and the use of the cars by assigned counseling staff personnel for the fiscal year 20XX. Analysis of these 37 leased cars disclosed that 24 cars were being used consistently for only short distances each day. In addition, 27 employees' personal cars, although not driven on agency business every day, were still driven sufficiently on agency business each month to justify using a leased car as opposed to reimbursing such employees at the rate of 30 cents per mile. Analysis of the entire situation, along with recommendations as to the reassignment of leased cars, demonstrated that the agency could realize a savings of more than $44,000 per year.

The operational review finding in response to this situation was as follows:

1. *Statement of Condition.* Our analysis of the use of leased cars by your assigned counseling personnel for the fiscal year 20XX disclosed the following:
   - Of 37 leased cars, we found that 24 of these were not being used sufficiently to justify the lease payment. It would be more economical to the company to allow these employees to use their own personal cars and reimburse them at the current rate of 30 cents per mile.

- For 27 employees who presently use their personal cars and are reimbursed at 30 cents per mile, the total reimbursement for the fiscal year exceeds the cost of leasing an automobile.

2. *Criteria.* It is normal business practice to lease automobiles for employees in situations in which the cost of the lease is expected to be less than the reimbursement for the use of their own cars.

3. *Cause.* We found that a procedure does not presently exist whereby the use of leased cars and personal automobiles on a reimbursement basis is analyzed periodically. Accordingly, the present situation has evolved over a number of years.

4. *Effect.* The present situation has resulted in the agency's paying excess costs of more than $44,000 per year, as shown in Schedule C.

5. *Recommendation.* We recommend that a procedure be implemented to analyze the use of leased and personal automobiles on an ongoing basis. To correct the present situation, we recommend the reassignment of leased cars according to Schedule D, which will result in a present savings to the agency of over $44,000 per year.

CONCLUSION

If the operational review team is successful, many of the findings will be accepted by not-for-profit management as the reviewers progress through their operational review. The reviewers present their findings to management as they are identified and developed. Management responds to each finding by agreeing and proceeding with the implementation of the recommended action, by agreeing but requesting further clarification, or by disagreeing. Because many, if not all, of the review findings are disposed of through this process as the operational review transpires, they do not need to be restated as part of a final report. If the operational review is conducted in this way, the final report becomes a summary of what has happened.

The following chapter discusses the next and final phase of the operational review: the reporting phase.

A Community Services Agency

The Santa Fe Rape Crisis Center (SFRCC)

BACKGROUND

SFRCC was started in 1973 by a handful of women who saw the need within the community for a rape crisis intervention hotline. The hotline volunteers handled 20 sexual assault cases out of their homes in that first year of operations. By 1976, when crisis hot line requests grew to a level that required a more structured system and increased resources, the agency was incorporated as a not-for-profit. A federal grant provided for part-time staff, and SFRCC increased its advocacy role in the community. SFRCC's services improved through coordination with community medical, legal, and judicial systems. With success in providing its rape crisis services, by 1979 the staff was promoted to full-time and a counselor was hired to provide psychological services, as well as a full-time program specialist to address the growing need for community education. SFRCC at present has a full-time staff of 26 employees and a 50-person volunteer base.

SFRCC is governed by a 20-member volunteer board of directors, which is responsible for setting policy and approving the budget and programs. SFRCC is funded by the Health and Environment Department of New Mexico, the City of Santa Fe, the United Way, the Crime Victims Reparation Commission, short-term grants, and private donations. Over 1,000 individuals are served by SFRCC each year.

MISSION AND PHILOSOPHY

SFRCC believes that any individual should be able to receive immediate, confidential, and appropriate care as a victim of sexual assault, and that all procedures should be performed with the informed consent of the victim and that all rights of the victim should be honored. SFRCC engages in a community-coordinated, systems-oriented approach to the prevention of sexual violence and to the treatment and rehabilitation of people affected by sexual violence. SFRCC provides legal advocacy to all victims entering the judicial system and medical advocacy to those undergoing medical procedures as a result of the sexual assault.

SERVICES PROVIDED

SFRCC has grown since its inception in 1973, increasing the original crisis intervention hotline and adding other programs and services such as:

- *Twenty-four hour crisis intervention and hotline.* A volunteer program staffed by a corps of approximately 50 volunteers who respond to crisis calls. These volunteers are trained advocates who provide guidance and assistance throughout the medical and legal process.
- *SANE (Sexual Assault Nurse Examiners) Unit.* A collaborative project with the community hospital, the SANE unit provides sexual assault nurse examiners, SFRCC advocates, and legal and law enforcement personnel who work as a team for all survivors of sexual violence throughout northern New Mexico. SANE offers a completely equipped, warm, and comfortable room away from the emergency services at the hospital to survivors and their families. The SANE nurses are able to provide expert testimony in subsequent legal proceedings.
- *StrongHeart SafeHouse.* This program works in collaboration with SANE nurses, law enforcement, the district attorney's office, and child protective services to create a nonthreatening, comforting, and emotionally supportive environment where children can tell their story to a team of trained forensic interviewers.
- *CARA (Counseling Against Rape and Assault).* A therapeutic counseling program providing services for children, adolescents, and adults who are survivors of sexual abuse. This program deals with survivors of incest and child sexual abuse and their families, as well as recent assault survivors.
- *NO MAS.* This program is the northern New Mexico branch of SFRCC located in the town of Espanola. The program provides immediate, confidential, and culturally sensitive care for survivors and their families and features preventive education and training for all northern New Mexico.
- *PARE (Preventing Abuse Reenactment).* An intensive outpatient program which offers assessment, evaluation, and treatment for sexually aggressive children aged 5 to 17. Many clients are *abuse reactive*, a term that refers to behaviors secondary to previous victimization.
- *Project AWARE.* A child sexual abuse prevention program that utilizes a revised version of the award-winning curriculum "Hands that Hurt, Hands that Heal." Fourth- through sixth-grade students in the public schools are empowered through the four-lesson program, inclusive for children with developmental and other disabilities, which focuses on respect, healthy boundaries, and personal safety.
- *Project GLYPH, A Youth Alliance Program.* This program is a comprehensive education and prevention program with the goal of sending a message to educators, students in middle and high schools, social service providers, parents, and youth providers that homophobia can no longer be tolerated in our community.
- *PASA (Partners Against Sexual Abuse).* A speaker's bureau of volunteer educators who speak with students in middle schools, high schools, and colleges. The program emphasizes healthy relationships, gender respect, communication, and prevention of sexual harassment and date rape.
- *Court Monitoring Project.* This program is a collaborative effort with the League of Women Voters. Trained volunteers from the League and community attend each court proceeding dealing with sexual violence. The results of their court

surveys are analyzed at the end of the year and the results are published to educate the community about sexual violence and working with the State Legislature to change and introduce laws to help bring about justice for survivors of sexual violence.

SFRCC ORGANIZATION

The SFRCC organizational chart is shown in Exhibit CS4.1. As mentioned above, it is governed by a policy setting volunteer board of directors (presently 15 members—20 authorized, plus the executive director) with Public Information, Nominations, Fund-Raising, Finance, Development, Executive, Space, and Administrative committees. An executive director, who is responsible for implementing board-established policies and for directing and overseeing ongoing operations reports directly to the board. Reporting to the executive director are the following 25 employees and volunteers:

- Client Services—clinical manager
  - Clinical Services
    - NO MAS—supervisor
      - Clinical Therapy—two therapists

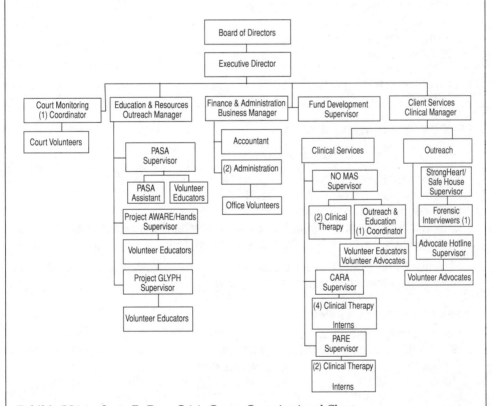

Exhibit CS4.1   Santa Fe Rape Crisis Center Organizational Chart

- Outreach and Education—coordinator
  - Volunteer educators
  - Volunteer advocates
- CARA—supervisor
  - Clinical Therapy—four therapists plus interns
- PARE—supervisor
  - Clinical Therapy—two therapists plus interns
- Outreach
  - StrongHeart Safe House—supervisor
    - Forensic Interviewer—one interviewer
  - Advocate hotline—supervisor plus volunteer advocates
- Education and Resources—outreach manager
  - PASA—supervisor
    - PASA assistant
    - Volunteer educators
  - Project AWARE/Hands—supervisor
    - Volunteer educators
  - Project GLYPH—supervisor
    - Volunteer educators
  - Court Monitoring—Supervisor
    - Court volunteers
- Finance and Administration—manager
  - Fund Development—supervisor
  - Accountant—one accountant
  - Administration—two office administrators
  - Office volunteers

SFRCC FINANCIAL CONDITION

SFRCC's financial information for the past fiscal year is shown as follows:

- Statement of Financial Position (Exhibit CS4.2)
- Statement of Activities (Exhibit CS4.3)
- Statement of Functional Expenses (Exhibit CS4.4)
- Expenditure Budget, showing budget versus actual for the past year, the proposed budget for the next year, and the percentage change (Exhibit CS4.5)

A quick analysis of this data, can bring forth to the review team the following potential areas for review and raise the following questions:

Statement of Financial Position

- The relatively large amount of cash on the Statement of Financial Position ($263,186) as to how it was built up and what SFRCC intends to do with it.
- Accounts receivable—indicating amounts due for services provided—SFRCC charges clients for services based on a sliding fee scale with an estimated allowance for doubtful accounts of $7,200. The entire concept of fees for ser-

Assets	
Cash and cash equivalents—unrestricted	$263,186
Accounts receivable, net of allowance for doubtful accounts	10,919
Contributions receivable	8,520
Grants receivable	67,504
Prepaid expenses	5,021
Deposits	3,401
Cash and cash equivalents—restricted	1,894
Property and equipment, net of accumulated depreciation	19,067
Total assets	$379,512
Liabilities and net assets	
Liabilities:	
Accounts payable	$ 8,675
Accrued expenses	17,352
Other payables	50,055
Accrued leave	5,608
Capital lease payable	7,285
Total liabilities	88,975
Net assets:	
Unrestricted	272,517
Temporarily restricted	18,020
Total net assets	290,537
Total liabilities and net assets	$379,512

Exhibit CS4.2 Santa Fe Rape Crisis Center Statement of Fiinancial Position

vices should be looked at. Total client service fees totaled only $26,000 for the past year.

- Contributions receivable—these are unconditional promises to give (i.e., contribution pledges)—such donations amounted to $159,800 for the past year (versus an expected budget of $60,000). This could indicate a change in fund raising activities or some special circumstance. The entire area of fund raising should be considered for review.
- Grants receivable—SFRCC has been awarded various grants and contracts from governmental agencies or pass-through entities. Such governmental grants equaled 48 percent ($444,034 of a total of $925,398 in total revenues) of total revenues indicating a possible reliance on outside grants. This reliance on governmental grants as well as the operations required to seek and operate within such grant guidelines is a critical area of operations to be included in the operational review.

	Unrestricted	Temporarily Restricted	Total
Revenue and other support:			
Contributions	$212,080	$112,755	$324,835
Contributed services	12,149	—	12,149
Governmental grants	—	444,034	444,034
Special events	102,206	—	102,206
Fees	31,280	—	31,280
Sales	103		103
Interest	10,791	—	10,791
Net assets released from restrictions	577,769	(577,769)	0
Total revenue and other support	946,378	(20,980)	925,398
Expenses:			
Program services	704,709	—	704,709
Supporting services:			
Management and general	126,600	—	126,600
Fund raising	59,962	—	59,962
Total expenses	891,271	0	891,271
Change in net asset	55,107	(20,980)	34,127
Net assets at beginning of year	217,410	39,000	256,410
Net assets at end of year	$272,517	$ 18,020	$290,537

Exhibit CS4.3   Statement of Activities for the Year Ended

- Property and equipment, net of accumulated depreciation—the total original cost of $99,508 for such furniture, fixtures, and equipment ($70,264) and leasehold improvements ($29,244) with accumulated depreciation of $80,441 or a net of $19,067 indicates a possibility of aging assets with possible requirements for replacement as well as the need for additional assets for agency growth.
- Other payables—of $50,055. The review team might want to spend some time looking at what constitutes such other payables and how such an amount has built up. This may indicate an operational area for further review or it might be quite legitimate for SFRCC's operations.
- Total net assets of $290,537 makes it evident that SFRCC is able to operate within its budget and provide a positive contribution to net assets each year ($34,127 in the past year). The review team should analyze what plans SFRCC has for using such positive net assets—that is, to expand operations and services provided, to make present operations more efficient and effective, to become less reliant on outside funding, to develop an endowment fund, and so on.

Statement of Activities
- Revenue and other support—looking at the sources of revenues, that is:

	Program Services	Supporting Services		
		Management & General	Fund Raising	Total
Payroll	$418,390	$ 87,972	$17,280	$523,642
Payroll taxes	31,347	6,591	1,295	39,233
Employee benefits	33,722	7,090	1,303	42,205
Insurance	6,107	1,527	—	7,634
Mileage and travel	4,045	850	167	5,062
Supplies	22,519	2,002	500	25,021
Printing	6,465	575	144	7,183
Postage	4,316	136	90	4,543
Telephone	14,861	991	660	16,512
Professional services	11,957	3,986	—	15,943
Outside services	11,374	3,791	—	15,165
Training	24,499	1,021	—	25,520
Board development	—	1,108	—	1,108
Occupancy	44,928	2,930	977	48,835
Equipment rent and repair	—	716	—	716
Advertising	1,689	844	844	3,377
Subawards	6,768	—	—	6,768
Special projects	46,890	—	—	46,890
Special events	—	—	25,963	25,963
Dues and subscriptions	601	—	—	601
License and permits	—	45	—	45
Bank fees	—	460	—	460
Miscellaneous	—	781	—	781
Interest	771	193		964
Depreciation	11,961	2,990	—	14,951
Donated Services	1,500	—	10,649	12,149
Total expenses	$704,709	$126,600	$59,962	$891,271

Exhibit CS4.4 Santa Fe Rape Crisis Center Statement of Functional Expenses for the Year Ended

Contributions, including foundation grants and other donations	$324,835	35.1%
Contributed services	12,149	1.3%
Government grants	444,034	48.0%
Special events	102,206	11.0%
Fees	31,280	3.3%
Sales	103	.1%
Interest	10,791	1.2%
Total revenues	$925,398	100.0%

The review team should consider a full review of all revenue sources considering such things as sources and dependencies on specific sources, optimization of

Expenses	FY99 Budget	FY99 Actual	FY00 Budget
Gross wages	501,388	477,144	592,206
Payroll taxes	38,356	35,676	45,313
Employee benefits	50,139	42,204	59,233
Insurance	7,000	7,634	6,000
Auto mileage	3,500	3,542	3,500
Clinical testing supplies	200	0	400
Therapy supplies	1,400	1,707	2,050
Office supplies	9,900	11,937	10,300
Educational supplies	10,000	10,734	5,660
Printing and reproduction	9,150	7,366	9,200
Postage and delivery	3,800	4,543	4,500
Telephone	13,000	11,176	12,240
Answering service	6,000	5,453	5,600
Beeper and cellular phone	440	1,085	600
Professional fees	5,000	15,943	10,000
Outside services	30,500	15,134	10,200
Awards and recognition	3,000	3,474	3,850
Volunteer training	3,500	3,448	4,450
Staff training	12,836	18,952	18,120
Board development	500	1,108	750
Executive director fund	800	781	800
Office rent/space rent	42,400	40,724	43,400
Utilities	3,500	3,761	3,700
Repairs and maintenance	2,200	4,350	2,200
Equipment rent	3,500	2,399	3,300
Advertising	2,900	3,377	3,000
Contract meeting	300	0	0
Travel/meals/lodging	2,000	1,972	1,650
Dues and subscriptions	250	701	525
Licenses and permits	125	45	50
Bank charges	500	460	100
Fundraiser expenses	12,500	33,933	25,450
Seminar expenses	2,000	0	15,000
Capital outlay	4,500	1,182	2,700
Take Back the Night	1,000	2,678	1,000
Train the Trainer, Hands	1,000	0	0
Special project expense	0	46,041	6,000
General allocation	0	0	0
Total expenses	**789,084**	**820,664**	**913,047**

Exhibit CS4.5 Santa Fe Rape Crisis Center Expenditure Budget

revenue sources, under-utilization of present revenue sources (e.g., contributed services, special events, fees, sales, and interest or investment income), other sources and so on.

- Expenses—looking at the major categories of expenses such as:

Program services	$704,709	79.1%
Management and general	126,600	14.2%
Fund raising	59,962	6.7%
Total expenses	$891,271	100.0%

The review team should consider looking at program service expenses to determine if such expenses are being spent most economically and efficiently so as to maximize the achieving of service delivery results. Management and general expenses should be reviewed as to efficient use of such expenditures so as to maximize the greatest share of expenses directly related to the providing of services. Fund-raising expenses need to be reviewed on the basis of results—that is, are these expenditures providing benefits of a sufficient multiple in terms of revenues to justify them.

Statement of Functional Expenses

Categories of expenses to be considered for analysis in the operational review include:

Personnel costs, including payroll, payroll taxes, employee benefits	$605,080	67.9%
Occupancy—too high or too low and necessary?	48,835	5.5%
Special projects—what is included here?	46,890	5.3%
Special events—what are they? Is cost justified?	25,963	2.9%
Training—necessary? Results achieved? Other ways?	25,520	2.9%
Supplies—what is necessary? How much is or can be donated?	25,021	2.8%
Telephone—basis for charges? Less expensive options? Overuse?	16,512	1.9%
Professional services—what kind? Necessary? Other sources?	15,943	1.8%
Outside services—what kind? Results? Other sources?	15,165	1.7%
Subtotal	$824,929	92.7%
All other expenses—looking for inappropriate expenses	66,342	7.3%
Total expenses	$891,271	100.0%

Revenue Budget

The review team should analyze the sources of revenues such as:

- Governmental grants (federal, state, and local), procurement process, award history, grant constraints and compliance, service support, and so on

- Private grants and contracts—foundations, corporations, private grantors and so on
- Donations—sources, fund raising, programs, and so on
- Client service fees—process, policies, billing and collections, and so on
- Fund raisers—what are they, could this be increased, efforts versus results, and so on
- Product sales (very small at present)—what is included, can this be increased?
- Interest income—is this being maximized on a prudent basis?
- Other sources of income—such as seminars, conferences, presentations, etc. Can these areas be increased as well as other possibilities?

Expense Budget

The review team also considers areas where actual expenses differ from budget:

- Personnel costs—why less than budget? What should they be? Budget of $589,883 versus actual of $555,024 or decrease of $34,859 or 6 percent
- Office supplies—increase of $2,037 or 21 percent
- Printing and reproduction—decrease of $1,784 or 19.5 percent
- Telephone—decrease of $1,824 or 14 percent
- Beepers and cellular phone—increase of $645 or 147 percent
- Professional fees—increase of $10,943 or 219 percent
- Outside services—decrease of $15,366 or 50 percent
- Staff training—increase of $6,116 or 48 percent
- Repairs and maintenance—increase of $2,150 or 98 percent
- Fund-raiser expenses—increase of $21,433 or 171 percent
- Capital outlay—decrease of $3,318 or 74 percent
- Special project expense—$46,041 versus no budget—what is this?

Questions that should be asked relative to these changes include:

- What should these expenses have been based on related activity levels?
- Do these budget versus actual changes relate to any operational changes?
- Do decreases from budget indicate more economical or efficient methods of operations? Can they be expected to continue? Can they be replicated as best practices in other operational areas of the agency?
- Can increased or decreased levels of expenses be expected to continue?
- Do any of these changes relate to ongoing changes in SFRCC operations?

OVERVIEW OF SITUATION

SFRCC has been in existence for over 25 years, since 1973, when it was started by a handful of women as a community rape crisis intervention hotline, handled by a group of volunteers out of their homes. It now has a 20-member board of directors, an executive director, a full-time staff of about 25 employees, and a 50-person volunteer base. In addition to the now 24-hour crisis intervention hotline staffed by a corps of approximately 50 volunteers, SFRCC also manages and oversees nine other programs. SFRCC started its hotline within the Santa Fe community, but now appears to be expanding its territory to all of New Mexico. SFRCC is also almost exclusively dependent on governmental, private foundation, organizational contributors, and other charitable contributors for its revenue. In fiscal year 1999, such revenues represented approximately 83 percent of total revenues from about 30 different donors. Some of these donors specify certain conditions that must be met by SFRCC or by a specific operating program. The loss of key donors would have an adverse effect on SFRCC's operations and specific operating programs.

OPERATIONAL REVIEW—AREAS TO CONSIDER

The case materials presented above present a picture of a successful community services organization. As is typical in many of these situations, a good community service idea—in this case, a rape crisis intervention hotline—conceived by a few dedicated people grew into a successful not-for-profit agency. The basic mission "that any individual should be able to receive immediate, confidential, and appropriate care as a victim of sexual assault" has blossomed into a relatively large social service agency with an annual budget approaching $1 million. Based on these case materials, the review team might want to consider the following areas for inclusion in their operational review of SFRCC.

- *Organizational mission.* SFRCC started out with a fairly narrow application of its mission—a community (Santa Fe)-based rape crisis intervention hotline. At present, it has grown into an agency which provides other related services. SFRCC needs to decide the direction it wants to take and then develop programs based on that direction. This situation may also indicate some deficiencies in SFRCC's planning and budget systems.
- *Services provided.* SFRCC presently has 10 operating programs under its auspices including the crisis intervention hotline. Some, if not all, of these programs are related to SFRCC's core mission. However, some of these programs may duplicate to some extent the services provided by other agencies while others possibly could be provided elsewhere. The review team should analyze this situation to determine which services SFRCC should be developing, which ones should be expanded, which ones should be curtailed, or possibly eliminated and so on.
- *Planning and budgeting.* Strategic and long-range planning, which helps to identify the direction for the organization is typically a major role for the board of directors and the executive director. The review team should analyze the manner in which this process operates at SFRCC and identify the specific focus for the agency.

Based on the above strategic definitions, the review team should then review short-term planning processes to determine that all SFRCC programs and operating departments fully understand the desired long-range direction and have identified short-term goals, objectives, and detail plans that correlate to the long-term direction.

The present budget process produces a typical line item budget for both revenues and expenses for the entire agency as well as budgets for each program. In this manner, SFRCC management can better determine the viability of such entities and whether expected benefits justify the costs and efforts required.

Budget reporting should also be based on flexible budgeting principles wherein such budgets are automatically adjusted based on actual activity levels.

- *Organizational concerns.* SFRCC is operating its 10 operating programs with limited staff together with a core of volunteers. It may be trying to accomplish too much with too little. The review team should determine the best manner to employ such personnel, whether additional personnel are needed, present personnel can be reduced or eliminated, other methods can be used to provide similar services, and so on. Areas to consider in such a review include:
  - Board of directors—role and responsibilities relative to setting policy and overall direction for SFRCC.
  - Executive director—working together with the board, other SFRCC management, staff personnel, volunteers, and the public. What are the expectations for this individual and the methods for determining the achievement of expected results?
  - Client services programs—what service-providing businesses should SFRCC be in, how should they provide such services and to what levels, what should be the fee structure and philosophy, where should they advocate and where should they provide direct services, and so on?
  - Education and outreach programs—what is the role of SFRCC in community education, how far should they delve, how effective are present programs, are there gaps in such services, are they the right programs, and so on?
  - Finance and administration—what is the level of services being provided, are they providing any value-added services, can such services be provided more economically and efficiently, and so on?
  - General—relationship of managers, coordinators, supervisors, therapists, administrative personnel, interns, volunteers, advocates, and so on to the purpose of SFRCC's existence. Is the organizational structure the most efficient in achieving desired results?
- *SFRCC financial condition.* At present, SFRCC appears to be in an acceptable financial position, with over $290,000 in total net assets and over $260,000 in cash. However, there are some questionable areas that should be examined by the review team, such as:
  - Assets
    - Relatively large cash position of over $260,000. What are plans for using?
    - Property and equipment—too much, too little, adequate facilities, and so on.
  - Liabilities
    - Other payables—review of what areas are included and how this amount was built up over time.
  - Revenues
    - Dependency on grants and contracts
    - Fees for services
    - Contributions and donations
    - Fund-raising activities
    - Compliance requirements to grants and contracts

In addition, the review team should determine whether SFRCC develops its plans for services and then develops its revenue plans or identifies revenue

sources and then develops services to match funding requirements—in other words, does effective service and revenue planning exist?
- Expenses
  - Program services
  - Management and general
  - Fundraising
  - Personnel costs
  - Other major expense categories
- *Management control and reporting.* Effective operations of such a community services agency requires that agency, department, and function management have both financial as well as operational information to effectively manage and control. With agreed-upon plans and flexible budget systems in operation, management needs to know on a continual basis whether operating activities are achieving desired results in the most economical and efficient manner. The review team should analyze such present control and reporting systems to determine if they are achieving such purposes and whether any changes need to be implemented.

CHAPTER 6

Reporting Phase

INTRODUCTION

In the reporting phase of an operational review, the review team communicates the results of its work to the intended not-for-profit management and operations personnel. The principal objectives of the operational review report are to (1) provide useful and timely information on significant operational deficiencies and other matters, and (2) recommend improvements in the conduct of operations.

The review report is the operational review team's opportunity to get not-for-profit management's undivided attention—an opportunity to show management the benefits of the operational review and what the operational review team has to offer. Accordingly, the operational review report has two functions:

1. To communicate the results of the operational review
2. To persuade and, when necessary, sound a call to action

This chapter discusses the principles and techniques for good reporting in an operational review. The reviewer normally prepares both an oral and written report for management review, based on the significant operational review findings developed during the field work and review finding development phases. As discussed in Chapter 5, specific review findings have been identified and developed for management review during the course of the review. If the review has been performed correctly, the review team has already presented these findings to management during the field work phase, and operations personnel have already begun to implement those steps necessary to correct the identified deficiencies. The review report then becomes more a summary of the operational review, documenting the following:

1. What the operational review team has accomplished,
2. What was found during the course of the operational review,
3. The extent of operational deficiencies, and
4. What operations personnel have done thus far to correct the situation.

In some instances, however, where operational review findings have not been addressed during the course of the review, the report (both oral and written) becomes the review team's vehicle to convince and persuade management to take corrective action. This is appropriate for reviews of short duration, of perhaps less than two weeks, or for a general overview type of review, where there is not sufficient elapsed time to present findings during the course of the review. Otherwise, the review team should present its findings as they are identified.

This chapter reviews the principles of good operational review reporting that should ensure the review team greater success in getting not-for-profit operations management and staff to implement recommended operational improvements. Remember, to be successful, the review team does not need to convince management to follow all recommendations—action on more than 50 percent of the significant findings is usually adequate.

> **OPERATIONAL REVIEW REPORTING IS NOT A**
> **COMMUNICATIONS EXERCISE**
> **BUT AN EXERCISE IN REPORTING RESULTS,**
> **TO PERSUADE AND TO SOUND A CALL TO ACTION**

INTERIM REPORTING

Operational review reports may be either informal or formal, and oral as well as written. The review team should issue a signed written report to appropriate not-for-profit management and staff and other interested parties after the field work is completed, as a record of the completed operational review. However, there is a need for reporting the progress of the review to management during the course of the review.

These interim reports may be oral or written, depending on the circumstances, and may be transmitted formally or informally. It is a good practice to review and submit findings to operations personnel in the five attribute format as they are identified during the actual review. This can be done by using the format shown in the review finding examples in Chapter 5, either showing the actual titles "Statement of Condition," "Criteria," "Cause," "Effect," and "Recommendations" or by merely separating each attribute into a paragraph. The review team can use a standard form or merely free form, leaving space to record management responses and comments. This gives operations and management personnel an opportunity to respond to the findings and recommendations quickly and to take whatever appropriate action is required— either to begin to implement the recommendations or to question some part of the finding.

In either case, this approach allows action to be taken when necessary, as opposed to waiting for the formal report to be issued and reviewed. This practice also allows the review team to include the views of management and operating staff in their final formal written report, both agreeing and opposing views. In addition, for balanced reporting, the reviewers' formal written report should acknowledge any outstanding accomplishments or any corrective action that operations has taken prior to completion of the operational review and issuance of the report.

Note that the reviewers can now refer to the detailed findings and recommendations previously issued and reviewed with operations in the formal report, or attach them as an appendix to the report. In effect, the final written report becomes a formal summary of actions already taken by operations personnel.

THERE IS NO NEED TO REPORT
IF THERE IS NOTHING TO REPORT

ORAL REPORTING

Oral reports or briefings should be given to operations and management personnel periodically, as determined by the length of the review and whether there is anything significant to report. For instance, an operational review scheduled for a three-month period might include periodic oral reporting on a biweekly basis. These progress reports should be specified in the original proposal or letter of understanding and included as part of the review team's budget. There is, of course, no need to hold such a meeting if there is nothing to report.

Oral reports are usually less formal than written reports and include a greater use of visuals such as photographs, slides, charts, and graphs. Oral reporting requires effective oral communication and presentation skills on the part of all review team members. To be most effective in communicating issues to operations personnel, those review team members involved in conducting the field work and developing the findings should make the presentation—not just review team management.

Oral reports have some distinct advantages over written reports, for example:

- Oral reports are immediate. They give prompt attention to current information to allow for timely corrective action.
- Oral reports evoke face-to-face responses. They can disclose client attitudes and convictions that may be important to the reviewers in finalizing their findings and recommendations.

- Oral reports allow the reviewers to counter operations' arguments and provide additional information that operations personnel may require.
- Oral reports can reveal inaccuracies in the review team's thinking, which can be corrected before decisions become final.

The review team may, in some cases, give oral briefings to operations personnel at various stages of the review. In most operational reviews, the reviewers present at least one internal oral briefing in addition to the final oral presentation. These oral briefings may take the form of scheduled periodic progress meetings or be called at the option of review or operations management when there is something significant to discuss or report.

These presentations need to be done professionally, as they are golden opportunities to convince management of the merits of operational reviews and the reviewers' competency. This is the reviewers' chance to persuade operations management to take the proper action so as to improve operations immediately—without waiting for a more formal written report. Often, the findings are presented at these briefings in attribute format.

**ORAL REPORTING EVOKES
FACE TO FACE RESPONSES**

WRITTEN REPORT

The review team does not generally close out the operational review with a final oral presentation alone, but normally will issue a written report as well. The more formal written report benefits operations personnel, as well as review team members. The written report provides official recognition of completion of the review and highlights, in writing, the review results. For review team members, the written report serves as a source of information concerning the work done and as a resource for future reviews.

Operations management judges the completed operational review work, in large part, by the quality of the reports. Operational review reports must be prepared according to certain basic principles to maintain high professional standards of operation and to effectively meet reporting objectives. A poor job of written reporting can discredit the reviewers' work accomplished on the operational review. It can also discredit the review staff and put them in a bad position for additional work, no matter how competently they performed the other aspects of the review.

The writer of the review report must keep in mind the intended recipients and other readers. A good rule to follow in achieving this objective is to present the report in a simpler format than the perceived reader's comprehension level. In conjunction with this principle of simplicity, the reviewers should consider using familiar words and phrases, specific descriptive examples, and visual displays such as charts, graphs, and flowcharts to enhance reader understanding.

A good way to ensure that responsible management personnel comprehend and understand the primary concerns is to develop the written report in an inverse format—that is, going from concepts to more specific details. Most people, particularly senior managers, do not want to read through all of the specific details and individual issues and concerns. They want to understand the top-level considerations and what action needs to be taken to correct a given operational deficiency. Therefore, the reviewers present the broad overview, the purpose and objectives of the operational review, and their opinions and the benefits to be derived, in conceptual terms.

The reviewers' findings should be specific and to the point, emphasizing the present effect and future benefits of implementing the recommendations. Recommendations should clearly state what actually needs to be done. Ideally, the reviewers' documented findings and related recommendations should be specific enough to give the person responsible for implementing the recommendation a clear description of what needs to be done. Remember too, the reviewers may be asked to help implement the recommendation.

Whether at the oral briefing or in the written report, each finding and recommendation should be reviewed in complete detail with operations management and staff to be sure of accuracy and understanding. This ensures mutual agreement on all reported findings and action to be taken.

THE WRITTEN REPORT
SUMMARIZES WHAT WAS DONE

SAMPLE REPORTS

Strict standardization is not recommended for operational review report formats. However, without some basic directions, there would be as many variations of reports as there are operational reviewers. There are typically two types of operational review reports—the letter report and the regular report.

1. The letter report, or short report, is designed to be used when the subject matter requires only a few pages of discussion. As a general rule, it should not be used if the report will be over five pages, contains exhibits or numerous appendices, covers a complex subject, or contains a group of different ideas or topics.

2. The regular report, or long report, is used for more lengthy reporting, particularly when a number of different areas or subjects are covered. It typically contains an introductory letter, plus a table of contents, and several report sections, each covering a major subject or area.

In the letter report, there is a "Summary of Findings and Recommendations" section, which gives a general description of each finding and the estimated savings. The detailed findings have either been presented previously or are documented separately or as an appendix to the report. In the regular report introductory letter, the "Summary of Findings and Recommendations" section merely references the findings and states the total amount of savings. The major findings are then summarized by section, as referenced in a table of contents.

A sample operational review report is shown in the Case Study following this chapter.

**OPERATIONAL REVIEWS
ARE THE CORNERSTONE
TO BEST PRACTICES
IN A PROGRAM OF CONTINUOUS IMPROVEMENTS**

Sample Operational Review Report

Dr. Lynn Anderson, President
Mercy College
College Boulevard
College, XX 99999

Dear Dr. Anderson:

Reider Associates is pleased to submit this report to Mercy College relative to our comments, findings, and recommendations as a result of our review and analysis of your business office systems and procedures. During the course of our review, we:

- Interviewed all business office personnel at your central administrative location as to their roles and functions.
- Reviewed business office systems and procedures set up to accomplish these functions.
- Performed a general review of manual and computerized systems to determine whether such systems were being used most efficiently and effectively.
- Identified areas that indicated more pervasive operating inefficiencies in other areas (or throughout the college).
- Reviewed use of personnel to determine if they are being used most effectively.
- Identified areas for positive improvements and implementation of best practices in overall functions as well as individual operating areas and use of personnel.

Specifically, we performed the following work steps:

1. Analyzed present business office systems and procedures.
2. Assisted operations personnel in implementing our best practice recommendations of an immediate and short-term nature as the start of the College's program of continuous improvements.
3. Documented the methodology for implementing long-term improvements.
4. Identified areas of personnel staffing economies in conjunction with recommended efficiencies of operations.

BACKGROUND

Mercy College has made major strides in the past few years resulting in increased student enrollments and the development and growth of a number of academic programs. However, basic systems and methods have remained relatively the same, with many of these no longer meeting the college's and students' needs. In fact, even with such growth, the college has been operating at a monetary operating deficit.

Mercy College is in existence to provide quality education and services to their students. However, the college is in a very competitive marketplace both within the state and around the country. With the present state of the economy, potential students are looking more intently at alternative options—from both an economic and quality education standpoint—prior to deciding on a college. Mercy College, as a small private college, must work harder to recruit potential students as well as to retain them. This means developing a uniqueness in the marketplace and establishing systems for maintaining academic and student service excellence. This, of course, costs more money.

To accomplish such a mission and meet its goals in the present environment of scarce resources, Mercy College needs to plan for and manage its resources more effectively. There are two main ways to increase monetary resources—either by increasing revenues or by decreasing (or not spending) expenditures. There needs to be effective planning both for revenue maximization as well as for use of funds. Typically, it costs something to create additional revenues, which sometimes retards doing what needs to be done, particularly with limited funds. However, a dollar not spent, without sacrificing what needs to be done to achieve desired results, goes directly to the fund balance or reserves. Accordingly, scarce resources need to be planned for and managed so as to use them most effectively based on a system of priorities and effective allocation.

We performed our operational review of business office operations to address these issues as well as to be responsive to the present needs of Mercy College. As we discussed, our comments, suggestions, and recommendations are for your review and consideration. You ultimately must decide the direction that Mercy College must take and whether these suggestions and recommendations are helpful in getting you there.

You and Mercy College senior management have been aware of the need for an operational review and analysis of business office procedures. While the scope of business office activities has greatly expanded in response to changing internal and external requirements, basic procedures have remained relatively stable. Additional procedures have been implemented solely to address specific situations. Accordingly, this method of operation has produced an operating environment characterized by individualized procedures that do not always efficiently meet operating and reporting needs. In recognition of this need, Mercy College management engaged Reider Associates to assist them in performing an operational review of such business office procedures.

SCOPE OF OUR REVIEW

For the purpose of identifying areas for improvements, our review and analysis of present business office systems and procedures included the following functions:

- Comptroller responsibilities and activities, including the comptroller, assistant comptroller, and secretary
- Business operations manager

- Payroll technician
- Accounts payable coordinator
- Restricted funds accounting
- Purchasing coordinator
- Accounts receivable
- Cashier
- Staff support—accounting technicians and secretarial

We reviewed the above functions according to the following general work steps:

1. *Personnel Interviews*

Met with business office management and operations personnel to analyze present operating procedures and associated areas for improvement, as well as to determine future requirements. These discussions and reviews provided us with a working knowledge of:

- Present operating procedures
- Timing and flow of current data
- Problem areas, particularly the critical ones
- Coordination and related communication networks between functions
- Information requirements, present and future needs

2. *Functional Activities*

Review of systems and procedures presently required to perform such business office oriented functions as:

- Business office organization structure and related functional job descriptions, including responsibility and authority relationships
- Business office planning systems, including the establishment of goals, objectives, and detail plans; and the integration of such plans with overall college planning systems
- Personnel practices including employee hiring, orientation, training, evaluation, promotion, and firing
- Business office policies and operating procedures

OBJECTIVES

The objectives of this operational review were to identify the work being performed by Mercy College business office personnel in order to formulate future operational requirements, as well as to make observations and recommendations as to the manner in which immediate and short-term improvements could be realized. The principal focus of our efforts was toward developing operating procedures that would provide optimum efficiencies in meeting Mercy College's requirements. We did not attempt to evaluate present personnel or their performance, but only to evaluate the tasks and functions being performed.

OUR APPROACH

Our approach to reviewing business office operating procedures involved an analysis of operations according to the existing organization structure. Accordingly, we divided our review into the business office functional activity areas:

- Management and supervision
- Payroll processing and coordination
- Accounts payable coordination
- Business office operations
- Accounting procedures and internal recordkeeping
- Management and operating information system
- Restricted funds accounting
- Purchasing coordination
- Accounts receivable coordination
- Cashiering function

At the conclusion of each of the above stages of analysis, we prepared a review of findings and recommendations, which were submitted to appropriate Mercy College management and operations personnel in oral presentations, together with written documentation. Accordingly, these presentation materials are not being included in this report. Basically, our review of findings discussed present deficiencies, suggested methods of improvement, and identified areas where economies and efficiencies could be achieved immediately or as a result of additional work efforts.

SUMMARY OF FINDINGS AND RECOMMENDATIONS

We are summarizing our major findings below for your review. The details of each finding have been submitted under separate cover for your information. We believe that should you implement all of these recommendations, Mercy College could realize an estimated annual savings of $410,000.

General Areas

During the course of our operational review of the business office operations, we identified various areas that have an impact on other functions or the college in general. Many times, in the conducting of an operational review, we pick up indications of inefficiencies or improper practices that are more pervasive than just the functions and activities being looked at—what we call "the tip of the iceberg" situations. We would like to bring them to your attention, as follows:

Organization

There appears to be an organizational structure set up in the typical top-to-bottom hierarchy based on the need to police and control, review, and redo, rather than on the need to achieve results based on clear expectations and criteria for accountability. Theoretically, it is better to develop a workplace where one knows what is expected of him or her and each one is motivated by clearly understood helpful systems in a self-motivated discipline system. To make this type of system work most effectively, you need to have clear performance and evaluation criteria, and the ability to determine whether effective results are being achieved. Within your constraints of limited resources, this allows you to accomplish desired results at less cost and to reward those individuals who contribute most positively on a merit basis rather than an across the board or years-in-service basis.

The art of management is to accomplish desired results with the least amount of resources using the most efficient methods. Based on our observations, there appears to be too much time spent on day-to-day crises and getting through the day and less emphasis on real management. For example, in the business office, there is a comptroller, an assistant comptroller, and a business operations manager, all with responsibilities for supervising other business office personnel. Not only is this a costly duplication of efforts, but such a practice tends to create a demoralizing and confusing atmosphere for employees. In addition, there are a number of other functions, such as payroll coordinator, accounts payable coordinator, restricted funds accountant, and accounts receivable/purchasing coordinator, and a great deal of their time is taken up with clerical- or mechanical-type functions rather than functional management and analysis tasks.

Systems and Procedures

The business office is presently using a XXXXXX minicomputer system with XXXX software for its accounting processing functions. This software is fairly old and does not incorporate many of the standard features to be found in currently available college accounting systems such as an integration of systems (e.g., accounting, student registration, financial aid, plant funds, etc.) and accounting data files (e.g., payroll, purchasing, accounts payable, student charges, budgets, accounts receivable, and general ledger), ability to manipulate data for user needs, report generation, and effective providing of management and operating data. Accordingly, business office personnel are spending a relatively large amount of time performing manual and clerical functions to make the system work as well as develop necessary and requested information. In fact, most "special reports" from management require an inordinate amount of time and often require the development of microcomputer spreadsheet and/or database procedures.

There are many college accounting and financial software packages presently available for operation on microcomputers. Most of your business office work stations are presently using microcomputers as data terminals into your present XXXX system. To support a new system, hardware costs can be kept to a minimum by using existing microcomputers and purchasing a file server (basically a microcomputer central processing unit and large hard disk storage unit) and network software. Before looking at software packages, you should develop your own systems specifications as to what you want the system to do—module by module and by data file. Then make sure the preferred software package can give you the flexibility to meet your defined needs and can be ultimately integrated with other operating functions. We believe the cost of necessary hardware and software will far outweigh the costs of present processing methods and the time required to provide operations and management information. In addition, it will provide the information necessary to manage and control college operations.

Planning and Budgeting

After reviewing the college's budget process, it appears to be more of a line item mathematical-type exercise (using last year as a base) than an effective budgeting system based on long-term, short-term, and detail planning concepts. It seems that management personnel are spending their time developing budgets based on incremental increases from last year's budget and actual spending regardless of what is actually needed to achieve results.

The budget should be the detailed plan depicting the manner in which scarce monetary resources will be acquired and used over a period of time. It is the quantitative manifestation of the next year of the college's strategic or long-term plan. The strategic plan is the defined direction from top management of where the college should be heading considering all of the various aspects such as:

• Makeup of student body—in state, out of state, undergraduate, graduate, continuing education, and so on
• Expansion and contraction of programs
• Use of facilities
• Student services
• Community outreach

The strategic plan should be backed up by organizational and departmental short-term plans identifying results to be accomplished in the coming period. Once such planning goals and objectives have been agreed upon by management and operations personnel, departmental personnel are then responsible for developing detail operating plans identifying the resources and activities necessary to accomplish these results. Until such detail plans are accomplished, there is no effective way to prioritize desired results and then allocate resources. This is budgeting.

Budgeting should include both revenue and expenditure planning, so that management at all levels agrees to the approach to be taken to produce revenues and expend funds to accomplish desired results. Some advantages to Mercy College of such a planning-oriented budget process include:

• Requires managers and others to focus on planning, and become proactive rather than reactive.
• Provides for communication of plans throughout the organization, creating an understanding of priorities and allocation of resources, fostering cooperation rather than competition.
• Reduces doubts as to what each employee, function, and activity is to do, how it is to be done, and what results are expected.
• Provides specific goals and objectives and detail plans, which serve as benchmarks for the subsequent evaluation of results achieved.
• Provides objective criteria for accountability in that each manager is evaluated based on working the plan and achieving results rather than spending or not spending their budget dollars.

The present budget system does not appear to relate results to resource allocations, creating an atmosphere in which some or all of the following budget "games" appear to be present:

• The "hammer" or punitive tool—blaming the budget or someone else when things go wrong.
• The "operational strait jacket," allowing minimum freedom or flexibility to operating management.

- The "excuse" for inaction—"It's not in the budget."
- The "spending" game—"If it's in the budget, I can spend it.
- Other games such as "high/low" negotiating, hoarding, cushioning, and management harassment or got-cha's.

The budget process in its proper place at the end of the planning process should be used as a positive force to assist Mercy College management in establishing expectations, measuring results, working toward long- and short-term goals and objectives, and identifying operational areas in need of improvement. In this context, Mercy College should consider the following factors in making the present budget process work for them:

- Revenue planning that defines revenue targets and develops detail plans as to how to reach them in all areas of Mercy College such as academic departments, use of facilities, development fund-raising office, outreach programs, noncredit continuing education, conferences, seminars and workshops, and so on.
- Prioritizing and allocating expenditure resources so that such funds are spent where they are most needed rather than on an incremental (usually across the board) increase system based on last year's budget.
- Adapting flexible budget concepts that take into account that conditions change and neither plans nor budgets are static but ever-changing. In fact, normally as soon as the budget is set, it is already obsolete and can hardly be set for the entire year.
- Using the automatic budget adjustment, which allows for budget changes as conditions change that are not in the control of the specific manager, for instance, a price increase of items that are needed to achieve results or a planned expenditure that is no longer needed.
- Evaluation of budgets based on movement toward achievement of detail plans, goals, and objectives. This eliminates the present need to monitor the detail spending related to line items and the consistent movement of dollars from one line item to another. The approved budget should not be permission to spend. However, agreed-upon plans are authority to take action.
- Results orientation rather than numbers focus. As most of your departmental budgets consist of 70 percent or more of personnel-related costs, which are set by contract, there is really little else to be concerned about. What is more important is how they will use their personnel and what additional resources are need to achieve results.

Management Information System

The present accounting and financial system does not contain the flexibility to provide the information to effectively monitor and control operations. It is not fully integrated between subsystem modules and the general ledger and is not designed to provide necessary operating statistics on an exception basis, such as:

- Cash requirements—excess cash to invest or borrowing needs
- Accounts payable—overdue with automatic notices
- Accounts receivable—becoming due or overdue
- Revenue shortfalls—present or future conditions

- Personnel statistics—absenteeism, overtime, overloads
- Cost analysis—by department, program, class, function

Key operating indicators (KOIs) should be defined for all academic and operating functions and investigated as to what is possible with the present system, and what is desired when you look at new software packages. The effective use of such KOIs and related exception reporting is usually much more effective than trying to analyze a universe of data, which many times operational personnel and accountants do not fully understand.

Committees and Meetings

It appears that management and other personnel are involved in numerous committees and meetings. This not only disrupts the main purposes for which they are employed, but it is also an indication of filling time on the part of the one calling the meeting and for those attending. Sometimes, it also indicates the inability to know what to do with one's time. Although there are many legitimate purposes for committees and meetings, it does not appear that many of these are really needed, particularly in your present condition. This entire area should be investigated as to the necessity of each committee and the abuse of meetings.

The overuse of such committees and meetings not only keeps these people from getting their jobs done, but also either necessitates their working additional hours or having someone else employed to perform their functions or secretaries and administrative assistants to maintain their schedules.

Specific Areas

The following comments, suggestions, and recommendations relate to our review of the specific functions within the business office. They are presented for your consideration, understanding that they emanate from a general review and need to be tempered with actual conditions such as present systems and personnel. They are presented in the order of the business office organization chart as shown in Exhibit CS5.1.

Comptroller

The comptroller is responsible for all business office operations, as well as being the director of support services with authority over physical plant, computer center, central mail operations, and the bookstore, and indirect responsibility for the financial aid office. This appears to be a strange mixture and overburdening of responsibilities. In light of what needs to be done, coupled with the amount of meetings required of the comptroller, it appears that she has been put in an impossible position. Typically, the responsibilities of a college comptroller of your size include:

- Financial analysis and planning—helping to set the future direction of the college and identifying the financial impact of the plans
- Accounting and auditing—maintaining accurate books and records, analyzing results, and evaluating performance
- Financing and capital structure—investigating and deciding on sources of funds to meet ongoing capital needs

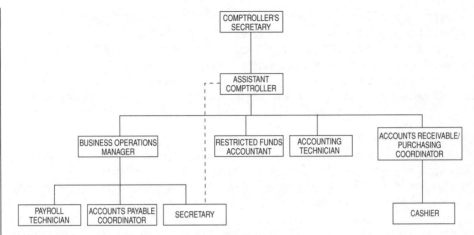

Exhibit CS5.1 Business Office Organizational Chart

- Controlling and reporting—establishing methods for maintaining financial control over operations and informing management about results (both favorable and unfavorable) and what, if anything, needs to be done to make improvements
- Asset management and protection—controlling and managing cash, accounts receivable, accounts payable, and fixed assets to ensure that assets are being properly used to benefit the college
- Information systems—managing and monitoring the information system to ensure that the system provides the operational data necessary for effective decision making

Based on discussions with the comptroller and a review of her responsibilities, it appears that these priorities have been shifted into other areas and her time is being grossly compromised. It would appear that these priorities need to be readjusted if positive improvements are to be made to support the growth of the college.

Comptroller's Secretary

The comptroller's secretary performs traditional secretarial duties such as typing correspondence using word processing software and related filing. In addition, she maintains the comptroller's calendar and appointments in a manually maintained schedule book. This could easily be computerized and shared between the two, eliminating clerical time and the possibility of double or conflicting entries.

The secretary is also involved in other clerical duties such as picking up and sorting the departmental mail. This appears to be a waste of high-priced and valued secretarial assistance which could be accomplished by a mail delivery system. It was also noticed that accounts receivable checks were included as part of the mail, which requires the secretary to date stamp, record each item on a check log, and then submit these materials to accounts receivable. You might consider providing a preaddressed return envelope which could alert the mail room to bring these receivable items directly to a control point for processing and immediate deposit. The returned portion of the billing statement would then be used to record the receipt against the accounts.

It appears that the secretary could be used to better advantage as more of an administrative assistant to the comptroller than as a more typical clerical secretary.

Assistant Comptroller

The assistant comptroller is responsible for managing the various business office functions and assisting the comptroller. After reviewing and discussing his functions, it does not appear that either of these areas are being addressed adequately. In fact, we are not quite sure why both a comptroller and an assistant comptroller are necessary, particularly with a business operations manager as well. You might want to consider whether the assistant comptroller can be used to straighten out these operations and develop more helpful systems and procedures.

Business Operations Manager

There appears to be some confusion between this role and that of the assistant comptroller. The other business office employees are not quite sure who to go to when they have a problem. This also creates confusion as to who has decision-making powers. It appears that accounts payable, payroll, and the business office secretary are to report to the business operations manager, while accounts receivable and the cashier report to the assistant comptroller. This is an expensive division of management and is probably unnecessary.

The business operations manager pointed out some problems with the present accounting software that need to be addressed because these are indicators of unnecessary manual efforts created by a nonresponsive system:

- Recordkeeping and printing of Form 1099s at the end of the year
- Vendor balance report—total dollars spent by vendor for year for purchasing purposes and Form 990 (over $30,000)
- Nonintegration of purchasing system with accounts payable, requiring separate entries for disencumbering
- Inability to print purchase orders, causing the business office secretary to manually type purchase orders and then enter them into the system

The business operations manager is also involved in the ongoing budget system by:

- Comparing purchase requisitions to a computer-produced budget report as the computer system is unable to make such a budget check, which is printed on the 15th and the 30th of the month. While this check may catch some requisitions that should not be processed, this manual checking misses any interim transactions and encumbrances and possibly could be stopped until new systems are implemented.
- Preparing and processing budget amendments, which appear to be mainly line item changes wherein a specific department has overspent on a line item. We are not sure what this accomplishes other than keeping the total departmental

budget in line. Time could be better spent analyzing whether the purchase is necessary in the first place.
- Reviewing check requests (helping accounts payable) for proper account approval, backup documentation, authorization, and so on. Oddly, these are not checked against the budget and are an area where personnel could be bypassing the purchasing system.

The business operations manager also manually prepares various journal entries based on computer-produced data in which the system does not automatically make the entries:

- Payroll transactions from the outside payroll processor. This entry is manually prepared and could go up to 12 pages. The information is available from the payroll processor but not in machine-usable form. Investigation should be made as to whether the payroll processor could either telecommunicate these data or provide a computer usable data file.
- Off-site program accounting transactions. This is another area where computerization could automatically transmit these transactions as they occur.
- Plant, restricted, and endowment fund transactions, which also could be easily computerized.
- Accounts receivable collection fees, which are computer entered against accounts receivable records, but does not create corresponding entries to the general ledger.

The business operations manager is presently spending time assisting the accounts payable operation due to the overload of paperwork and present systems, such as reviewing check requests, large vendor reconciliations, prepayment processing, and so on. You should consider best practice systems for reducing the number of check requests, purchase orders, and accounts payable transactions, such as elimination of low-dollar purchases (e.g., under $200) with a direct cash systems, purchase credit cards, vendor charges and so on; elimination of repetitive check requests, purchase orders, and vendor transactions through blanket purchase order releases; and direct vendor purchases for approved budget purchases.

He is also involved in closing out the accounting system subledgers to the general ledger due to the inability of the system to automatically close. Cash receipts are done daily, accounts payable twice a month to update budget reports, and accounts receivable monthly. Note that with a fully integrated system, each of these subsystems and the general ledger would be up-to-date with each entry.

The business operations manager and the comptroller review the budget reports on a monthly basis, looking for questionable items resulting in budget line item adjustments based on an "overspent" message. This appears to be chasing mice to keep total departmental budgets in line as opposed to identifying what is happening and taking corrective action. Keep in mind that under flexible budget concepts, many times budgets need to be increased based on activity-level changes and the charge may be actually an automatic budget adjustment.

In summary, the business operations manager is performing many unnecessary clerical and computer routines due to present systems and the lack of an integrated computer system. It would be more advantageous to free up his time for more systems analysis and evaluation tasks.

Payroll Operations

The payroll technician works part time (20 hours a week) coordinating payroll processing with an outside payroll processor. An online submission system to and from the payroll processor does not exist, which necessitates the manual feeding of data through the preparation of various input forms. Through discussions with the payroll processor, it was determined that such online processing is possible and is used by many of their other customers. Such online processing should be implemented immediately.

The payroll technician still maintains certain data files in the College's accounting system such as the master payroll file, deduction file, and vacation and sick leave file. This is a duplication of efforts with the service provided by the outside payroll processor. The move to online processing would allow access to these files maintained by the payroll processor.

The payroll technician prepares a budget salary schedule monthly using a computer spreadsheet routine. This procedure should be incorporated into the College's systems specifications for a new computer system.

Accounts Payable

Purchases emanate either from a purchase requisition or a check request from the various departments as they see fit. This has created a larger number of purchases than appears to be necessary. There is no central purchasing function to exercise overall control to take advantage of purchasing economies such as:

- Blanket purchase orders for large volumes of items or dollars wherein prices can be negotiated downward and releases processed against a single purchase order (e.g., maintenance supplies, copy paper, office supplies, etc.).
- Traveling requisitions for repetitively ordered items rather than individual purchase requisitions each time the item is ordered.
- Preapproved purchases based on agreed-upon plans and budgets, eliminating the need for purchase requisitions.
- Telephone ordering system whereby the user can order small purchases and repetitive items without having to go through the purchasing and accounts payable systems.
- Combined purchases for items like books, in which volume discounts increase based on the total order, reducing the number of purchase orders.

Due to the present system, particularly with the inability of the present system to computer produce a purchase order, the clerical volume greatly exceeds what should be necessary. In effect, the accounts payable coordinator is being overwhelmed with paper. The business operations manager is providing some assistance, and the business office secretary is typing and entering purchase order data and assisting in filing. All of this is a waste of time that could be used better in the analyzing and evaluation function.

Compounding these problems is the lack of a centralized receiving area, which results in items being delivered to each and every area. Because payments cannot be processed until receipt is verified, vendor invoices are waiting in accounts payable, increasing processing volumes and problems. The accounts payable coordinator estimates that this entails about 30 to 40 percent of all vendor invoices. Conversely, there are receipts without invoices caused by departments requesting the vendor to submit their invoices directly to the department. This is due to many departments maintaining their own private "budget control" systems due to the lack of confidence in central accounting functions.

The entire purchasing and accounts payable area needs to be streamlined and better controlled. Mercy College is not achieving meaningful purchasing economies, and the present system is not providing adequate controls and is resulting in an overburden of clerical activities and paperwork.

Business Office Secretary

The secretary provides basic secretarial-type duties to the business office such as telephone receptionist, word processing, mail sorting, and so on. She is also presently processing purchase requisitions into the computer purchasing system. However, she is first typing the purchase order using a typewriter and then entering the data into the computer system because the present software does not produce a purchase order. This is not only a duplication of effort but also provides the opportunity for picking up the wrong data. For the time being (until new computer procedures are implemented), a mock printout from the present system should be used as the purchase order.

Restricted Funds Accountant

The restricted funds accountant is responsible for maintaining and controlling the college's restricted funds such as:

- Multicultural Education Program
- Upward Bound
- Center for Academic Development
- Financial aid
- Other private restricted grants and gifts

He is responsible to prepare all necessary federal reports (e.g., Department of Education) for grant reimbursement as well as any other necessary reporting.

Mercy College does not have an approved indirect cost allocation plan. Presently, indirect cost rates are set for each program within the individual federal contract. This may be adequate for the level of present federal contracts. However, the college should actively go after more federal monies, as once you are in the federal system you are obligated with reporting, recordkeeping, and audit requirements. The more federal funds, the greater the economy of scale in charging indirect costs to federal programs. Each dollar paid by the federal contracts releases the same amount to the college for other purposes.

This accountant is also responsible for student loan funds (e.g., Stafford loans with independent lenders and Perkins revolving funds). In addition, he is responsible for the endowment fund of which about 55 percent is unrestricted and 45 percent is restricted (mostly for scholarships). It does not appear that records as to restrictions (i.e., specific purposes) are complete.

This entire area of restricted and endowment funds needs to be defined as to its requirements and incorporated into the college's systems specifications for more sophisticated computer systems.

Accounting Technician

The accounting technician is responsible for a number of functions that help support business office operations such as:

- Review cash receipts as processed by the cashier.
- Maintaining of cash balance via a manual log. Again, this should be provided by the computer system.
- Reconcile cash accounts to monthly bank statements.
- Cash flow report weekly using spreadsheet (this should be computerized). In the interim, determine how useful this is—can it be eliminated?
- Special projects using a spreadsheet or database system where present system cannot provide information.

The accounting technician should be spending more time analyzing and less time doing.

Accounts Receivable/Purchasing Coordinator

Accounts receivable mainly consists of student payments that are due. The student registration system, student account, financial aid, payment system appears to be overly cumbersome with the student being shunted from one area to the other. Because Mercy College is in the student service business, this entire process should be examined so that it is more student-oriented.

The coordinator is now seeing all students at the time of registration to determine the amount of tuition based on each student's registration form. She then records room and board charges manually and prepares a financial aid voucher. This information is then entered into the student account system and the amount due is calculated. The student then goes to the cashier to make payment.

Mercy College presently has differential rates per credit—that is, a different rate for traditional students, graduate students, nontraditional students, and off-site students—each with different payment terms. For instance, traditional students pay on the front end with a 3 percent discount or in 10 monthly payments with an extra $40 fee. Graduate, nontraditional, and off-site students can pay all up front or in three installments. With Mercy College's present cash position, these pricing and payment policies should be reviewed. The one advantage that colleges generally have related to cash flow is that they receive the bulk of their money prior to providing the services. Mercy College is losing some of this advantage.

Those students not paying immediately are required to sign a promissory note, which is kept in a loose-leaf binder. These notes are not on the computer system and require the coordinator to manually post to the note. In addition, the book needs to be reviewed manually for those not paid or delinquent. The coordinator also needs to prepare the accounts receivable monthly aging schedule using a spreadsheet application together with manually aging each receivable.

The accounts receivable coordinator is also recognized as the purchasing coordinator. It appears that what she does in this role is to handle the ordering of departmental envelopes, stationery, and business cards, as well as advising and possessing catalogs as to business furniture and equipment and office supplies. This should, of course, be part of a central purchasing function together with more autonomy for the operating departments.

Cashier

The cashier is responsible for recording and receiving all payments. These include student payments at registration, subsequently in person, and received in the mail. As the present system is set up, the cashier must check for a number of items at registration such as signatures (e.g., accounts receivable and financial aid), installment payment approved, overload conditions, and amount due. If the student pays in full, the cashier calculates the 3 percent discount and writes up a payment slip for accounts receivable to enter. It appears that all of this can be integrated through a well-designed computer system, which would not only make the registration process easier for students but would also provide greater control over cash receipts.

Mail receipts for subsequent student payments are processed by accounts receivable against the student records and then sent to the cashier for cash receipts processing. It would appear that these types of transactions can be captured as received, allowing the funds to be directly deposited into the bank.

Other receipts and checks are also funneled through the one cashier. Again, the goal is to get such cash receipts deposited as quickly as possible. It does not appear that present procedures are accomplishing this—other alternatives need to be investigated.

Summary

We believe through cross-training and redefinition of job responsibilities, business office personnel can be better used for processing-type functions as well as analysis and control. Presently, clerical functions are being performed by more highly paid and capable people, and skilled accounting personnel are being used as computer data entry clerks rather than as analyzers, evaluators, and controllers. Through the correct use of personnel, in conjunction with systems improvements, the business office can be operated at less cost, more efficiently, and with increased results.

OTHER AREAS

During the course of our review, we identified other areas that were not necessarily part of business office operations but that we believe should be brought to your attention.

- The accounting chart of accounts appears to be extremely cumbersome. You might want to look at a simpler system that makes it easier for users to provide account coding, to input into the computer system, and for reporting.
- Price, cost, volume considerations. The college presently has different prices for credit courses (e.g., traditional, graduate, nontraditional, and off-site). These

should correspond to the college revenue plan based on expected number of students and costs for providing such services. Sound cost principles require that such tuition pricing recover direct costs, indirect costs, allocated costs, recovery of overhead costs, and a contribution to fund balance or reserves. Such cost principles should be based on expected student volumes or a breakeven point concept.

- Central services concepts might provide the college with some economies. For instance, centralized purchasing, copying (with large copying better controlled at less cost), word processing, and centralized secretarial and administrative services (as opposed to the proliferation of such personnel throughout the college).
- Registration system and related payment options needs to be revamped so that the college gets its money as quickly as possible on the front end without causing inconvenience to the students. Rather than a 3 percent discount for paying all at once, consider a larger discount with a stiffer penalty (e.g., more than just a $40 fee) based on the cost of money for installment payments.
- External reporting and special requests. There appears to be a large amount of manual, spreadsheet, and database manipulation to provide such reporting. Until such time as these requests can be incorporated into a more flexible computer system, the college should look at each such request as to its benefit versus the time and cost involved. It appears that sometimes even with such efforts, the data is still inaccurate and may cause improper decisions.
- External audit. You presently require a federally mandated organization-wide audit due to receiving more than the threshold amount of federal awards. The present audit fees are not being paid with these federal funds to the extent possible. As previously mentioned, the college should be going after more federal moneys and then developing an indirect cost allocation plan. The trick here is to get federal monies to pay as much as possible, so that the college can free up these unexpended funds for other purposes.

In addition, we reviewed the past audit report and while all of the required reports for federal purposes were there, the college does not appear to be getting any worthwhile operational suggestions and recommendations. The auditor's findings and comments all relate to internal controls over federal moneys. The college should be clear in negotiating the next audit contract that this type of assistance is expected.

- Revenue planning seems to be deficient, with little backup to expected revenue numbers. For instance, what is the plan to provide the number of students by department, program, off-site and so on. In addition, what are the fund-raising and development office's detail plans as to federal and other grants, gift giving, wills, insurance beneficiaries, fund raising, and so on?

As in most purely line item budget systems, revenues tend to be overestimated with minimal backup support, and expenditures tend to be underestimated after much justification and calculation efforts. A more effective integrated planning and budgeting system will allow Mercy College to better manage its needs more effectively through proper prioritizing and scarce resource allocations. Such a system will also allow the college to control ongoing operations more effectively and permit flexibility based on continuing changing requirements throughout the year.

- Proposed integrated computer system. The computerized integrated financial and accounting control and management reporting system that we are proposing involves a communications process in which data are recorded initially and revised as needed, in order to support management and staff decisions for planning, operating, and controlling college operations. Our conceptual design attempts to maximize the use of common data to satisfy the information requirements of Mercy College staff at various levels. It attempts to strike an economic balance between the value of the information to be carried and the cost of operating the system. Accordingly, our objective is not simply to mechanize, but to design an effective computerization plan that will provide Mercy College personnel with the necessary data to manage and operate.

  Proposed computerization will also afford the opportunity for additional personnel cost savings in the purchasing, accounts payable, payroll, accounts receivable, general ledger, and management and operating analysis and reporting functions. Mercy College management should review future departmental and personnel functions for possible eliminations, combining, shifting, and downgrading. A personnel plan should be developed to coordinate procedural changes with personnel requirements on an ongoing basis as changes are implemented.

  We believe that to successfully implement the proposed computer systems in a timely manner, in addition to simultaneously completing our other computer processing–related recommendations, will require at least one additional experienced computer programmer to be hired.

  We also believe that the most efficient and practical course of action for Mercy College management to take, with regard to computer processing, is to establish the following priorities:

- Implement our recommended business office function improvements, based onthe priorities previously established.
- Simultaneously program and implement the financial and accounting systems presently being designed.
- System design and program the proposed integrated college computer system.

  We believe that the present computer system (with some additional file servers and data terminals) is capable of performing the processing described above. Present computer usage is relatively low at present and can be appreciably increased with minimal impact on overall computer operations. Additionally, manual control functions should be reduced, providing for a streamlining of operations. After the recommendations described above have successfully been accomplished and are operational, Mercy College management should reappraise computer equipment needs with respect to total processing.

We appreciate the courtesies and cooperation extended to us by Mercy College management and business office personnel during the course of this operational review. We are, of course, prepared to discuss any aspects of this review or specific items mentioned in this report with you, should you so desire. In addition, we are available to provide additional consultative assistance in the operational review of other functional areas, as well as work with you in the implementation of recommendations mentioned in this report. We appreciate the opportunity to assist Mercy College management in accomplishing the results of this operational review and look forward to continued good relations between Reider Associates and Mercy College.

Very truly yours,

Rob Reider, President
REIDER ASSOCIATES

Index